D1432711

Postfix
The Definitive Guide

Other networking resources from O'Reilly

Related titles

sendmail
qmail
sendmail Cookbook
Programming Internet Email
Essential System
  Administration
TCP/IP Network
  Administration
Running Mac OS X Panther

Mac OS X Panther for Unix
  Geeks
Mac OS X Panther in a
  Nutshell
Mac OS X Panther Pocket
  Guide
Learning Unix for Mac OS X
  Panther
Applescript: The Definitive
  Guide

networking.oreilly.com

networking.oreilly.com is a complete catalog of O'Reilly books on networking and related technologies, including sample chapters and code examples.

oreillynet.com is the essential portal for developers interested in open and emerging technologies, including new platforms, programming languages, and operating systems.

Conferences

O'Reilly & Associates brings diverse innovators together to nurture the ideas that spark revolutionary industries. We specialize in documenting the latest tools and systems, translating the innovator's knowledge into useful skills for those in the trenches. Visit *conferences.oreilly.com* for our upcoming events.

Safari Bookshelf (*safari.oreilly.com*) is the premier online reference library for programmers and IT professionals. Conduct searches across more than 1,000 books. Subscribers can zero in on answers to time-critical questions in a matter of seconds. Read the books on your Bookshelf from cover to cover or simply flip to the page you need. Try it today with a free trial.

Postfix
The Definitive Guide

Kyle D. Dent

O'REILLY®

Beijing · Cambridge · Farnham · Köln · Paris · Sebastopol · Taipei · Tokyo

Postfix: The Definitive Guide
by Kyle D. Dent

Published by O'Reilly Media, Inc., 1005 Gravenstein Highway North, Sebastopol, CA 95472.

O'Reilly & Associates books may be purchased for educational, business, or sales promotional use. On-line editions are also available for most titles (*safari.oreilly.com*). For more information, contact our corporate/institutional sales department: (800) 998-9938 or *corporate@oreilly.com*.

Editor:	Andy Oram
Production Editor:	Reg Aubry
Cover Designer:	Ellie Volckhausen
Interior Designer:	David Futato

Printing History:

December 2003:	First Edition.

 This book uses RepKover™, a durable and flexible lay-flat binding.

ISBN: 0-596-00212-2
[C]

Table of Contents

Foreword

All programmers are optimists—these words of wisdom were written down almost thirty years ago by Frederick P. Brooks, Jr.* The Postfix mail system is a fine example of this. Postfix started as a half-year project while I was visiting the network and security department at IBM Research in New York state. Although half a year was enough time to replace the mail system on my own workstation, it was not nearly enough to build a complete mail system for general use. Throughout the next year, a lot of code was added while the software was tested by a closed group of experts. And in the five years that followed the public release, Postfix more than doubled in size and in the number of features. Meanwhile, active development continues.

One of the main goals of Postfix is wide adoption. Building Postfix was only the first challenge on the way to that goal. The second challenge was to make the software accessible. While expert users are happy to Read The Friendly Manual that accompanies Postfix, most people need a more gentle approach. Truth be told, I would not expect to see wide adoption of Postfix without a book to introduce the concepts behind the system, and which gives examples of how to get common tasks done. I was happy to leave the writing of this book to Kyle Dent.

Just like Postfix, I see this book as a work in progress. In the time that the first edition of the book was written, Postfix went through several major revisions. Some changes were the result of discussions with Kyle in order to make Postfix easier to understand, some changes added functionality that was missing from earlier versions, and some changes were forced upon Postfix by the big bad ugly world of junk email and computer viruses. Besides the changes that introduced new or extended features, many less-visible changes were made behind the scenes as part of ongoing maintenance and improvement.

* Frederick P. Brooks, Jr.: *The Mythical Man-Month: Essays on Software Engineering*, Addison Wesley, 1975.

This book describes Postfix Version 2.1, and covers some of the differences with older Postfix versions that were widely used at the time of publication. As Postfix continues to evolve, it will slowly diverge from this book, and eventually this book will have to be updated. While it is a pleasure for me to welcome you to this first edition, I already look forward to an opportunity to meet again in the near future.

—Wietse Venema
Hawthorne, New York
September 19, 2003

Preface

I'm always astounded when I think about the early designers of Internet technologies. They were (and many still are) an amazing group of people who developed software and technologies for a network that was minuscule, by comparison with today's Internet. Yet their work scaled and has continued to function in not only a much larger but in a very different environment. The expansion hasn't been completely without growing pains, but that doesn't diminish this amazing feat. Sendmail is an example of one of the early technologies that was written for a different universe, yet is still relevant and handles a large portion of email today.

Postfix has an advantage in that it was built with an awareness of the scope and hostile environment it would have to face. In fact, its creation was motivated by the need to overcome some of the problems of software written in a more innocent age. What a difference a little hindsight can make.

I first started using Postfix when I was working with systems in a security-sensitive environment. The promise of more flexibility and better security caught my interest as soon as I heard about it. I was not disappointed. It didn't take long before I was hooked, and preferred using Postfix everywhere. This book is my attempt to create a reference and a guide to understanding how Postfix works. Its main goal is to explain the details and concepts behind Postfix. It also offers instructions for accomplishing many specific tasks.

Documenting a piece of software that is still under active development is a bit like trying to stop running water. Sadly, this book will be incomplete even before it is out. I've tried to structure the information in the book in such a way as to exclude things that might become irrelevant or quickly out-of-date, so that what you find in the book will be good information for a long time to come. However, you may have to supplement this book with online documentation, web sites, and the Postfix mailing list for coverage of the latest features.

Audience

Postfix is a network application written for Unix. The more you know about networking and Unix, the better equipped you will be to manage a Postfix server. This book tries to explain things in such a way as to be understandable to users new to Unix, but it is unrealistic to think that you could learn to administer a Postfix server without having (or at least acquiring) some Unix knowledge. The book focuses on Postfix itself. Other concepts are explained as needed to understand the functions and configuration of Postfix. If you're new to Unix, you should certainly consult other texts for general Unix information. *Unix System Administration Handbook* by Evi Nemeth, et al. (Prentice-Hall) is an excellent choice, and includes a helpful section on email. The relevant RFCs mentioned in this book can also be very helpful for understanding the details of a subject.

Organization

Chapters 1 through 3 provide background information on Postfix and email, chapters 4 through 7 discuss general aspects of running a Postfix server, and Chapters 8 through 15 each present a specific topic that you may or may not need, depending on how you use Postfix:

Chapter 1, *Introduction*
> Introduces Postfix and some general email concepts. Also discusses some of the design decisions that went into Postfix.

Chapter 2, *Prerequisites*
> Covers required topics for understanding other concepts in the book. Anyone with a basic understanding of Unix and email can safely skip this chapter.

Chapter 3, *Postfix Architecture*
> Explains the pieces of the modular architecture of Postfix and how Postfix handles email messages.

Chapter 4, *General Configuration and Administration*
> Covers a wide range of topics for configuring and managing a Postfix server.

Chapter 5, *Queue Management*
> Explains how the Postfix queue manager works, and presents the tools used to work with the queue.

Chapter 6, *Email and DNS*
> Discusses how DNS is used for email routing. Presents considerations for configuring DNS to work with Postfix.

Chapter 7, *Local Delivery and POP/IMAP*
> Covers how Postfix makes local deliveries and how it operates in conjunction with POP and IMAP servers.

Chapter 8, *Hosting Multiple Domains*
Discusses using Postfix to receive email for virtual domains.

Chapter 9, *Mail Relaying*
Discusses operating Postfix as a mail relay or gateway system.

Chapter 10, *Mailing Lists*
Discusses setting up mailing lists in Postfix, and using Postfix with mailing-list managers. Provides examples with Majordomo and Mailman.

Chapter 11, *Blocking Unsolicited Bulk Email*
Discusses Postfix controls for blocking unwanted mail messages.

Chapter 12, *SASL Authentication*
Covers using SASL libraries to provide SMTP authentication for clients to relay messages through your Postfix server.

Chapter 13, *Transport Layer Security*
Covers using the TLS patch to provide encrypted communications between clients and your Postfix server.

Chapter 14, *Content Filtering*
Discusses setting up external content filters with Postfix.

Chapter 15, *External Databases*
Covers using external data sources for Postfix lookup tables.

Appendix A, *Configuration Parameters*
Presents an alphabetical listing of Postfix configuration parameters.

Appendix B, *Postfix Commands*
Presents a list, with brief explanations, of the command-line utilities that come with Postfix.

Appendix C, *Compiling and Installing Postfix*
Discusses compiling and installing Postfix from source files.

Appendix D, *Frequently Asked Questions*
Presents a list of frequently asked questions about Postfix.

Conventions Used in This Book

Items appearing in this book are sometimes given a special appearance to set them apart from the regular text. Here's how they look:

Italic
Used for commands, email addresses, URIs, filenames, emphasized text, first references to terms, and citations of books and articles.

`Constant width`
Used for literals, constant values, code listings, and XML markup.

Constant width italic
> Used for replaceable parameter and variable names.

Constant width bold
> Used to highlight the portion of a code listing being discussed.

 These icons signify a tip, suggestion, or general note.

 These icons indicate a warning or caution.

Comments and Questions

Please address comments and questions concerning this book to the publisher:

> O'Reilly & Associates, Inc.
> 1005 Gravenstein Highway North
> Sebastopol, CA 95472
> (800) 998-9938 (in the United States or Canada)
> (707) 829-0515 (international or local)
> (707) 829-0104 (fax)

O'Reilly maintains a web page for this book, that lists errata, examples, and any additional information. You can access this page at:

> *http://www.oreilly.com/catalog/postfix/*

To comment or ask technical questions about this book, send email to:

> *bookquestions@oreilly.com*

For more information about O'Reilly books, conferences, Resource Centers, and the O'Reilly Network, see O'Reilly's web site at:

> *http://www.oreilly.com/*

Acknowledgments

I would first like to thank Wietse Venema for Postfix, of course, but also for his many contributions to the Internet community. Having had the honor to work with him on this book, it is apparent to me that he brings the same level of intelligence and attention to detail to all of his endeavors. This book has benefited greatly from his considerable input.

I have always admired O'Reilly & Associates as a company. After having had the experience of working with them, my admiration has not diminished in the least. My editor, Andy Oram, excellently personifies the goals of the company. I've enjoyed discussions with him, and his comments were always very helpful. I appreciate his enormous patience. Lenny Muellner helped me get going with text-processing tools and I'd like to thank David Chu for his timely assistance when needed. I would also like to thank Robert Romano for turning my crude diagrams into the professional figures you find in the book, and Reg Aubry for guiding the book through the production process.

Several technical reviewers assisted me not only in staying honest and correct in the details, but they also often offered useful stylistic suggestions. Thanks to Rob Dinoff, Viktor Dukhovni (a.k.a. Victor Duchovni), Lutz Jänicke, and Alan Schwartz. I wish I had such a team looking over my shoulder for everything I do.

I would also like to acknowledge the many members of the postfix-users@postfix.org list. It is an active list with a low noise-to-signal ratio, populated by a group of remarkably capable and helpful people. Its members not only help the user community, but have contributed through their comments and discussions to the evolution of Postfix itself.

Finally, I owe a large debt of gratitude to my wife and first editor, Jackie. She subjected my initial drafts to scrupulous tests for lucidity and sanity (shocking how often they failed). This book is much improved from her patient and valuable input. She is an all-around good egg who remained cheerful even when faced with reading and rereading several rewrites.

## CHAPTER 1

Introduction

Internet email history goes back as far as the early 1970s, when the first messages were sent across the Arpanet, the predecessor of today's Internet. Since that time, email has been, and continues to be, the most widely used application on the Internet. In the olden days, email delivery was relatively simple, and generally consisted of moving mail files from one large host to another large host that served many users. As the Internet evolved and the network itself became more complex, more flexible tools were needed to move mail between different networks and different types of networks. The Sendmail package, released in the early 1980s, was designed to deal with the many variations among mail systems. It quickly assumed a dominant role for mail delivery on the Internet.

Today, most Internet sites use the SMTP mail protocol to deliver and receive mail messages. Sendmail is still one of the most widely deployed SMTP servers, but there have been problems with it. Sendmail's monolithic architecture has been the primary cause of numerous security issues, and it can be difficult to configure and maintain.

Postfix was originally conceived as a replacement for the pervasive Sendmail. Its design eliminates many opportunities for security problems. Postfix also eliminates much of the complexity that comes with managing a Sendmail installation. Postfix administration is managed with two straightforward configuration files, and Postfix has been designed from the beginning to handle unexpected hardware or software problems gracefully.

Postfix Origins and Philosophy

Postfix was written by Wietse Venema, who is widely known for his security tools and papers. It was made available as open source software in December 1998. IBM Research sponsored the initial release and has continued to support its ongoing development. (IBM calls the package Secure Mailer.) There were certain goals from the beginning that drove the design and development of Postfix:

Reliability

Postfix shows its real value when operating under stressful conditions. Even within simple environments, software can encounter unexpected conditions. For example, many software systems behave unpredictably when they run out of memory or disk space. Postfix detects such conditions, and rather than make the problem worse, gives the system a chance to recover. Regardless of hazards thrown its way, Postfix takes every precaution to function in a stable and reliable way.

Security

Postfix assumes it is running in a hostile environment. It employs multiple layers of defense to protect against attackers. The security concept of least privilege is employed throughout the Postfix system, so that each process, which can be run within an isolated compartment, runs with the lowest set of privileges it needs. Processes running with higher privileges never trust the unprivileged processes. Likewise, unneeded modules can be disabled, enhancing security and simplifying an installation.

Performance

Postfix was written with performance in mind and, in fact, takes steps to ensure that its speed doesn't overwhelm other systems. It uses techniques to limit both the number of new processes that have to be created and the number of filesystem accesses required in processing messages.

Flexibility

The Postfix system is actually made up of several different programs and subsystems. This approach allows for great flexibility. All of the pieces are easily tunable through straightforward configuration files.

Ease-of-use

Postfix is one of the easier email packages to set up and administer, as it uses straightforward configuration files and simple lookup tables for address translations and forwarding. The idea behind Postfix's configuration is the notion of least surprise, which means that, to the extent it's possible, Postfix behaves the way most people expect. When faced with design choices, Dr. Venema has opted for the decision that seems most reasonable to most humans.

Compatibility with Sendmail

With Sendmail compatibility, Postfix can easily replace Sendmail on a system without forcing any changes on users or breaking any of the applications that depend on it. Postfix supports Sendmail conventions like */etc/aliases* and *.forward* files. The Sendmail executable program, `sendmail`, is replaced with a Postfix version that supports nearly all of the same command-line arguments but runs in conjunction with the Postfix system. While your Sendmail-dependent programs continue to work, Postfix has been evolving independently of Sendmail, and doesn't necessarily implement all email features in the same way.

Email and the Internet

Unlike most proprietary email solutions, where a single software package does everything, Internet email is built from several standards and protocols that define how messages are composed and transferred from a sender to a recipient. There are many different pieces of software involved, each one handling a different step in message delivery. Postfix handles only a portion of the whole process. Most email users are only familiar with the software they use for reading and composing messages, known as a *mail user agent* (MUA). Examples of some common MUAs include mutt, elm, Pine, Netscape Communicator, and Outlook Express. MUAs are good for reading and composing email messages, but they don't do much for mail delivery. That's where Postfix fits in.

Email Components

When you tell your MUA to send a message, it simply hands off the message to a mail server running a *mail transfer agent* (MTA). Figure 1-1 shows the components involved in a simple email transmission from sender to recipient. MTAs (like Postfix) do the bulk of the work in getting a message delivered from one system to another. When it receives a request to accept an email message, the MTA determines if it should take the message or not. An MTA generally accepts messages for its own local users; for other systems it knows how to forward to; or for messages from users, systems, or networks that are allowed to relay mail to other destinations. Once the MTA accepts a message, it has to decide what to do with it next. It might deliver the message to a user on its system, or it might have to pass the message along to another MTA. Messages bound for other networks will likely pass through many systems. If the MTA cannot deliver the message or pass it along, it bounces the message back to the original sender or notifies a system administrator. MTA servers are usually managed by Internet Service Providers (ISPs) for individuals or by corporate Information Systems departments for company employees.

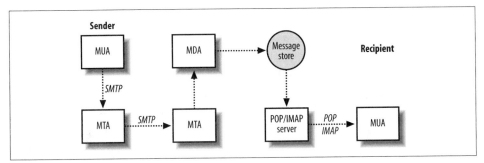

Figure 1-1. Simple Internet message flow

Ultimately, a message arrives at the MTA that is the final destination. If the message is destined for a user on the system, the MTA passes it to a *message delivery agent* (MDA) for the final delivery. The MDA might store the message as a plain file or pass it along to a specialized database for email. The term *message store* applies to persistent message storage regardless of how or where it is kept.

Once the message has been placed in the message store, it stays there until the intended recipient is ready to pick it up. The recipient uses an MUA to retrieve the message and read it. The MUA contacts the server that provides access to the message store. This server is separate from the MTA that delivered the message and is designed specifically to provide access for retrieving messages. After the server successfully authenticates the requester, it can transfer that user's messages to her MUA.

Because Internet email standards are open, there are many different software packages available to handle Internet email. Different packages that implement the same protocols can interoperate regardless of who wrote them or the type of system they are running on. If you are putting together a complete email system, most likely the software that handles SMTP will be a different package than the software that handles POP/IMAP, and there are many different software choices for each aspect of your complete email system.

Major Email Protocols

The communications that occur between each of these email system components are defined by standards and protocols. The standards documents are maintained by the Internet Engineering Task Force (IETF) and are published as Request For Comments (RFC) documents, which are numbered documents that explain a particular technology or protocol.

The *Simple Mail Transport Protocol* (SMTP) is used for sending messages, and either the *Post Office Protocol* (POP) or *Internet Mail Application Protocol* (IMAP) is used for retrieving messages. SMTP, defined in RFC 2821, describes the conversation that takes place between two hosts across a network to exchange email messages. The IMAP (RFC 2060) and POP (RFC 1939) protocols describe how to retrieve messages from a message store. The IMAP protocol was developed after POP and offers additional features. In both protocols, email messages are kept on a central server for message recipients who generally retrieve them across a network.

Note that the MUA does not necessarily use the same system for POP/IMAP as it does for SMTP, which is why email clients have to be configured separately for POP/IMAP and SMTP. An ISP might provide separate servers for each function to their customers, and corporate users who are away from the office often retrieve their messages from the company POP/IMAP server, but use the SMTP server of a dial-up ISP to send messages. MTA software running on SMTP servers constantly listens for requests to accept messages for delivery. Requests might come from MUAs or other MTA servers.

SMTP and email submission

SMTP is commonly used for email submission and for transmissions of email messages between MTAs. When an MUA contacts an MTA to have a message delivered, it uses SMTP. SMTP is also used when one MTA contacts another MTA to relay or deliver a message. Originally, SMTP had no means to authenticate users, but extensions to the protocol provide the capability, if required. See Chapter 7 for more information on authenticating SMTP users.

POP/IMAP and mailbox access

When users want to retrieve their messages, they use their MUA to connect to a POP or IMAP server to retrieve them. POP users generally take all their messages from the server and manage their mail locally. IMAP provides features that make it easier to manage mail on the server itself. (See Chapter 12 for more information on using Postfix with POP and IMAP servers.) Many servers now offer both protocols, so I will refer to them as POP/IMAP servers. POP and IMAP have nothing to do with sending email. These protocols deal only with how users retrieve previously delivered and stored messages.

Not all users need POP/IMAP access to the message store. Users with shell access on a Unix machine, for example, might have their MUA configured to read their email messages directly from the mail file that resides on the same machine.

The Role of Postfix

Postfix is an MTA and handles the delivery of messages between servers and locally within a system. It does not handle any POP or IMAP communications.

Figure 1-2 illustrates a simple example of message transmission where Postfix handles the responsibilities of the MTA and local delivery. As the MTA, Postfix receives and delivers email messages over the network via the SMTP protocol. For local delivery, the Postfix local delivery agent can deposit messages directly to a message store or hand off a message to a specialized mail delivery agent.

This example shows Postfix as the SMTP server at both ends of the email transaction; however, since Postfix is based on Internet standards, the other email server in this example could easily be any other standards-compliant server. Postfix can communicate with any other server that speaks SMTP (and even some that are not quite fluent). In our example, Heloise wants to send a message to Abelard from her address (*heloise@oreilly.com*) to his address (*abelard@postfix.org.*) Heloise uses her email client to compose her message, which passes it to her MTA (using SMTP). As it happens, her MTA is a Postfix server that allows her to relay messages. After accepting the message from Heloise's email client, the Postfix server determines where Heloise's message needs to go, based on Abelard's email address. Using DNS (see Chapter 6 for more information on DNS and email) it figures out which SMTP

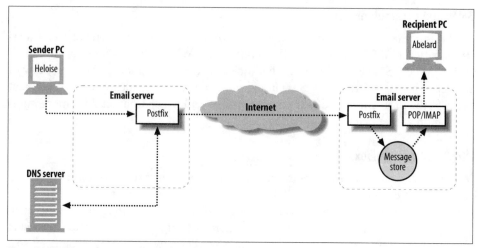

Figure 1-2. Example network email message delivery

server should accept messages for Abelard's domain (*postfix.org*) and contacts that server (using SMTP). Abelard's Postfix server accepts the message and stores it until Abelard is ready to pick it up. At this point Postfix's job is done. When Abelard is ready to retrieve his messages, his email client, using POP or IMAP, picks up Heloise's message.

This example leaves out the details of the complicated tasks involved when Postfix delivers mail. In the case of messages with multiple recipients, Postfix has to figure out where to deliver copies for each recipient. In case one or more recipients cannot receive mail due to a networking or systems problem, Postfix has to queue the message and retry delivery periodically. From a user's point of view, the Postfix piece of the operation is nearly invisible. From the Internet mail system's point of view, Postfix handles most aspects of email message delivery.

Postfix Security

Email systems are necessarily exposed to possible attacks because their function requires that they accept data from untrusted systems. The challenge is to build systems that are resistant to attack, and any good security strategy includes multiple layers of protection. This is particularly true for public systems in a potentially hostile environment. Postfix takes a proactive and multilayered approach to security. The Postfix architecture limits the severity of vulnerabilities, even if there are design or coding errors that might otherwise create major vulnerabilities in a monolithic privileged program.

Modular Design

The modular architecture of Postfix forms the basis for much of its security. Each Postfix process runs with the least amount of privilege necessary to get its particular job done. Many of Sendmail's security problems were exacerbated because Sendmail ran as a privileged process most of the time. Postfix operates with the minimum privilege necessary to accomplish a particular task. Postfix processes that are not needed on a system can be turned off, making it impossible to exploit them. For example, a network firewall system that only relays mail and does not need local delivery can have all the Postfix components for local delivery turned off. Postfix processes are insulated from each other and depend very little on any interprocess communication. Each process determines for itself what it needs to know.

Shells and Processes

In most cases, the delivery of mail does not require a Unix shell process, but when a configuration does make use of one, Postfix sanitizes information before placing it into environment variables. Postfix tries to eliminate any harmful characters that might have special meaning to a shell before making any data available to the shell.

Most Postfix processes are executed by a trusted master daemon. They do not run as user child processes, so they are immune to any of the security problems that rely on parent-child inheritance and communications. These attacks that use signals, shared memory, open files, and other types of interprocess communication are essentially useless against Postfix.

Security by Design

A buffer overflow is another common type of attack against applications. In this type of attack, crackers cause a program to write to memory where it is not supposed to. Doing so might allow them to change the path of execution in order to take control of the process. I've already mentioned that Postfix processes run with as little privilege as possible, so such an attack would not get very far; moreover, Postfix avoids using fixed-size buffers for dynamic data, making a successful buffer overflow attack highly unlikely.

An important security protection available on Unix systems is the ability to *chroot* applications. A chroot establishes a new root directory for a running application such as /var/spool/postfix. When that program runs, its view of the filesystem is limited to the subtree below /var/spool/postfix, and it cannot see anything else above that point. Your critical system directories and any other programs that might be exploited during an attack are not accessible. Postfix makes it very simple to cause its processes to run within a chroot (see more about chrooting in Chapter 4). By doing so, you cause Postfix to run in its own separate compartment. Even if Postfix is somehow subverted, it will not provide access to many of the methods an attacker typically employs to compromise a system.

Because Postfix is designed to run even under stressful conditions, denial-of-service (DOS) attacks are much less effective. If a system runs out of disk space or memory due to a DOS attack or another type of problem, Postfix is careful not to make the situation worse. It backs off from what it is trying to do to allow the system to recover. Postfix processes are configured to use a limited amount of memory, so they do not grow uncontrollably from an onslaught of messages.

The difficulty in planning for security is that you don't know what the next attack will be or how it will be carried out. Postfix is designed to deal with adverse conditions no matter what their cause. Its built-in robustness is a major factor in the degree of security that Postfix provides. Indeed, Dr. Venema has said that he is not so much interested in security as he is in creating software that works as intended, regardless of the circumstances. Security is just a beneficial side effect.

Additional Information and How to Obtain Postfix

You can get more information about Postfix at the official web site: *The Postfix Home Page* (*http://www.postfix.org/*). The site contains the source code, documentation, links to add-on software, articles, and additional information about Postfix. There is also information about joining an active mailing list that discusses all aspects of Postfix.

If you don't have a copy of Postfix already, you can obtain the source code from the Postfix web site. It is, however, quite possible that there is a precompiled package for your platform that may be more convenient for you. If that is the case, you can obtain the Postfix package for your operating system and use your system's normal tools for software installation and configuration. You should check the normal repositories you use to get software for your system.

There are many good reasons to build Postfix for yourself: there may not be a prepackaged bundle for your platform, you might not trust the packager of the bundle to have done everything correctly for your environment, you might need support for add-ons that are not built into a package, you might need a more current version than is available in packages, or you might just enjoy the task. If you have any experience compiling software, you'll have no trouble building Postfix. It's one of the easier open source packages to compile.

The Postfix web site has a download link that displays a list of mirrors from which you can get the software. You should select the mirror that is closest to you. Postfix is available as either an Official Release package or as an Experimental Release package. Even though it's called experimental, you should consider the code to be very stable. Experimental releases contain new features that might still change before they become official. Some new features are available only in an experimental release, but you should feel comfortable using them. Just be aware that they may evolve slightly in later releases until their feature sets are considered stable enough for the official release. No Postfix software is released that hasn't gone through extensive testing and review. Read through the *RELEASE_NOTES* file that comes with the package to learn what the differences are between the current official and experimental releases.

CHAPTER 2

Prerequisites

This chapter presents some basic Unix and email concepts that you need in order to follow explanations and examples presented later in the book. If you are already familiar with email administration, you can safely skip the material here and move on to the next chapter. This chapter does not give a systematic or comprehensive overview of either email or Unix administration. There is already an enormous amount of information available on both topics. This chapter simply presents an assortment of items that are referred to later in the book, with the expectation that readers already understand them.

Unix Topics

There's no question that the more familiar you are with Unix, the better a Postfix administrator you'll be. Postfix is very much a Unix program working in conjunction with the underlying operating system for many of its functions. If you're new to Unix, you should study an introductory text. In the meantime, this section presents some fundamental concepts that you will need to understand to follow explanations in the book.

Login Names and UID Numbers

The list of recognized users on a system is stored in the *etc/passwd* file. Every user should have a unique login name and user ID number (commonly written as uid or UID). The UID, not the user's login name, is the important attribute for identity and ownership checks. The login name is a convenience for humans, and the system uses it primarily to determine what the UID is. Some Postfix configuration parameters require UIDs rather than login names when referring to user accounts. Postfix sometimes takes on the identify of different users. A process is said to be using the rights or privileges of that account when assuming its identity.

Pseudo-Accounts

A pseudo-account is a normal Unix system account except that it does not permit logins. These accounts are used to perform administrative functions or to run programs under specific user privileges. Your system most likely came installed with several pseudo-accounts. Account names such as *bin* and *daemon* are common ones. Generally, these accounts prevent logins by using an invalid password and nonexistent home directories and login shells. For Postfix administration, you need at least one pseudo-account for Postfix processes to run under. You may need additional ones for other functions, such as mailing-list programs and filters.

Standard Input/Standard Output

Nearly all processes on a Unix system have a standard input stream and a standard output stream when they start. They read data on their standard input and write data on their standard output. Normally, standard input is the keyboard and standard output is the monitor, which is how users interact with running programs. Standard input and output can be redirected so that programs can get input from, and send output to, a file or another program. This is often how batch mode programs operate. For the purpose of email, you should be aware of standard input and output because your mail system may have to interact with other programs over their standard inputs and outputs. A mail filter program, for example, might accept the contents of an email message on its standard input and send the revised contents to its standard output. Programs usually also have a standard error stream that, like standard output, is normally a user's monitor, but it can also be redirected. Standard input/output/error are often written as *stdin*, *stdout*, and *stderr*. For more information, consult an introductory book on Unix.

The Superuser

The administrative login on Unix systems is the *root* account. It is also referred to as the superuser account, and you should treat it carefully. You should log in as the *root* user only when its privileges are required to accomplish a particular task. Administering Postfix sometimes requires *root* privileges. If you do not have superuser access on your system, you cannot administer Postfix.

Command Prompts

When working with an interactive shell, you are normally greeted with a command prompt that indicates the system is ready for you to enter a command. By convention, user command prompts are shown as either the $ character or the % character, while the *root* prompt is presented as the # character. You should use the *root* account only when it is necessary. In examples in this book, a normal user prompt is shown as $, and that for *root* is shown as #. If the example shows the prompt as #, you know that you must execute the command as *root*.

Long Lines

It is common usage in Unix to break long commands into multiple lines with a back-slash (\) at the end of the line, which indicates that two or more lines continue as if they were a single line. The continuation backslash can be used at a command prompt and in shell scripts, and it is commonly used in configuration files (but not in Postfix configuration files—see Chapter 4). In this book, lines that don't fit on the page are continued with backslashes. If you follow the examples, you can type lines exactly as shown with the backslashes, or simply combine the continued lines into a single one.

ManPages

Documentation for Unix systems is kept in an online manual known as *manpages*. You can read the documentation for a particular item by issuing the man command with the item as its argument. For example, to read about the mailq command, simply type:

```
$ man mailq
```

A description of the command is presented on your screen, one page at a time. Press the spacebar to continue scrolling through the information.

Manpages have a standard organization showing the syntax of the command, all options, and descriptions of behavior and other context. Some users find manpages daunting, but you'll do yourself a great service by getting comfortable with manpages. All Unix and Postfix commands as well as many other features are documented in manpages. See an introductory Unix text or your system documentation to learn more about manpages.

Email Topics

Internet email is a complex subject with many aspects. There are important principles that apply when administering an email system regardless of the MTA you are working with. This section presents a few concepts that will help in understanding later explanations in the book, but you are urged to learn as much about Internet email as possible from the many resources available in books and online.

RFCs

RFCs, or Request for Comments documents, define the standards for the Internet. There are several RFCs relating to Internet email, all of which are relevant to you if you are administering an email system on the Internet. The two most commonly referenced RFCs for email are RFC 821 and RFC 822, which deal with how email messages are transferred between systems, and how email messages should appear.

These documents were put into effect more than 20 years ago. They were updated in April 2001 with the proposed standards RFC 2821 and RFC 2822, although you will still see many references to the original documents. RFC documents are maintained by the Internet Engineering Task Force, whose site is available at *http://www.ietf.org/*.

Email Agents

Chapter 1 introduced several of the email agents involved in message composition to final delivery. For convenience, Table 2-1 contains a summary of these agents.

Table 2-1. Email agents

Agent	Name	Purpose
MUA	Mail User Agent	Email client software used to compose, send, and retrieve email messages. Sends messages through an MTA. Retrieves messages from a mail store either directly or through a POP/IMAP server.
MTA	Mail Transfer Agent	Server that receives and delivers email. Determines message routing and possible address rewriting. Locally delivered messages are handed off to an MDA for final delivery.
MDA	Mail Delivery Agent	Program that handles final delivery of messages for a system's local recipients. MDAs can often filter or categorize messages upon delivery. An MDA might also determine that a message must be forwarded to another email address.

The Postmaster

An email administrator is commonly referred to as a *postmaster*. An individual with postmaster responsibilities makes sure that the mail system is working correctly, makes configuration changes, and adds/removes email accounts, among other things. You must have a *postmaster* alias at all domains for which you handle email that directs messages to the correct person or persons. RFC 2142 specifies that a *postmaster* address is required.

Reject or Bounce

If a receiving MTA determines during the SMTP conversation (see "The SMTP Protocol" later in the chapter) that it will not accept the message, it *rejects* the message. At that point the sending system should generate an error report to deliver to the original sender. Sometimes the MTA accepts a message and later discovers that it cannot be delivered—perhaps the intended recipient doesn't exist or there is a problem in the final delivery. In this case, the MTA that has accepted the message *bounces* it back to the original sender by sending an error report, usually including the reason the original message could not be delivered.

The MTA that accepts a message takes responsibility for the message until it is delivered or handed off to another MTA. When a system is responsible for a message and cannot deliver or relay it, the responsible system informs the sender that the mail is undeliverable.

Envelope Addresses and Message Headers

A common source of confusion for email users is the fact that the To: address in email message headers has nothing to do with where a message is actually delivered. The envelope address controls message delivery. In practice, when you compose a message and provide your MUA with a To: address, your MUA uses that same address as the envelope destination address, but this is not required nor is it always the case. From the MTA's point of view, message headers are part of the content of an email message. The delivery of a message is determined by the addresses specified during the SMTP conversation. These addresses are the *envelope addresses*, and they are the only thing that determine where messages go. See "The SMTP Protocol" later in the chapter for an explanation of the SMTP protocol.

Mailing lists and spam are common examples of when the envelope destination address differs from the To: address of the message headers. For more information, see RFC 2821 and RFC 2822. Also see "Email Message Format" later in the chapter for more information about the format of email messages. If you follow the SMTP session in Example 2-2, try substituting any address you want in the To: field of the message contents to see that it has no effect on where the message is delivered.

Local Parts of Email Addresses

RFC 2822 describes the format of email addresses in great detail. It specifies how things such as quoting and comments should work in email addresses. If we ignore the more obscure details, a simple email address is generally composed of three parts: the *local part* (which is usually a username), the @ separator, and the *domain name*. The local part might also be an alias to another address or to a mailing list. The local part is sometimes referred to as the lefthand side (LHS), and the domain is sometimes called the righthand side (RHS). For more information, see RFC 2822.

Email Message Format

Since RFC 822 was the document that originally described how Internet email messages should be formatted, messages are commonly referred to as "in the RFC 822 format" or as an "RFC 822 message." You should understand the basics of the format since it is referred to in this book and you will likely see it elsewhere. I'll use the newer proposed standard and refer to "RFC 2822 messages."

RFC 2822 messages

RFC 2822 specifies the format of both email messages and email addresses as they appear in message headers (but not envelope addresses). The specification describes the format for transmission, but many implementations use the same or a similar format to store messages. A message is comprised of two parts: the *header* and the *body*. The header contains specific fields with names such as To, From, or Subject followed by a colon (:). After the colon comes the contents of the field. One message header field can span multiple lines. Lines that continue a field start with whitespace characters (space or tab characters) to show that they are continuations of the previous line.

The standard document provides a lot of detail about the header fields and what they should be used for. There are rules about how fields relate to each other and when one or another must be used, but in the simplest case, the only required fields are the Date: and the From: fields. The standard also provides for customized fields that a particular email implementation might want to create for its own use.

The header fields are separated from the message body by an empty line. The body of a message contains the contents of the message itself. The body is purposely free-form, but should contain only ASCII characters. Some defined headers have a pre-scribed structure that is more restricted than the body. Binary files, such as images or executables, must be converted in some way to ASCII characters, so they can be sent in compliance with the standard. Other standards such as MIME encoding or traditional uuencoding deal with converting such files for mailing. Example 2-1 shows a typical message with headers and body.

Example 2-1. Email message format

```
Return-Path: <info@oreilly.com>
Delivered-To: kdent@mail.example.com
Received: from mail.oreilly.com (mail.oreilly.com [192.168.145.34])
        by mail.example.com (Postfix) with SMTP id 5FA26B3DFE
        for <kdent@example.com>;
        Mon, 8 Apr 2003 16:40:29 -0400 (EDT)
Date: Mon, 8 Apr 2003 15:38:21 -0500
From: Customer Service <info@oreilly.com>
To: <kdent@example.com>
Reply-To: <info@oreilly.com>
Message-ID: <01a4e2238200842@mail.oreilly.com>
Subject: Have you read RFC 2822?

This is the start of the body of the message. It could continue
for many lines, but it doesn't.
```

The fields in the example are mostly self-explanatory. The Received: header is not required by RFC 2822, but every MTA that handles a message normally prepends a Received: header to the message, as discussed in RFC 2821, which is described in the following section.

The SMTP Protocol

The SMTP protocol is defined in RFC 2821. The protocol is actually quite simple to follow, and was designed to be easily comprehensible both to humans and computers. A client connects to an SMTP server, whereupon the server begins the SMTP conversation, which consists of a series of simple commands and replies, including the transmission of the email message. The best way to understand the protocol is to see it in action. You can easily try it yourself once you have your mail server set up. Using a Telnet client, you can pose as a delivering MTA. Example 2-2 shows the steps and the basic commands to deliver a message.

Example 2-2. Email message delivery

```
$ telnet mail.example.com 25
Trying 10.232.45.151
Connected to mail.example.com.
Escape character is '^]'.
220 mail.example.com ESMTP Postfix
HELO mail.oreilly.com
250 mail.oreilly.com
MAIL FROM:<info@oreilly.com>
250 Ok
RCPT TO:<kdent@example.com>
250 Ok
DATA
354 End data with <CR><LF>.<CR><LF>

Date: Mon, 8 Apr 2003 15:38:21 -0500
From: Customer Service <info@oreilly.com>
To: <kdent@example.com>
Reply-To: <service@oreilly.com>
Message-ID: <01a4e2238200842@mail.oreilly.com>
Subject: Have you read RFC 2822?

This is the start of the body of the message. It could continue
for many lines, but it doesn't.
.
250 Ok: queued as 5FA26B3DFE
quit
221 Bye
Connection closed by foreign host.
$
```

The SMTP session depicted in Example 2-2 is actually the delivery that produced the sample message in Example 2-1. To follow the example yourself, start by using a Telnet client to connect to the mail server on port 25 at *mail.example.com*. You should connect to your own Postfix server and type in your own email addresses for the envelope addresses. Port 25 is the well-known port for SMTP servers. After the Telnet messages:

```
Trying 10.232.45.151
Connected to localhost.
Escape character is '^]'.
```

the server greets you with its banner:

```
220 mail.example.com ESMTP Postfix
```

SMTP server replies, such as the greeting message, always start with a three-digit response code, usually followed by a short message for human consumption. Table 2-2 provides the reply code levels and their meanings. The first digit of the response code is enough to know the status of the requested command. In documentation the response codes are often written as 2xx to indicate a level 200 reply.

Table 2-2. SMTP response codes

Code level	Status
2xx	The requested action was successful. The client may continue to the next step.
3xx	Command was accepted, but the server expects additional information. The client should send another command with the additional information.
4xx	The command was not successful, but the problem is temporary. The client should retry the action at a later time.
5xx	The command was not successful, and the problem is considered permanent. The client should not retry the action.

After receiving the welcome banner, introduce yourself with the HELO command. The hostname after the HELO command should be the name of the system you're connecting from:

    HELO mail.oreilly.com

The server replies with a success. So you may continue:

    250 mail.oreilly.com

Indicate who the message is from with the MAIL FROM command:

    MAIL FROM:<info@oreilly.com>

The server accepts the sending address:

    250 Ok

Indicate who the message is to with the RCPT TO command:

    RCPT TO:<kdent@example.com>

The server accepts the recipient address:

    250 Ok

Now you are ready to send the content of the message. The DATA command tells the server that you have an RFC 2822 message ready to transfer:

    DATA

The server replies that it accepts the command and is expecting you to begin sending data:

    354 End data with <CR><LF>.<CR><LF>

At this point, you can transfer the entire contents of your message. The contents of messages start with the message headers. When the message itself is finished, indicate the end by sending a single period on a line by itself.

The server acknowledges the end of your message and replies that the transfer was successfully completed:

```
250 Ok: queued as 5FA26B3DFE
```

At this point the server has taken responsibility for the message. If you wanted to continue with more commands, you could do so now. Since you have no other messages to deliver to this server, you can start to disconnect with the quit command:

```
quit
```

The server replies with a success and disconnects:

```
221 Bye
```

Finally, the Telnet client tells you that the connection has ended returns to the command prompt:

```
Connection closed by foreign host.
$
```

This was, of course, the simplest example of an SMTP transaction. The basic protocol provides additional commands and has been extended to allow for many enhancements. RFC 1869 provides a framework for adding additional features to the basic SMTP protocol. The enhanced protocol is referred to as ESMTP. A client indicates its willingness to use the enhanced protocol by beginning with the EHLO command instead of HELO. If the server also supports enhancements, it replies with a list of the features it provides.

Many enhancements have been specified in various RFCs. You can learn about them by searching for SMTP information on the IETF web site (*http://www.ietf.org/*). There are many other resources available on the Web regarding the SMTP and ESMTP protocols.

## CHAPTER 3

Postfix Architecture

You can easily manage and operate Postfix without understanding everything about how it works. If you're ready to dive right in, you can skip this section and start at the beginning of the next chapter. It might be difficult to digest all of the material here if you don't have much experience with Postfix yet, but this chapter will give you an overview of the various pieces, which might come in handy as you start to work with Postfix. Later, after you have more experience with Postfix, you might want to return to this chapter to try to absorb more of the details.

Postfix Components

The architecture of Postfix is quite different from that of a monolithic system such as Sendmail, which traditionally uses a single large program for its handling of email messages. Postfix breaks down tasks into separate functions using individual programs that each perform one specific task. Most of these programs are daemons, which are processes that run in the background on your system. The master daemon is started first, and it invokes most other processes, as needed. Postfix daemons that are invoked by the master daemon process their assigned tasks and terminate. They might also terminate after a configured amount of time or after handling a maximum number of requests. The master daemon is resident at all times, and gets its configuration information at startup from both *main.cf* and *master.cf*. See Chapter 4 for more information on Postfix configuration files.

Figure 3-1 depicts a high-level picture of the Postfix architecture. Broadly speaking, Postfix receives messages, queues them, and finally delivers them. Each stage of processing is handled by a distinct set of Postfix components. After a message is received and placed into the queue, the queue manager invokes the appropriate delivery agent for the final disposition of the message. The next few sections in this chapter discuss the details of each of the stages.

Figure 3-1. Broad view of the Postfix architecture

How Messages Enter the Postfix System

Messages come into Postfix in one of four ways:

1. A message can be accepted into Postfix locally (sent from a user on the same machine).

2. A message can be accepted into Postfix over the network.

3. A message that was already accepted into Postfix through one of the other methods is resubmitted for forwarding to another address.

4. Postfix generates messages itself when it has to send notifications of undeliverable or deferred delivery attempts.

There is always the possibility that a message is rejected before it enters the Postfix system, or that some messages are deferred for later delivery.

Local Email Submission

The various Postfix components work together by writing messages to and reading messages from the queue. The queue manager has the responsibility of managing messages in the queue and alerting the correct component when it has a job to do.

Figure 3-2 illustrates the flow when a local email message enters the Postfix system. Local messages are deposited into the *maildrop* directory of the Postfix queue by the postdrop command, usually through the sendmail compatibility program. The pickup daemon reads the message from the queue and feeds it to the cleanup daemon. Some messages arrive without all of the required information for a valid email message. So in addition to sanity checks on the message, the cleanup daemon, in conjunction with the trivial-rewrite daemon inserts missing message headers, converts addresses to the user@domain.tld format expected by other Postfix programs, and possibly translates addresses based on the canonical or virtual lookup tables (see Chapter 4 for more information on lookup tables).

The cleanup daemon processes all inbound mail and notifies the queue manager after it has placed the cleaned-up message into the incoming queue. The queue manager then invokes the appropriate delivery agent to send the message to its next hop or ultimate destination.

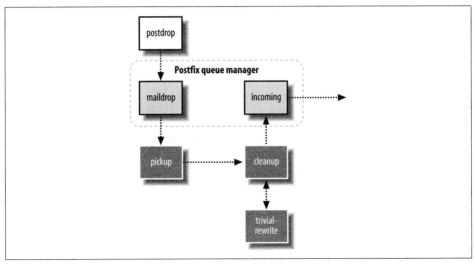

Figure 3-2. Local email submission

Email from the Network

Figure 3-3 illustrates the flow when a network email message enters the Postfix system. Messages received over the network are accepted by the Postfix smtpd daemon. This daemon performs sanity checking and can be configured to allow clients to relay mail on the system or deny them from doing so. The smtpd daemon passes the message to the cleanup daemon, which performs its own checks then deposits the message into the incoming queue. The queue manager then invokes the appropriate delivery agent to send the message to its next hop or ultimate destination.

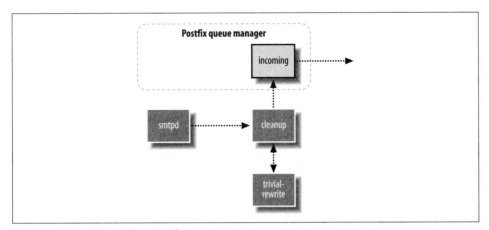

Figure 3-3. Email from the network

Postfix Email Notifications

When a user message is deferred or can't be delivered, Postfix uses the defer or bounce daemons to create a new error message. The error message is handed off to the cleanup daemon. It performs its normal checks before depositing the error message into the incoming queue, where it is picked up by the queue manager.

Email Forwarding

Sometimes, after processing an email message, Postfix determines that the destination address actually points to another address on another system. It could, at that point, simply hand off the message to the SMTP client for immediate delivery, but to make sure that every recipient is processed and logged correctly, Postfix resubmits it as a new message where it is handled like any other locally submitted message.

The Postfix Queue

The Postfix queue manager does the bulk of the work in processing email. Postfix components that accept mail have the ultimate goal of getting the email message to the queue manager. This is done through the cleanup daemon, which notifies the queue manager when it has placed a new message into the incoming mail queue. Once the queue manager has a new message, it uses trivial-rewrite to determine the routing information: the transport method to use, the next host for delivery, and the recipient's address.

The queue manager maintains four different queues: incoming, active, deferred, and corrupt. After the initial cleanup steps, the incoming queue is the first stop for new messages. Assuming system resources are available, the queue manager then moves the message into the active queue, and calls on one of the delivery agents to deliver it. Messages that cannot be delivered are moved into the deferred queue.

The queue manager also has the responsibility of working with the bounce and defer daemons to generate delivery status reports for problem messages to be sent back to the sender, or possibly the system administrator, or both. In addition to the message queue directories, the Postfix spool directory contains *bounce* and *defer* directories. These directories contain status information about why a particular message is delayed or undeliverable. The bounce and defer daemons use the information stored in these directories to generate their notifications. See Chapter 5 for more detailed information on how the queue manager works.

Mail Delivery

Postfix uses the concept of address *classes* when determining which destinations to accept for delivery and how the delivery takes place. The main address classes are *local*, *virtual alias*, *virtual mailbox*, and *relay*. Destination addresses that do not fall into one of these classes are delivered over the network by the SMTP client (assuming it was received by an authorized client). Depending on the address class, the queue manager calls the appropriate delivery agent to handle the message.

Local Delivery

The local delivery agent handles mail for users with a shell account on the system where Postfix is running. Domain names for local delivery are listed in the mydestination parameter. Messages sent to a user at any of the mydestination domains are delivered to the individual shell account for the user. In the simple case, the local delivery agent deposits an email message into the local message store. It also checks aliases and users' .forward files to see if local messages should be delivered elsewhere. See Chapter 7 for more information on local delivery.

When a message is to be forwarded elsewhere, it is resubmitted to Postfix for delivery to the new address. If there are temporary problems delivering the message, the delivery agent notifies the queue manager to mark the message for a future delivery attempt and store it in the deferred queue. Permanent problems cause the queue manager to bounce the message back to the original sender.

Virtual Alias Messages

Virtual alias addresses are all forwarded to other addresses. Domain names for virtual aliasing are listed in the virtual_alias_domains parameter. Every domain has its own set of users that do not have to be unique across domains. Users and their real addresses are listed in lookup tables specified in the virtual_alias_maps parameter. Messages received for virtual alias addresses are resubmitted for delivery to the real address. See Chapter 8 for more information on virtual aliases.

Virtual Mailbox Messages

The virtual delivery agent handles mail for virtual mailbox addresses. These mailboxes are not associated with particular shell accounts on the system. Domain names for virtual mailboxes are listed in the virtual_mailbox_domains parameter. Every domain has its own set of users that do not have to be unique across domains. Users and their mailbox files are listed in lookup tables specified in the virtual_mailbox_maps parameter. See Chapter 8 for more information on virtual mailboxes.

Relay Messages

The smtp delivery agent handles mail for relay domains. Email addresses in relay domains are hosted on other systems, but Postfix accepts messages for the domains and relays them to the correct system. Relay configurations are common when Postfix accepts mail over the Internet and passes it to systems on an internal network.

Domain names for relay domains are listed in the relay_domains parameter. See Chapter 9 for more information on relaying.

Other Messages

Messages that do not fit into one of the address classes are generally destined for other domains hosted elsewhere on the network. Postfix accepts such messages only from authorized clients, such as systems that run on the same local network. When a message has to be delivered across the network, the queue manager calls the smtp delivery agent. The smtp agent determines which host or hosts can receive the message and makes a connection to each in turn until it finds one to accept it. If there are temporary problems delivering the message, the smtp delivery agent notifies the queue manager to mark the message for a future delivery attempt and store it in the deferred queue. Permanent problems cause the queue manager to bounce the message back to the original sender.

When a destination system that has been unavailable comes back online, Postfix is careful not to overwhelm it with all its pending messages. Whether delivering previously deferred messages or new messages, Postfix, at first, makes only a limited (configurable) number of connections to a receiving system. After Postfix has detected successful deliveries to a particular site, it slowly increases (up to a configurable limit) simultaneous connections to it. If Postfix detects any trouble from the receiving site, it starts to back off deliveries immediately.

Other Delivery Agents

There are other Postfix delivery agents that can be configured to handle messages for a particular class or destination. Other delivery agents must be configured in the *master.cf* file. They are invoked either through the *class*_transport parameter or through an entry in a transport table, listed in the transport_maps parameter. Two common alternate delivery agents are the lmtp and pipe agents.

Delivery via LMTP

The LMTP protocol is similar to SMTP, but it is used for deliveries between mail systems on the same network. (See Chapter 7 for more information on LMTP.) For example, if a message has to be delivered to a different software package, which might be running on the same machine or another system on the local area network, the queue manager calls the lmtp delivery agent. The most common example for using LMTP is when a POP/IMAP server stores messages in a proprietary format. (Recall that POP and IMAP are protocols for users to retrieve their messages.) The POP/IMAP server, in this case, has its own proprietary format for storing messages, so Postfix uses the LMTP standard to hand off the message to the POP/IMAP server. If there are any problems delivering the message, the lmtp delivery agent notifies the queue manager to mark the message for a future delivery attempt and store it in the deferred queue.

Pipe delivery

Postfix offers the option of delivering messages to another program through the pipe daemon. The pipe daemon delivers messages to external commands. A common use for the pipe daemon is to have email delivered to an external content filter or another communications medium, such as a FAX machine. If there are any problems delivering the message, the pipe daemon notifies the queue manager to mark the message for a future delivery attempt and store it in the deferred queue.

Tracing a Message Through Postfix

Let's follow a typical message through the Postfix system. Figure 3-4, Figure 3-5, and Figure 3-6 illustrate the process as the message goes from the originating system to a destination MTA, which, in turn, forwards it to the final MTA, where it is held until the user is ready to read it. In Figure 3-4, Helene (*helene@oreilly.com*) wants to send a message to Frank (*frank@postfix.org*). Helene has an account on a system that runs Postfix. Her email client lets her compose the message, and then it calls the Postfix sendmail command to send it. The Postfix sendmail command receives the message from Helene's email software and deposits it into the *maildrop* directory. The pickup daemon then retrieves the message, performs its sanity checks, and feeds the message to the cleanup daemon, which performs the final processing on the new message. If Helene's email client did not include a From: address, or did not use a fully-qualified hostname in the address, cleanup makes the necessary fixes to the message.

Once finished, cleanup places the message into the incoming queue and notifies the queue manager that a new message is ready to be delivered. If the queue manager is ready to process new messages, it moves the message into the active queue. Because this message is destined for a user on an outside system, the queue manager has to alert the smtp agent to handle the delivery of the message.

The smtp agent uses DNS (see Chapter 6) to get a list of email systems that can accept mail for the domain *postfix.org*. The smtp delivery agent selects the most preferred MX host from the list and contacts it to deliver Helene's message.

Figure 3-5 shows Frank's email server at *postfix.org* also running Postfix, although the system could be using any other standards-compliant MTA. The Postfix smtpd on Frank's server takes the message from Helene's smtp delivery agent. After the smtpd daemon verifies that it should, in fact, accept this message, it passes the message through to the cleanup daemon, which performs its checks before depositing the message into the incoming queue.

The queue manager moves the message to the active queue, performs its processing, and determines that it should call on the local agent to make the final delivery of the message. The local delivery agent finds that *frank* is an alias and resubmits the message through the cleanup daemon for delivery to the new address.

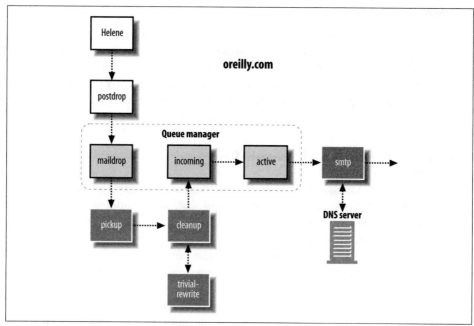

Figure 3-4. Tracing message delivery 1

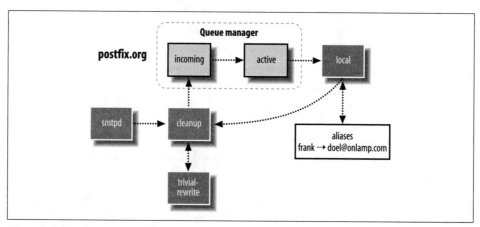

Figure 3-5. Tracing message delivery 2

Both cleanup and the queue manager call upon the trivial-rewrite daemon when processing messages. trivial-rewrite helps with converting email addresses to a standard format and determining the transport type and next hop for delivery.

When a new message has to be delivered to another network, the queue manager calls on smtp, which checks the DNS for mail servers that can accept mail for the domain *onlamp.com*. In Figure 3-6, the MTA at the *onlamp.com* system (once again by a happy coincidence, it's a Postfix system) eventually hands the message to the local delivery agent, which deposits it into the message store on that system. At this point Postfix has finished its job. Frank can now read the message using his own email client, which might pull it directly from the local message store or might use another protocol, such as POP or IMAP, to get the message for him to read.

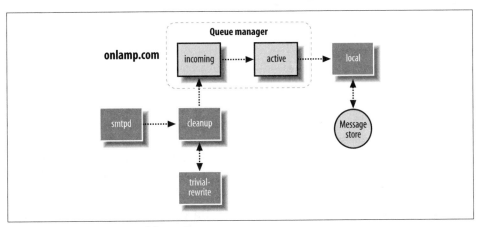

Figure 3-6. Tracing message delivery 3

There are several variations that might have occurred in our simple example. Perhaps the message could not be delivered at any step for some temporary reason, in which case the delivery agent alerts the queue manager, which places the message into the deferred queue and attempts another delivery at a later time. Another possibility is that *doel* is not an actual account on the system but an account in an IMAP email system. In this case, the queue manager might deliver the message through the lmtp agent or via a specialized command configured through the pipe delivery agent.

There are many variations and potential complications for Postfix to deal with. Fortunately, the architecture is robust enough to deal with nearly all situations, and flexible enough to easily accommodate changes in the future.

CHAPTER 4

General Configuration
and Administration

One of the truly remarkable things about Postfix is that, in many cases, it works as soon as you install it, with little or no change to its configuration. In the first section of this chapter, we'll walk through checking the configuration and starting Postfix for the first time. Later sections discuss Postfix configuration details.

By default, Postfix is configured as a traditional Unix mail server, sending and receiving messages for all the accounts on the system. Your users can send and receive messages using any email client software available on your system.

In most environments, Postfix works in conjunction with a variety of other software systems. You should build each piece of your email system and test each one as a separate module before trying to integrate them all together. As you add each module, test the system before moving on to the next piece.

At this point you should have Postfix installed on your system. You might install Postfix from a packaged bundle for your platform or compile it yourself. See Appendix C for help with compiling Postfix, if you're building it yourself. Check your normal software sources for any Postfix packages that might be available. If you haven't yet installed Postfix, either get a package for your system or follow the instructions in Appendix C to build it. When you have finished with the installation, come back to this chapter for the final configuration.

I will assume, in examples throughout the book, that your installation of Postfix uses the default directories:

/etc/postfix
    Configuration files and lookup tables

/usr/libexec/postfix
    Postfix daemons

/var/spool/postfix
    Queue files

/usr/sbin
    Postfix commands

I will also assume that you or your installer created a *postfix* user and *postdrop* group. This user and group should not be used for any other purpose on your system. If you have changed any of the defaults, or if your Postfix package did, keep that in mind when you read the examples presented in the book.

Starting Postfix the First Time

There are two important issues to deal with before starting Postfix for the first time. The first is how your system identifies itself. Postfix uses a configuration parameter called myhostname, which must be set to the fully qualified hostname of the system Postfix is running on. Once Postfix knows the fully qualified hostname, it can use that hostname to set default values for other important parameters, such as mydomain. If the parameter myhostname is not set, Postfix defaults to the hostname reported by the system itself. There is a complete discussion of myhostname later in the chapter. You can see what name your system reports with the Unix hostname command:

```
$ hostname
mail.example.com
```

A fully qualified hostname is comprised of both the individual hostname and the domain in which it resides. Some systems are configured with their simple hostname, rather than its fully qualified version:

```
$ hostname
mail
```

If your system is configured with just its simple hostname, Postfix cannot determine what the fully qualified name is. You must therefore explicitly set the myhostname parameter. You can do this quite easily with the postconf Postfix command. The postconf command is a Postfix utility that provides an easy way to get a variety of information about your Postfix system. One of its functions is to display or change a specific configuration parameter. You can use it to set the myhostname parameter:

```
# postconf -e myhostname=mail.example.com
```

The -e option tells postconf to edit the configuration with the parameters and values specified. If your system is configured with its fully qualified hostname, you don't have to do anything to the Postfix configuration.

The second important issue before starting Postfix for the first time is to make sure that your system's *aliases* database is in the correct format. There are certain required aliases that you should configure when operating your mail server in a production environment. We'll discuss the *aliases* file later in this chapter. For now, be aware that it is a text file that must be mapped into an indexed, binary format. Your existing *aliases* binary format might be different from what Postfix uses by default on your system. You can rebuild the indexed file with the newaliases command:

```
# newaliases
```

This command doesn't require any arguments, and it simply recreates your alias database without making any changes to your actual alias file.

Having accomplished these two critical items, you are now ready to start Postfix. Execute the following command:

```
# postfix start
```

If Postfix encounters any problems at start up, it reports them to your terminal. After some initial setup, Postfix detaches from the terminal and can no longer report problems to the screen. It will, however, continue to send a lot of information to your system log. Whenever you start or reload Postfix, be sure to check your system's log to make sure that there are no reported errors or warnings. See "Logging" later in this chapter for information on Postfix logging and how to find the log file it uses.

Under most circumstances, Postfix will start without any problems, and you should now be the proud administrator of a currently running, fully functional Postfix system. See Chapter 7 for information about configuring Postfix to work with a POP/IMAP server, so that your users do not need shell access to your mail system. You should also review Chapter 6 for important information on DNS and email.

To read about stopping and restarting Postfix, see "Starting, Stopping, and Reloading Postfix" later in this chapter. The rest of this chapter discusses Postfix configuration and administration.

Configuration Files

The directory */etc/postfix* contains Postfix configuration files. The two most important files used in the configuration of Postfix are *master.cf* and *main.cf*. These files should be owned by, and only writable by, the root user. They should be readable by everyone. Whenever you make changes to these files, you have to reload Postfix for your changes to go into effect:*

```
# postfix reload
```

The master daemon is the overall process that controls other Postfix daemons for mail handling. The master daemon uses the *master.cf* file for its configuration information. The *master.cf* file contains a line for each Postfix service or transport. Each line has columns that specify how each program should run as part of the overall Postfix system. See Chapter 3 for information on Postfix's architecture and how various components interact with each other. In many installations, you will never have to change the default *master.cf* file. See "master.cf" later in the chapter for information on when and how to make changes to *master.cf*.

---

* If you change the inet_interfaces parameter, you must stop and start Postfix.

The main.cf Configuration File

The *main.cf* file is the core of your Postfix configuration. Nearly all configuration changes occur in this file. The default *main.cf* file lists only a portion of the nearly 300 Postfix parameters. Most Postfix parameters do not need to be changed, but the flexibility is there when it's required. All Postfix parameters are listed and described in the various sample configuration files. The sample files are located in the directory specified by the `sample_directory` parameter, which is usually the same directory as your *main.cf* file. Both the *main.cf* file and the sample files that come with the Postfix distribution contain comments that explain each of the parameters.

 Throughout this book, when the text says to modify a parameter, it always refers to a parameter in your *main.cf* unless a different file is indicated.

You can edit *main.cf* with the `postconf` command, as you saw earlier in the chapter, or you can change the file directly with any text editor[*] (such as vi or emacs). The file contains blank lines, comment lines, and lines that assign values to parameters. Comment lines start with the # character and continue to the end of the line. Blank and comment lines are ignored by Postfix. Parameters can appear in any order within the file, and are written as you would expect:

```
parameter = value
```

A parameter definition must start in the first column of the line. The spaces around the equals sign are optional.

Here is an example parameter assignment with a comment:

```
# The myhostname value must be a fully qualified hostname.
myhostname = mail.example.com

# The rest of the file continues below...
```

You cannot have a comment on the same line as a parameter. The following example is incorrect and, with some parameters, could cause unexpected behavior that might be difficult to track down:

```
#
# This is a bad parameter assignment. Never do this.
#
myhostname = mail.example.com   # must be fully qualified hostname
```

Do not use quotation marks around values. They have no significance in the Postfix configuration, so they would be considered part of the value, which is probably not what you want.

---

[*] Postfix expects configuration files to contain normal Unix-style line endings. If you edit your configuration files from another platform, such as Windows or Mac, make sure that your editor uses the correct line endings for Unix.

Line continuation

A line that starts with whitespace (tabs or spaces) is considered a continuation of the previous line. This allows you to continue long parameter values onto multiple lines. The parameter assignment:

```
mydestination = example.com oreilly.com ora.com postfix.org
```

is the same as:

```
mydestination = example.com
    oreilly.com
    ora.com
    postfix.org
```

Configuration variables

You can refer to the value of a defined parameter by putting a $ in front of the parameter name:

```
mydomain = example.com
myorigin = $mydomain
```

This causes the value of myorigin to be "example.com."

You can reference a value in the file even before it has been set. The following example works as well as the previous one:

```
myorigin = $mydomain
mydomain = example.com
```

Multiple values

Many parameters can have more than one value. Multiple values can be separated by commas, spaces, tabs, or new lines. Remember that when you separate values with new lines there must be spaces or tabs in front of the values to indicate a continuation of the previous line:

```
mydestination = $mydomain, example.com, oreilly.com
mydestination = $mydomain example.com oreilly.com
mydestination = $mydomain
        example.com
        oreilly.com
```

These three assignments to mydestination are effectively the same.

Certain parameters allow you to place multiple values in a text file and then point the parameter to that file in *main.cf*. A value that starts with a forward slash is assumed to be a pointer to a file. If your system receives mail locally for many destinations, you may want to keep the list of destinations in a separate file. Then point the mydestination parameter to that file:

```
mydestination = /etc/postfix/destinations
```

The parameters that can use external files to store values are those that accept lists where the order of the listed items is not significant, such as `mynetworks`, `mydestination`, and `relay_domains`. Check the documentation for a particular parameter to see if it supports this feature.

If you have thousands of items in a list, it can be more efficient to keep them in a lookup table instead. Lookup tables are described in the next section.

Whenever you make a change to *main.cf*, you must reload Postfix for your changes to go into effect:

```
# postfix reload
```

See "Starting, Stopping, and Reloading Postfix" later in the chapter for more information about stopping and starting Postfix.

Lookup Tables

Rather than using complicated rewriting or pattern transformation rules as Sendmail does, Postfix makes use of simple, yet flexible, lookup tables. Many parameters point to lookup tables to obtain important configuration information. One such parameter is `canonical_maps`. It's used to rewrite email addresses in messages. Consider a site that uses account names internally for email addresses, but wants any publicly visible addresses to have the form *firstname.lastname@example.com*. For example, the address *kdent@example.com* should appear as *kyle.dent@example.com*. A `canonical_maps` lookup table provides the mapping from a *key* (*kdent@example.com*) to a *value* (*kyle.dent@example.com*).

There are many parameters that use lookup maps, but they all work on the same principle. An email message (or client) provides some kind of key used to look up a value. Based on the value, Postfix takes some action or makes some change.

Lookup table format

Postfix lookup tables are usually Unix database files, which are specially indexed files that provide faster access to the stored items. Lookup tables start as simple text files, with each key and value on the same line separated by spaces or tabs:

```
#
# canonical mappings
#
kdent@example.com       kyle.dent@example.com
```

Each entry has a unique key. The keys are often referred to as the LHS, or lefthand side of an entry, and the values are referred to as the RHS, or righthand side of an entry. Keys in lookup tables are not case-sensitive. The files can contain comment and blank lines just like *main.cf*, and line continuation works by putting whitespace at the beginning of carry-over lines. Lookup tables also do not treat quotation marks with any special significance.

Once you have created a text file with all of your mappings, you have to execute the `postmap` command against it to create the actual indexed version of the file:

```
# postmap /etc/postfix/canonical
```

Whenever you change your text file you must execute `postmap` against it.

The `postmap` command can also be used to query lookup tables. Use the `-q` option to query a value:

```
# postmap -q kdent@example.com /etc/postfix/canonical
kyle.dent@example.com
```

Database formats

Different types of Unix database files have different internal formats. The format you use depends on the database libraries available on your system. Normally Postfix supports one or more of three types: `btree`, `dbm`, and `hash`. Depending on your system libraries, you may have fewer or more than these three types available. It's important to know which map type you use. The `postconf` command with the `-m` option lists all of the map types supported by your installation of Postfix:

```
$ postconf -m
static
pcre
nis
regexp
environ
proxy
btree
unix
hash
```

The output of this command lists all map types, some of which are used for access to other kinds of storage. But you should find at least one of the three database types (`btree`, `dbm`, and `hash`).

The `default_database_type` parameter tells you which database type Postfix uses by default:

```
$ postconf default_database_type
default_database_type = hash
```

 All of the examples in this book use the `hash` type, but if your installation is using something different, be aware of that as you follow the examples.

If you don't specify a database type with `postmap`, it automatically uses your default type. In general, you can just use the default type configured on your system, but you must know what it is when assigning lookup tables to mapping parameters.

When you assign a lookup table to a parameter, you must specify both the map type and the path to the lookup table. The format of lookup maps is:

```
parameter = type:name
```

where *type* is the storage access method and *name* is the resource containing keys and values. With indexed datafile lookups, *name* is the filename. The canonical example is assigned as follows:

```
canonical_maps = hash:/etc/postfix/canonical
```

You can assign multiple lookup tables to a parameter. Postfix searches the tables in the order listed, stopping as soon as it finds a match. Some table lookups are recursive, depending on the parameter. The canonical_maps parameter in these examples is one such parameter. With recursive lookups, once a value is found, Postfix tries to match it against all of the keys again until a key matches itself or is not found.

You may have noticed that when postmap indexes files, it creates additional files. postmap creates either one additional file with the extension *.db*, or two additional files with the extensions *.dir* and *.pag*, depending on your database format. When you assign the lookup table to its parameter, specify the path and filename without any extensions.

Search order

Since keys are often email addresses, Postfix automatically parses addresses, breaking them up into their parts. You can have keys that match a full address, just the domain portion, or just the local part. The way Postfix searches for addresses or portions of addresses depends on the type of mapping parameter. Certain maps might sensibly include the simple local part of an address, such as canonical_maps. Others would not expect a local part key, such as transport_maps. The order in which Postfix searches for a match differs slightly, depending on which type of parameter it's working with. Check the lookup table's manpage to see which search order it follows.

The search order where local parts are expected, such as with canonical_maps, relocated_maps, and virtual_alias_maps, is as follows:

1. The complete address. Example: *kdent@example.com*

2. The local part alone. Example: *kdent*

3. The domain portion only, specified with the @ character. Example: *@example.com*

For lookup tables where it doesn't make sense to have a local part, such as with transport_maps, Postfix searches for matches in the following order:

1. The complete address. Example: *kdent@example.com*

2. The domain by itself. Example: example.com

3. The domain specified with an initial period, which matches any subdomain. Example: .example.com

If you always want domains to match themselves plus any subdomain, you can simplify your lookup tables somewhat by setting the parent_domain_matches_subdomains parameter. The parameter, by default, contains many lists. To add transport_maps to the list, append it as follows:

```
parent_domain_matches_subdomains =
    debug_peer_list
    fast_flush_domains
    mynetworks
    permit_mx_backup_networks
    qmqpd_authorized_clients
    relay_domains
    smtpd_access_maps
    transport_maps
transport_maps = hash:/etc/postfix/transport
```

Now, a domain entry in the */etc/postfix/transport* matches itself and all of its subdomains automatically. You no longer need any entries such as the third item, .example.com, from the preceding list.

Lookup tables and simple lists

Some parameters that normally take a simple list, such as mydestination, can also be specified with a lookup table. The LHS keys are the items in the list. You still have to provide a RHS value for each key, but the value is simply ignored. You can specify any text you want. It's a good place to provide yourself a comment. Using a lookup table for a straight list is useful when you have thousands of items; otherwise, a simple text file is more than adequate and probably has better performance. If you use a lookup table for lists of network IP addresses, you cannot use the network/netmask notation to specify an entire subnet. You must list each address individually. Check the documentation to see if a list parameter supports the lookup table feature.

Regular expression tables

Postfix provides a special lookup table type using *regular expressions* that offers even more flexibility for matching keys in lookup tables. Regular expressions are used in many Unix utilities. They provide a powerful tool for specifying matching patterns. There are two types of regular expression libraries that you might use with Postfix, depending on which libraries are available on your system.

By default, Postfix uses POSIX extended regular expressions, which I'll refer to as *regexp*. POSIX, which stands for Portable Operating System Interface, is a standard that encourages portability across different operating systems. It includes specifications for regular expressions. Postfix also supports Perl-compatible regular expressions, which I'll refer to as *pcre*. If you're used to regular expressions in Perl, you'll find that regexp patterns are a bit different. If you want pcre support, be sure you have a pcre library to link with when building Postfix. With the pcre format, some features differ from regexp, and the performance is usually better. It's possible that your Postfix distribution already includes pcre support. You can check by executing the postconf command with the -m option, as you did earlier in the chapter.

If pcre is listed among your map types, then you can use Perl-style regular expressions for your regular expression lookup tables. But don't rush to add pcre support if you don't have it; the default regexp is quite powerful and usually adequate for administrators who need regular expressions. Install pcre only if you know of particular Perl-style regular expression features you need.

Both Perl-style and POSIX regular expressions are very well-documented in many places. Any book on Perl should include information on its regular expressions, and if you have Perl installed on your system, you should find a manpage called perlre(1). Documentation for regexp usually appears in a manpage called re_format(7). If your system does not include the manpage, you should be able to find it on the Web. *sed & awk* by Dale Dougherty and Arnold Robbins (O'Reilly) contains information on POSIX regular expressions.

To use regular expression tables, specify either regexp or pcre as the map type when assigning tables to map parameters:

    body_checks = regexp:/etc/postfix/re_body_checks

Entries in re_body_checks are conventionally specified—with the regular expression pattern between two forward slashes—as the key, followed by whitespace, followed by the mapped value:

    /pattern/   value

The most common use of regular expression tables is with the header_checks and body_checks parameters for blocking spam. See Chapter 11 for more information.

Other Formats

Postfix can make use of other backend systems for its lookup tables. (Later chapters discuss using MySQL and LDAP lookup tables.) When you make use of these external sources for lookup values, you should start with one of the simple database formats, such as dbm or hash. Make sure your configuration works as expected. After setting up your external data source, verify that it returns the same results as your simple tables.

The postmap with the -q option is an important tool for testing any kind of lookup table. For example, the following two commands should return the same values when you test your MySQL database:

    $ postmap -q hash:/etc/postfix/transport

    $ postmap -q mysql:/etc/postfix/transport.cf

See Chapter 15 for more information on using Postfix with external data sources.

Alias Files

Alias files are a special case of Postfix lookup tables because they use a Sendmail-compatible format. The file has traditionally been called *aliases*, and its location depends on your platform, but it is normally within the */etc* directory or a subdirectory below it. By default, Postfix is configured to point to your original *aliases* file, so if you are migrating from Sendmail, your existing aliases continue to work.

Locating aliases

Historically, email systems used a single alias database. Postfix lets you have as many as you want. Multiple alias files can help in organizing your configuration information. Typically, administrators configure multiple alias files for convenience when configuring separate mailing lists. The alias_maps parameter points to your alias files.

If your system supports NIS, which is a network database of users (including their aliases), then by default Postfix includes NIS among your alias maps. A typical default alias_maps looks like the following:

```
alias_maps = hash:/etc/aliases, nis:mail.aliases
```

If your system includes support for NIS, but you're not using it, you should change the parameter so that it points to your *aliases* file only:

```
alias_maps = hash:/etc/aliases
```

You may want to locate your *aliases* file in your Postfix configuration directory for consistency. Some administrators prefer to have all of the email configuration files located together. Simply reassign alias_maps to point to the new location:

```
alias_maps = hash:/etc/postfix/aliases
```

You should also reassign alias_database so that your newaliases command continues to work correctly (see the next section):

```
alias_database = hash:/etc/postfix/aliases
```

Building alias database files

Since the format of alias maps differs from that of Postfix lookup tables, you cannot use postmap to build the alias database from your text file. Instead, Postfix provides the postalias command. Its command-line syntax is the same as that of postmap, allowing you to create or query alias maps. To build an alias database from your *aliases* file, execute the following:

```
# postalias /etc/aliases
```

Another Sendmail compatibility command related to alias files is the newaliases command. It provides a convenient way to rebuild your alias databases. The Postfix installation includes a replacement version of the command that follows the same syntax as the original. It's normally executed with no arguments and determines which alias files to rebuild from the alias_database parameter. The alias_database parameter differs from alias_maps in that it includes only standard Unix database-mapped files (those that should be indexed by newaliases), whereas alias_maps might also contain other map types such as nis. newaliases uses the default_database_type parameter discussed earlier to determine which database format to use.

Alias file format

The text file for alias databases is much like Postfix lookup tables, except for the alias definition itself. Alias files can have blank and comment lines that are ignored. Comments are marked by a # at the beginning of the line and cannot be on the same line as an alias definition. A single alias definition can be broken onto multiple lines by starting continuation lines with whitespace.

The form of an alias definition consists of the name being aliased, followed by a colon, followed by one or more targets for the aliased name. Aliases can be directed to different types of targets (discussed below). Multiple targets are separated by commas. Both aliases and targets should be quoted if they contain whitespace or any special characters such as a #, :, and @:

```
alias: target1, target2, ...
```

The LHS aliases are always local addresses, so you cannot specify a domain name with an alias key. The target is often one or more addresses, but can be any of the following:

Email addresses
> Any RFC 2822 address is allowed, meaning target addresses can be local or forwarded to another site for delivery. For example:
> ```
> kyle.dent:        kdent, kdent@oreilly.com
> ```

Filename
> Specify the full path to a file. New messages are appended to the file specified. Delivery occurs to the file as it would to any local mailbox. See Chapter 7 for information on local delivery to mailboxes and on specifying different mailbox formats. For example:
> ```
> info:   /usr/local/mail/info_box
> ```

Command
> Specify a pipe character and a command. See Chapter 14 for more information on delivery to commands. For example:
> ```
> info:   "|/usr/local/bin/autoreply"
> ```

:include:
> An included file contains a list of additional alias targets. The targets in the file can be any valid target type as described here, but by default filenames and commands are not allowed. The next section discusses configuration parameters to override these default restrictions. For example:
> ```
> info:   :include:/usr/local/mail/info_list
> ```

Normally, when Postfix makes a local delivery it assumes the identity of the recipient of the message. With aliases, Postfix uses the identity of the owner of the alias file, except when the file is owned by root. When a delivery would occur as root, Postfix uses the identity of the account configured with the default_privs parameter instead.

Alias restrictions

You can control which kinds of targets are allowed in your alias files with the parameters allow_mail_to_commands and allow_mail_to_files. Each of these parameters takes a list of the aliasing mechanism that permits its action. Aliasing mechanisms are "alias," the alias file we've been discussing; "include," the include target, and "forward," which is the *.forward* file discussed in Chapter 7.

The default setting for the two parameters is to allow delivery to commands and files from both alias and *.forward* files, but not from include files, for security considerations. If you want to disallow delivery to commands and files from your aliases database entirely, set the parameters to blank:

```
allow_mail_to_commands =
allow_mail_to_files =
```

If you would like to make delivery to commands and files available in all the alias mechanisms, set the parameters as follows:

```
allow_mail_to_commands = alias, forward, include
allow_mail_to_files = alias, forward, include
```

This setting is equivalent to the default behavior for Sendmail. However, it could expose access to possibly vulnerable mailing-list managers that might be coerced into adding a filename or command as a destination address. If you don't need the additional include option for files and commands, it's best to accept the Postfix default.

Important aliases

There are several common aliases that are configured by default. By convention, these system aliases point to the root account. You want to make sure that root's mail is read regularly. This is normally accomplished by creating an alias for root to the normal login account of the person or persons responsible for system administration.

RFC 2142 defines several mailbox names that all domains should have, depending on which services they run on the Internet. At a minimum, you should have a *postmaster* alias, and you should review the RFC to see if there are other aliases you want to create.

Important Configuration Considerations

We saw at the beginning of this chapter how Postfix requires only minimal configuration changes to work. Depending on how you plan to use your Postfix system, you may want to consider some of the more common options. This section discusses how your system identifies itself, and then covers the very important topic of relay control.

Configuring Your MTA Identity

There are four parameters dealing with your system's hostname and domain that you want to consider, no matter how you use Postfix: myhostname, mydomain, myorigin, and mydestination.

myhostname and mydomain

We discussed the purpose and importance of the myhostname parameter earlier in this chapter. If myhostname is not specified, Postfix uses the function gethostname to determine what your system's hostname is. If your system correctly reports the fully qualified hostname, you can leave myhostname unspecified in the configuration file. Some systems may not be configured correctly or may not report the fully qualified version of the hostname. In these cases, you can set either myhostname to the fully qualified hostname or mydomain to your system's domain. If mydomain is explicitly set, Postfix automatically sets myhostname to the domain name specified and the local hostname reported by gethostname to create the fully qualified hostname.

If you set myhostname to the system's fully qualified hostname but omit mydomain, Postfix uses the value of myhostname, minus the first component of the fully qualified hostname, to automatically set mydomain. A value of *mail.example.com* for myhostname causes mydomain to be *example.com* unless you explicitly set it to something else. Similarly, a hostname of *mail.ny.example.com* causes the value to be *ny.example.com*. If your system does not report its fully qualified name, and you have not set either the mydomain or myhostname parameters, Postfix reports the problem in your log file. See "Logging" later in this chapter.

myorigin

When your users send or receive mail through the Postfix system with no domain name specified in the envelope or header addresses, the parameter myorigin determines what domain name should be appended. The default is to use the value of myhostname. If Postfix is running on a system whose hostname is *mail.example.com*, messages from the user *kdent* have a From: address of *kdent@mail.example.com*. However, frequently users want their mail to be sent from the domain name without any extra host information (*kdent@example.com* instead of *kdent@mail.example.com*). If that is the case, set myorigin to $mydomain:

```
myorigin = $mydomain
```

mydestination

The mydestination parameter lists all the domains your Postfix system should accept mail for and deliver to local users. By default Postfix accepts mail destined for $myhostname and localhost.$mydomain. If you want your system to accept mail for your entire domain and not just the single host it is running on, add $mydomain to the list:

```
mydestination = $myhostname, localhost.$mydomain, $mydomain
```

Now your mail server can act as a gateway receiving all mail for the domain.

Relay Control

In addition to accepting mail and delivering messages to your local users, Postfix also relays messages to other systems. It's very important to restrict who is allowed to relay messages through your system. Systems on your own network may require the ability to send messages anywhere, but you do not want to provide the rest of the world with the same service. Relay control is an important topic in email administration because of the prevalence of Unsolicited Bulk Email (UBE), or spam. (See Chapter 11 for more information on UBE.) A common practice among spammers is to find a well-connected system that allows them to relay their mail. You want to prevent anyone who is not authorized from using your system to relay mail. If you leave yourself configured as an open relay, not only will you be contributing to the spam problem, but your own machine may become unusable as it is abused by spammers. Furthermore, you may find that other systems start refusing mail from you as they discover that your system is the source of spam. They'll refuse the spam as well as any legitimate messages your own systems send. Mail servers that permit anyone to relay mail are called *open relays*.

Restricting relay access

By default Postfix is not an open relay. The parameters mynetworks_style and mynetworks determine what other systems can use your mail server to send messages. The default configuration allows relaying only from other machines that are connected to the same IP subnet as your server. You can limit or broaden the range of addresses that should be allowed to relay by setting the parameter mynetworks_style. If you prefer to limit relaying to the local machine only, set mynetworks_style to "host". You can also set mynetworks_style to "class" to allow relaying by any host within the same class A, B, or C network as your server. For many networks a class setting opens relaying to too many systems. If you aren't familiar with IP address classes, stick to the default "subnet" or more restrictive "host" settings.

Alternatively, you can explicitly indicate the hosts that should be allowed to relay mail by setting mynetworks. If you set mynetworks, the mynetworks_style parameter is ignored. You can list individual IP addresses or specify subnets using the network/netmask notation—for example, 192.168.100.0/28. This parameter is handy if you need to provide mail relay to hosts outside of your network because you can list specific IP addresses regardless of their relationship to your own subnet. If, for example, you want to provide relaying to remote users, you simply add an IP address to your list. In this case, your remote users need a static IP address, or at least an address assigned from a limited range of addresses. If your remote users do not have static IP addresses, then you have to configure some kind of SMTP authentication.

SMTP authentication

All of the techniques for SMTP authentication introduce their own complexities. You would be wise to consider simpler options before selecting an authentication technique. Is it possible to get static IP addresses for your remote users? Can your remote users avail themselves of another SMTP server? Perhaps your users' remote access provider offers an SMTP server as well.

Your first inclination may be to use UBE controls to permit mail relaying when a message's envelope sender address is from the local domain. Don't do this. Envelope addresses are trivial to fake, and spammers know to use local addresses for this purpose. Configuring your mail server in this way makes you an open relay.

Dynamic IP solutions

Chapter 12 discusses using SASL for SMTP authentication. SASL is a general protocol that defines how a server and client can exchange authentication credentials. It requires that additional libraries be linked to your SMTP server. There are three alternatives to SASL that all work similarly: *pop-before-smtp*, *DRAC* (Dynamic Relay Authorization Control), and *WHOSON*. Each of these methods is designed to work with clients that have dynamically assigned IP addresses. They require that a user first log in to a POP/IMAP server, thereby supplying the client's currently assigned IP address to your system or network. The client IP address is fed to the SMTP server, which then permits mail relaying by the client system for some configurable time limit. This technique is mostly transparent to end users, but it does require that they first check for new messages (logging into the POP/IMAP server) before trying to send out any messages.

Both pop-before-smtp and DRAC work with Postfix by dynamically updating a Postfix lookup table, adding new addresses as users authenticate, and deleting others when the time period expires. Postfix doesn't require any special libraries or configuration. You simply configure it to check the lookup table that is updated when users log in via your POP/IMAP server. Your POP/IMAP server, on the other hand, may require changes and recompiling to work. DRAC differs from pop-before-smtp in that it can work over a network, while pop-before-smtp requires that the POP/IMAP server be installed on the same system as the SMTP server.

WHOSON is actually a protocol that provides an interface to both the POP/IMAP and SMTP servers. You have to run a WHOSON server on your network, and you must obtain a patch that adds a new lookup type to Postfix. After building Postfix with the patch, it can communicate with the WHOSON server to determine if a particular client IP address should be allowed to relay mail.

Certificate authentication

Another option to consider is client-side certificate authentication. (See Chapter 13 for a full discussion of Transport Layer Security and certificates.) We normally think of certificates as a means to encrypt communications, but they can also be used as a strong method of authentication. However, they do require management of certificates and support for the TLS protocol.

None of these add-ons is an ideal solution. They require additional code compiled into your existing daemons that may then require special write access to system files. They also require additional work for busy system administrators. If you cannot use any of the nonauthenticating alternatives mentioned earlier, or your business requirements demand that all of your users' mail pass through your system no matter where they are on the Internet, SASL is probably the solution that offers the most reliable and scalable method to authenticate users.

Administration

Running a mail server is an ongoing task. You cannot start it and forget about it. There are periodic administrative tasks, and you should regularly check for any problems your system might have. This section discusses many of those tasks and how to accomplish them with Postfix.

Postfix provides a utility through the `postfix` command to validate many aspects of your installation. The command checks for configuration problems, looks at directory and file ownership, and creates any missing directories. Executing:

```
# postfix check
```

should report no messages on a correctly installed system. If there are any problems, the command reports them to you both on the screen and in your log file.

Logging

Since Postfix is a long-running program, you should regularly check your system's log file for warnings or messages. Things can change on your system that might impact Postfix. Almost all Postfix activity, successful or not, is logged. Whenever you start or reload Postfix, it is a good idea to check your log file for messages.

Postfix logging is accomplished by using your system's *syslog* daemon. System log files are an aspect of system administration that vary across versions of Unix, so you may have to consult your own system documentation to fully understand Postfix logging.

In general, the syslog daemon (syslogd) receives messages from various system processes and writes them to their final destination (often a file). syslogd organizes messages according to their importance and the application or facility that generated the message. The file */etc/syslog.conf* tells syslogd where to write each type of message. The logging facility used by Postfix is mail. If you don't know where to find messages logged by Postfix, the file */etc/syslog.conf* should point you in the right direction. Some operating systems, by convention, log nearly everything to a single file, such as */var/log/syslog*, while others prefer to separate messages by applications or services, so that Postfix messages go to a file like */var/log/maillog*. For the latter type of systems, you might find an entry like the following in */etc/syslog.conf*:

```
mail.*          -/var/log/maillog
```

Once you locate your mail log file, check it regularly. You'll probably want to check it at least daily, but decide for yourself, depending on the volume of mail your server handles and your existing log rotation scheme. You can use the following command to find Postfix messages that might be of interest:

```
$ egrep '(reject|warning|error|fatal|panic):' /var/log/maillog
```

assuming that your log file is */var/log/maillog*. If not, substitute the name of your own mail log file.

Starting, Stopping, and Reloading Postfix

You saw earlier in the chapter how to use the postfix command to start Postfix:

```
# postfix start
```

Once Postfix is running, if you make any changes to *main.cf* or *master.cf*, have Postfix reread its configuration by executing postfix with the reload argument:

```
# postfix reload
```

Postfix gracefully terminates running processes after they have finished any tasks they are working on, rereads its configuration files, and continues to receive mail without interruption.

The most important thing when starting or reloading Postfix is to check your system log to see if Postfix reports any errors or warnings.

You can stop Postfix with the stop argument. Running processes will still finish any tasks they're working on and then terminate:

```
# postfix stop
```

You should not stop and start Postfix when a reload will suffice. Also, do not stop, restart, or reload frequently, since any of these actions can impact performance.

Running Postfix at System Startup

Most systems automatically start Postfix when they boot up because of Postfix's built-in Sendmail compatibility. Sendmail is typically launched at startup with a command like:

```
sendmail -bd -q15m
```

The Postfix sendmail command understands nearly all of the same options as Sendmail, so if your server already has scripts that start Sendmail, those same scripts will start Postfix. One common Sendmail option ignored by Postfix is -q, which is used by Sendmail to specify the time between queue scans. The time between queue scans for Postfix is set in the *main.cf* file with the queue_run_delay parameter, which defaults to 1000 seconds.

Your system may have a configuration option to turn on automatic startup of Sendmail. After you install Postfix, turning on this option should be sufficient to cause Postfix to start at system initialization. Different versions of Unix have different idioms for configuring a server to start a process at system initialization. If your system's Sendmail start script doesn't work, or you prefer to use a Postfix-specific script, you can easily create a start script.

Do it yourself

The requirements and conventions for initialization scripts vary among the different versions of Unix, so you should consult your system's documentation to see where and how to add startup options. On System V–type systems, you can install a script like the one shown in Example 4-1.

Example 4-1. Sample SysV-style init script

```
#!/sbin/sh
#
# Set the path to your own logger and postfix commands.
#
LOGGER="/usr/bin/logger"
POSTFIX="/usr/sbin/postfix"
rc=0

if [ ! -f $POSTFIX ] ; then
    $LOGGER -t $0 -s -p mail.err "Unable to locate Postfix"
    exit(1)
fi
if [ ! -f /etc/postfix/main.cf ] ; then
    $LOGGER -t $0 -s -p mail.err "Unable to locate Postfix configuration"
    exit(1)
fi

case "$1" in
    start)
        echo -n "Starting Postfix"
        $POSTFIX start
```

Example 4-1. Sample SysV-style init script (continued)

```
        rc=$?
        echo "."
        ;;

    stop)
        echo -n "Stopping Postfix"
        $POSTFIX stop
        rc=$?
        echo "."
        ;;

    restart)
        echo -n "Restarting Postfix"
        $POSTFIX reload
        rc=$?
        echo "."
        ;;

    *)
        echo "Usage: $0 {start|stop|restart}"
        rc=1

esac
exit $rc
```

Depending on your environment, you may also want to add additional pre- and post-checks to this example. You should install your script in the correct directory for your system, commonly */etc/init.d*, although HP-UX, for example, uses */sbin/init.d*. Once the script is in place, you also have to create a symlink to it in the appropriate run level directory for your server (often */etc/rc2.d*). For example, if you named the above script *postfix*, create a symlink such as the following:

```
# ln -s /etc/init.d/postfix /etc/init.d/rc2.d/S95postfix
```

You should consult your system documentation for the details on your platform.

Queue Management

The Postfix queue is also an important part of email administration. See Chapter 5 for information on the Postfix queue manager.

master.cf

The Postfix master daemon launches all of the other Postfix services as they are needed. The various services, and how they are run, are specified in the *master.cf* file.

The master configuration file works like other Postfix configuration files. A comment is marked by a # character at the beginning of a line. Comments and blank lines are ignored. Long lines can continue onto subsequent lines by starting the carry-over lines with whitespace.

Example 4-2 shows a sample file. Each column contains a specific configuration option. A dash in a column indicates the default setting for that column. Some default values come from parameters in the *main.cf* file.

Example 4-2. Sample master.cf file

```
#==================================================================
# service type private unpriv chroot wakeup  maxproc command + args
#  name          (yes)  (yes) (yes) (never)  (100)
#==================================================================
smtp      inet  n    -       y    -       -    smtpd
pickup    fifo  n    -       n    60      1    pickup
cleanup   unix  n    -       n    -       0    cleanup
qmgr      fifo  n    -       n    300     1    qmgr
rewrite   unix  -    -       n    -       -    trivial-rewrite
bounce    unix  -    -       n    -       0    bounce
defer     unix  -    -       n    -       0    bounce
flush     unix  n    -       n    1000?   0    flush
proxymap  unix  -    -       n    -       -    proxymap
smtp      unix  -    -       y    -       -    smtp
relay     unix  -    -       y    -       -    smtp
          -o smtp_helo_timeout=5 -o smtp_connect_timeout=5
showq     unix  n    -       n    -       -    showq
error     unix  -    -       n    -       -    error
local     unix  -    n       n    -       -    local
virtual   unix  -    n       n    -       -    virtual
lmtp      unix  -    -       n    -       -    lmtp
maildrop  unix  -    n       n    -       -    pipe
   flags=DRhu user=vmail argv=/usr/local/bin/maildrop -d ${recipient}
cyrus     unix  -    n       n    -       -    pipe
  user=cyrus argv=/cyrus/bin/deliver -e -r ${sender}
  -m ${extension} ${user}
uucp      unix  -    n       n    -       -    pipe
  flags=Fqhu user=uucp argv=uux -r -n -z -a$sender -
  $nexthop!rmail ($recipient)
```

The following list describes each column in the file, including its default setting:

service name

> The name of the component. The rules for naming a service depend on the type of service, as specified in the transport type column (see below).

transport type

> Valid transport types are inet, unix, and fifo. Each of these indicates a method of communication for this service.

> The inet type refers to network sockets. A network socket component can communicate with other processes on the same machine or other machines on the network. Network sockets use a combination of a system's IP address and the port used for connecting. They are commonly written in combination as the host or IP address and the port, separated by a colon. The name of an inet transport in *master.cf* is a socket specified as the host and port. The name can be written as just the port if it's on the local system. You can use a hostname or an IP

address for the host, and the port can be the actual port number, or its symbolic name. (Symbolic names for ports come from the */etc/services* file. See your system documentation.)

The unix type refers to Unix domain sockets, and fifo refers to named pipes. Both are used for communication between processes on the same machine. Both Unix domain sockets and FIFOs use special files for their communications. The names for unix and fifo components follow the same naming rules as for valid Unix filenames without directories. Postfix creates special communications files using the service name. Unix domain sockets and named pipes are standard Unix interprocess communications tools. If you would like more information about them, refer to a text on Unix programming.

Table 4-1 shows examples of valid service names for the various transport types.

Table 4-1. Example service names

Service name	Transport type	Description
smtp	inet	Name for the smtpd daemon. The name is the symbolic name for the SMTP port.
127.0.0.1:10025	inet	A component that listens on the loopback interface on port 10025.
465	inet	A component that listens on the local host on port 465.
maildrop	unix	A component that is invoked through Postfix's pipe daemon.
pickup	fifo	A Postfix FIFO component.

private

Access to some components is restricted to the Postfix system itself. This column is marked with a y for private access (the default) or an n for public access. inet components must be marked n for public access, since network sockets are necessarily available to other processes.

unpriv

Postfix components run with the least amount of privilege required to accomplish their tasks. They set their identity to that of the unprivileged account specified by the mail_owner parameter. The default installation uses *postfix*. The default value of y for this column indicates that the service runs under the normal unprivileged account. Services that require root privileges are marked with n.

chroot

Many components can be chrooted for additional security. The chroot location is specified in the queue_directory parameter in *master.cf*. The default is for a service to run in a chroot environment; however, the normal installation marks all components with an n so they are not chrooted when they run. Chrooting a service adds a level of complexity that you should thoroughly understand before taking advantage of the added security. See "chroot" later in the chapter for more information on running Postfix services in a chroot environment.

wakeup

Some components require a wake-up timer to kick them into action at the specified interval. The `pickup` daemon is one example. At its default setting of 60 seconds, the `master` daemon wakes it up every minute to see if any new messages have arrived in the maildrop queue. The other services that require a wake-up are the `qmgr` and `flush` daemons. A question mark character (?) can be added at the end of the time to indicate that a wake-up event should be sent only if the component is being used. A 0 for the time interval indicates that no wake-up is required. The default is 0, since only the three components mentioned require a wake-up. The values as they are set in the Postfix distribution should work for almost all situations. Other services should not have `wakeup` enabled.

maxproc

Limits the number of processes that can be invoked simultaneously. If unspecified here, the value comes from the parameter `default_process_limit` in *main.cf*, which is set to 100 by default. A setting of 0 means no process limit. You may want to adjust `maxproc` settings if you run Postfix on a system with limited resources or you want to optimize different aspects of the system.

command

The actual command used to execute a service is listed in the final column. The command is specified with no path information, because it is expected to be in the Postfix daemon directory specified by the `daemon_directory` parameter in *main.cf*. By default the directory is */usr/libexec/postfix*. All of the Postfix commands can be specified with one or more -v options to turn on increasingly more verbose logging information, which can be helpful if you must troubleshoot a problem. You can also enable information for a debugging program with the -D option. See the *DEBUG_README* file that comes with the Postfix distribution for more information on debugging if necessary.

Each of the Postfix daemons has its own set of options that can be specified after the command itself. (See the manpages for the individual daemons to learn about the available options.) You can specify only Postfix commands in the command column. If you want to execute your own commands, use the Postfix `pipe` daemon. See the Postfix `pipe` manpage for more information.

Time Units

Some Postfix parameters accept a length of time for their values. Time values in Postfix can be specified with the appropriate abbreviation to indicate their units: s (seconds), m (minutes), h (hours), d (days), or w (weeks). If no time unit is specified, each time parameter has a default unit that it assumes for the given value. You should check the documentation to see what the default value is for a given parameter, or always be sure to specify a unit with the time.

If *main.cf* offers configuration information for a component, you can override that information in *master.cf* by providing an alternative in an -o option. To create a specialized smtp client service, for example, add another entry to *master.cf* such as the following:

```
smtp-quick unix -    -    n    -    -    smtp
    -o smtp_connect_timeout=5s
```

There can be no spaces between the parameter and the equals sign and the assigned value. As configured in the example, smtp-quick is a specialized smtp service that doesn't wait as long for a server to respond when it tries to connect. This SMTP client follows the configuration in *main.cf*, but uses a different value for the smtp_connect_timeout parameter. You'll see more examples later in this chapter and elsewhere in the book.

Receiving Limits

The smtpd daemon can enforce a number of limits on incoming mail. The limits are configurable through several parameters in the *main.cf* file. You can limit the size of messages, the number of recipients for a single delivery, and the length of lines in a message. You can also limit the number of errors to allow from a single client before breaking off communications.

To limit the number of recipients for a single message, use the smtpd_recipient_limit parameter. The default is 1,000 recipients, and it should be adequate for normal operation.

The message_size_limit parameter limits the size of any message your system will accept. The default is 10 MB. If you have limited disk space or memory, you might want to lower the value. On the other hand, if your users commonly receive large attachments, you may have to increase it.

Increasingly frequent errors from the same client might indicate a problem or an attack. Postfix keeps a counter of errors, and handles potential problem clients by introducing delays with each error. The delays can help protect your system from misconfigured or malignant clients. As the number of errors increases so does the length of each delay. The length of the initial delay is specified by smtpd_error_sleep_time with a default of one second. After the number of errors exceeds the value set for smtpd_soft_error_limit, Postfix increases the delay by one second for every error, so that with each error, there is a slightly longer delay. Finally, when the error count hits the value set in smtpd_hard_error_limit, Postfix gives up on the client and disconnects.

If a malicious program connects to your mail server and sends garbage commands, attempting to crash your server, the bogus commands appear to Postfix as errors from a misbehaving client. Assume the following values for the delay parameters:

```
smtpd_error_sleep_time = 1s
smtpd_soft_error_limit = 10
smtpd_hard_error_limit = 20
```

With these settings, Postfix initially waits one second (smtpd_error_sleep_time) after each error before responding to the client. After 10 (smtpd_soft_error_limit) such probes, Postfix starts increasing the length of each delay. After 11 errors, Postfix waits 11 seconds. After 12 errors, Postfix waits 12 seconds, and so on. Once the number of errors hits 20 (smtpd_hard_error_limit), Postfix disconnects, cutting off the malicious program. If the program connects again, it simply gets the same treatment each time it starts creating problems.

Rewriting Addresses

Postfix tries to make sense of addresses in email and writes them using the standard RFC 2822 format. Certain address rewriting occurs automatically.

You saw earlier in the chapter how Postfix appends myorigin to a local name that has no domain part. Postfix also appends the value of mydomain to addresses that include only the host portion without the domain name. This fixes addresses that look like *kdent@host* so they become *kdent@host.example.com*.

Canonical Addresses

Postfix provides another type of address rewriting that lets you map disparate addresses into a standard format for your entire site. The canonical_maps parameter points to a lookup table of address mappings. (While the word *canonical* has many meanings, among computer professionals it means "the usual, standard, or normal.") If different mail systems on your network create addresses in different ways, you can relay them all through your Postfix gateway and have it fix up the addresses into your standard format. Canonical maps are often used to change addresses from an internal format to a public one. Include entries like the following in your canonical table:

```
#
# /etc/postfix/canonical
#
pabelard@example.com    peter.abelard@example.com
hfulbert@example.com    heloise.fulbert@example.com
```

They can also rewrite addresses completely.

```
#
# /etc/postfix/canonical
#
pabelard@example.com    abelard@oreilly.com
hfulbert@example.com    heloise@oreilly.com
```

Turning Off Address Completion

Postfix's expansion of incomplete email addresses is sometimes the source of confusion for end users. If your system is hosting the domain *example.com* and receives an email message where the From: message header contains an incomplete address like:

```
From: Marketing
To: kdent@example.com
```

Postfix performs its normal repairs, and the message header becomes:

```
From: Marketing@example.com
To: kdent@example.com
```

Incomplete addresses, such as in this example, are often employed by spammers. When naive users see the adjusted address, they assume that the spam originated on your server. It is possible to configure Postfix so that it doesn't append your domain. You probably don't want to do so unless your mail system is used strictly as a mail gateway and no messages are sent from the machine itself. Many applications expect RFC 2822 conforming addresses, and you may run into problems if your addresses are not complete.

To prevent Postfix from appending the domain in myorigin or mydomain to partial addresses, you can change the parameters append_at_myorigin and append_dot_mydomain:

```
append_at_myorigin = no
append_dot_mydomain = no
```

Under most circumstances you do not want to do this. Postfix itself assumes addresses are in the correct format, as do many other applications that handle email messages. A better solution is to reject messages that do not include complete email addresses. For more information on problem email, see Chapter 11.

In *main.cf*, point the canonical_maps parameter to the *canonical* file:

```
canonical_maps = hash:/etc/postfix/canonical
```

Be sure to execute postmap against your *canonical* file and reload Postfix so that it recognizes your changes to *main.cf*:

```
# postmap /etc/postfix/canonical
# postfix reload
```

The canonical_maps parameter affects all of the addresses, including envelope and message headers. If Postfix finds a match, it makes the change. If you want your changes to affect only sender or recipient addresses, Postfix provides the additional parameters sender_canonical_maps and recipient_canonical_maps. They both work the same as canonical_maps, but only on their respective classes of addresses. If you use either of these two parameters in addition to canonical_maps, Postfix first fixes the addresses according to sender_canonical_maps and recipient_canonical_maps, and then canonical_maps.

Masquerading Hostnames

Address masquerading refers to the idea that you can hide the names of internal hosts, and make all addresses appear as if they originated from the gateway system itself. You may have internal systems that use your Postfix server as a gateway. When mail is sent from these systems and the sender addresses include the fully qualified hostname, you may want addresses to appear with the domain name only. The `masquerade_domains` parameter strips hostnames down to their simpler domain names.

The parameter takes a list of domains. Any address whose fully qualified hostname matches the domain portion is stripped down to just the domain name:

```
masquerade_domains = example.com
```

Addresses that look like *heloise@server1.example.com* and *frank@server2.example.com* are converted to *heloise@example.com* and *frank@example.com*.

You can list multiple domains and subdomains. Postfix processes addresses against masquerade domain names in the order you list them. Consider a network that includes the two subdomains, *acct.example.com* and *hr.example.com*. You want addresses from these domains to show the subdomain, but you want addresses from any other domain or host in the network to show the parent domain. Set `masquerade_domains` as follows:

```
masquerade_domains = acct.example.com hr.example.com example.com
```

With this setting, the address *heloise@sys3.acct.example.com* matches *acct.example.com*, so that it becomes *heloise@acct.example.com*. The address *frank@db.hr.example.com* matches *hr.example.com*, and becomes *frank@hr.example.com*. Finally, *helene@server1.example.com* matches the last value, *example.com*, to become *helene@example.com*.

If you want to preserve a domain name that would otherwise be stripped down, you can preface the domain with an exclamation point:

```
masquerade_domains = !it.example.com, example.com
```

In this case, the domain *it.example.com* will not be rewritten, so the address *kdent@it.example.com* stays as it is.

You can exclude specific account names from masquerading. For example, if you want an address like *root@db.example.com* to stay intact, add the account to the `masquerade_exceptions` parameter:

```
masquerade_exceptions = admin, root
```

When you use masquerading, it is normally applied to all envelope and header addresses but not envelope recipient addresses. This allows mail addressed to a specific host to be delivered from the mail gateway to that particular system, while still rewriting addresses for messages sent from the host. If you prefer to have all addresses masqueraded, set the `masquerade_classes` parameter to include the complete list of address classes recognized by Postfix:

```
masquerade_classes = envelope_recipient, envelope_sender,
        header_sender, header_recipient
```

Be aware that if you set masquerade_classes this way, a gateway mail system may no longer know where to deliver a message that was originally addressed to *kdent@server1.example.com* once it has been rewritten as *kdent@example.com*.

Relocated Users

The relocated_maps parameter points to a lookup table where you can store a list of addresses or domains that have moved to another location:

```
relocated_maps = hash:/etc/postfix/relocated
```

The lookup table uses the old address as the key and its new location as the value. When a message is delivered to a relocated address, Postfix rejects the delivery attempt with a message that includes the user's new address as specified in the lookup table. You can also list just a domain name to have all recipients at that domain rejected with your specified message.

The file */etc/postfix/relocated* contains entries like:

```
kdent@ora.com        kdent@oreilly.com
heloise@ora.com      hfulbert@oreilly.com
@example.com         oreilly.com
```

Messages sent to either *kdent@ora.com* or *heloise@ora.com* are rejected with an error message that gives their respective new addresses. Any messages sent to *example.com* are rejected regardless of what the local part is. The message reports that the address has moved to *oreilly.com*.

Unknown Users

A local address that is not listed in relocated or other maps, and is not an account on the system is an unknown user. Normally, when Postfix receives mail for an unknown user, it rejects it. If you prefer to capture all of the messages sent to nonexistent accounts, you can use the luser_relay parameter. Set it to any email address to have messages destined for unknown users sent to the address you provide. You must also set local_recipient_maps to blank to prevent Postfix from rejecting mail for unknown users:

```
luser_relay = catchall
local_recipient_maps =
```

Assuming catchall is a legitimate address (alias or user account) on your system, it will receive all messages sent to nonexistent users. Be careful when using luser_relay, since spammers often launch dictionary attacks, where they try enormous lists of addresses hoping to find a legitimate one at your site. If luser_relay is configured, it will catch all of the spam.

chroot

Postfix provides multiple layers of security. One such layer is the option to permit most Postfix services to run within a *chroot* environment. The Unix chroot function allows a process to change its view of, and access to, its filesystem by changing its root directory to a new path other than the normal /.

The chroot feature is particularly beneficial for processes that must communicate with external, potentially hostile clients. If an attacker somehow manages to subvert the smtpd daemon, for example, the attacker gains only very limited access to the filesystem. Configuring for a chroot environment is an advanced Postfix feature that adds a layer of complexity that you or your administrators may not want to deal with. Generally, chroot is not needed, except for sites that use Postfix in a highly secure environment or on particularly exposed servers, such as dedicated firewall systems and bastion hosts.

All of the Postfix processes that use chroot change their root directory to the directory specified in the queue_directory parameter, which is normally */var/spool/postfix*. When a process runs chrooted, the directory */var/spool/postfix/pid*, for example, becomes */pid* to that process, and the process cannot access any files other than those below its new root.

To chroot individual components, edit your *master.cf* file. Change the fifth column to y. The chroot option is possible with all components except the pipe, virtual, local, and proxymap services. In Example 4-2, chroot is enabled for the SMTP clients and server.

Since chroot changes the environment of the process, all of the resources the chrooted daemon needs must be available below the new root directory. Unfortunately, the specific resources Postfix daemons might need depend on your platform. In general, Postfix might require resources that provide user information (*/etc/passwd*), name resolution configuration (*nsswitch.conf* or *resolv.conf*), timezone information, or shared libraries. Some platforms also require certain device files. There are platform-specific scripts that come with the Postfix distribution. They're available in the *examples/chroot-setup/* subdirectory below the main distribution directory.

Executing the correct script should be sufficient to set up the chroot environment on your system. If there is not a script for your platform, you may have to experiment a little to find everything you need. Consider all of the resources mentioned above and review the example scripts for other platforms. Watch your logs for error messages after you chroot a process. An entry like the following:

```
postfix/smtp[1575]: fatal: unknown service: smtp/tcp
```

shows that Postfix cannot determine what port the smtp service uses. This problem is fixed by placing the */etc/services* file into the chroot, by copying it to */var/spool/postfix/etc/services*. Other symptoms show up in the log complaining of similar types of problems.

If the normal Postfix log doesn't give enough information, you may have to run a trace to see where the program fails. Look for tools such as truss, strace, and tusc on your system. These tools can be used to see where a service fails when it tries to run in a chroot. If you discover the failure is due to a missing component, copy the component into the chrooted environment. See the *DEBUG_README* file that comes with Postfix for instructions on attaching tracing tools to Postfix.

Once you have Postfix running in a chroot, you need to make sure you keep your chroot resources in sync with the normal system files. If your chroot requires */etc/passwd*, for example, whenever the system */etc/passwd* changes, the chroot version must be updated, too. Creating link files doesn't work because symlinks cannot cross the chroot boundary, and hard links do not work across filesystems.

Documentation

The Postfix distribution ships with a lot of documentation. Depending on your installation package, you may or may not have all of the documents. You should have at least the manpages and sample configuration files. The sample files are located in the directory specified by the sample_directory parameter, which is usually the same directory in which your *main.cf* file resides. All of the Postfix parameters are documented in one or more of the sample files.

When Postfix was installed, the manpages should have been installed in a sensible place on your system. If they are in a directory where your system expects to find them, you only have to type, for example:

```
$ man postfix
```

to have the manpage displayed on your screen. If your system replies with an error message such as:

```
$ man postfix
No manual entry found for postfix.
```

then either the pages are not installed or they are not in a location your system expects to find them. Read the documentation for your system to find out about setting your MANPATH variable or moving the manpages to a more standard location for your platform.

There are many manpages for various Postfix commands, daemons, and lookup tables. All of the documentation is also available as HTML files. If the HTML files are not installed on your system, you can find them on the Postfix web site at *http://www.postfix.org/*. The online documentation always refers to the current release of Postfix.

CHAPTER 5

Queue Management

The queue manager daemon qmgr is in many ways the heart of your Postfix system.[*] All messages, both outbound and inbound, must pass through the queue. It's a good idea to understand the queue and how Postfix uses it in case you have to trouble-shoot a problem.

The queue manager maintains five different queues: incoming, active, deferred, hold, and corrupt. Postfix uses a separate directory for each queue below the path specified in the queue_directory parameter. By default the path is */var/spool/postfix*, which gives you a directory structure like the following:

```
/var/spool/postfix/active
/var/spool/postfix/bounce
/var/spool/postfix/corrupt
/var/spool/postfix/deferred
/var/spool/postfix/hold
```

The qmgr daemon running in the background handles most of the queue management tasks automatically. The commands postsuper and postqueue are used by administrators for manual queue management tasks. This chapter looks at how qmgr and the command-line tools work, as well as Postfix parameters that affect the queue.

How qmgr Works

Figure 5-1 illustrates how messages move through the queue. The incoming queue is where messages first enter Postfix. The queue manager provides protection for the queue filesystem through the queue_minfree parameter. The default value is 0. You can make sure the disk that stores your queue doesn't run out of space by setting a limit.

---

[*] You may see references to nqmgr in older configuration files and documentation. Earlier Postfix versions shipped with two queue manager daemons, qmgr and nqmgr. The original qmgr was replaced by the current one, which has a better scheduling algorithm. nqmgr was the name of the current queue manager daemon while it coexisted with the original. Once it was ready for promotion as sole queue manager for Postfix, it was renamed qmgr.

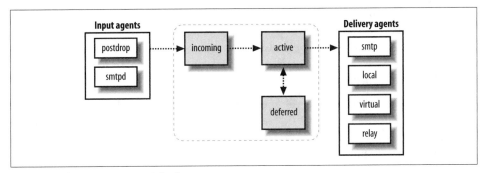

Figure 5-1. Message movement in the queue.

From the incoming queue, the queue manager moves messages to the active queue and invokes the appropriate delivery agent to handle them. For the most part, if there are no problems with delivery, movement through the queue is so fast that you won't see messages in the queue. If Postfix is trying to deliver to a slow or unavailable SMTP server, you may see messages in the active queue. Postfix waits 30 seconds to decide if a remote system is unreachable.

A message that cannot be delivered is placed in the deferred queue. Messages are deferred only when they encounter a temporary problem in delivery, such as a temporary DNS problem or when a destination mail server reports a temporary problem. Messages that are rejected, or encounter a permanent error, are immediately bounced back to the sender in an error report and don't stay in the queue.

Deferred Mail

Messages in the deferred queue stay there until they are either delivered successfully or expire and are bounced back to the sender. The bounce_size_limit parameter determines how much of a message that could not be delivered is bounced back to the sender in the error report. The default is 50,000 bytes.

Once a message has failed delivery, Postfix marks it with a timestamp to indicate when the next delivery attempt should occur. Postfix keeps a short-term list of systems that are down to avoid unnecessary delivery attempts. If there are deferred messages scheduled for a redelivery attempt, and there is space available in the active queue, the queue manager alternates between taking messages from the deferred and incoming queues, so that new messages are not forced to wait behind a large backlog of deferred ones.

Queue Scheduling

Postfix periodically scans the queue to see if there are deferred messages whose timestamps indicate they are ready for another delivery attempt. Subsequent failed attempts at delivery cause scheduled delays to double, so Postfix waits longer each time before it attempts to deliver a message. You can configure the maximum delay with the `maximal_queue_lifetime` parameter. When the time has expired, Postfix gives up trying to deliver the message and bounces it back to the sender. By default the period is five days (5d). You can set it to any length of time, or to 0 to have undeliverable mail returned immediately.

Queue scans occur at an interval specified by the `queue_run_delay` parameter. By default the parameter is set to 1,000 seconds (1000s). With this setting, every 1,000 seconds, Postfix checks the deferred queue to see if there are any messages due for another delivery attempt.

The parameters `minimal_backoff_time` and `maximal_backoff_time` set minimum and maximum time limits on how often Postfix attempts to redeliver deferred messages. Each time a message is deferred, the queue manager increases the amount of time it waits to attempt to deliver that message again. The calculated increase of time is never allowed to exceed `maximal_backoff_time` (default 4,000 seconds) and is never less than `minimal_backoff_time` (default 1,000 seconds). If you find that you have a large backlog of deferred messages, you may want to increase the `maximal_backoff_time` so that Postfix doesn't expend system resources in trying to deliver messages to unavailable servers.

Message Delivery

The queue manager arranges for the delivery of messages by invoking the appropriate delivery agent. Postfix is careful not to overwhelm destination systems and provides several parameters to control resources for outgoing messages. For most situations the default settings are correct, but if you are experiencing resource problems or you are trying to optimize deliveries, you may want to experiment with the queue manager configuration.

Outgoing messages might be delivered over any of the transports available in the *master.cf* file. Each transport can have a limit on its total number of processes, specified in the `maxproc` column (see "master.cf"). If a value is not specified there, Postfix uses `default_process_limit` for its limit.

The `initial_destination_concurrency` parameter limits the number of messages initially sent (default is five). You can increase the value, but it can't go higher than the `maxproc` value or `default_process_limit` for the transport used. After the initial delivery of messages, if there are more messages in the queue for a particular destination, Postfix increases the number of concurrent delivery attempts, as long as it doesn't detect any problem from the destination system at the current load. Postfix continues to increase the number of simultaneous deliveries up to the number specified in the `default_destination_concurrency_limit` parameter, which is 20 by default. In general, you don't want to increase the concurrency limit, or you risk overwhelming the receiving system.

You can override the default_destination_concurrency_limit value for any transport by setting a parameter of the form *transport*_destination_concurrency_limit. For example, you can limit concurrent connections to external systems with the parameter smtp_destination_concurrency_limit, or limit local deliveries with local_destination_concurrency_limit.

There are also parameters of the form *transport*_destination_recipient_limit that control how many recipients Postfix specifies for a single copy of an email message. If a transport-specific parameter is not configured, it takes its default value from default_destination_recipient_limit. If the number of recipients for a message exceeds the limit, Postfix breaks up the list of recipients into smaller groups of addresses and sends separate copies of the message to each group of addresses.

Corrupt Messages

The corrupt queue is simply used to store damaged or otherwise unreadable messages. If a message is too damaged to do anything with it, Postfix places it here. If you want to investigate an issue, the problem message is available in this queue where you can view it manually, if necessary. Corrupt messages are very rare. If you have them, they may be a symptom of an underlying operating system or hardware problem.

Error Notifications

Postfix can report certain errors by sending error messages to an administrator. Postfix classifies errors for notification, as shown in Table 5-1. The notify_classes parameter in *main.cf* contains the list of error classes that should generate error notices. By default the parameter includes "resource" and "software" errors.

Each class of error can be configured to send the notification to a particular email address, using parameters of the form *class*_notice_recipient. By default they all go to *postmaster*. Table 5-1 provides a list of possible error classes, along with the parameters that indicate who should receive the error notices.

Table 5-1. Email error notices

Error class	Description	Notice recipient parameter
bounce	Send headers for all bounced messages.	bounce_notice_recipient
2bounce	Send undeliverable bounced messages.	2bounce_notice_recipient
delay	Send headers of delayed messages.	delay_notice_recipient
policy	Send the transcript of any SMTP transaction when a message is rejected due to anti-spam restrictions.	error_notice_recipient
protocol	Send the transcript of any SMTP transaction that had errors.	error_notice_recipient

Table 5-1. Email error notices (continued)

Error class	Description	Notice recipient parameter
resource	Send notice that a message could not be delivered because of system resource problems.	error_notice_recipient
software	Send notice that a message could not be delivered because of software problems.	error_notice_recipient

If you would like to receive all problem notices, set the parameter as follows:

```
notify_classes = bounce, 2bounce, delay, policy, protocol,
    resource, software
```

Queue Tools

Postfix provides command-line tools for displaying and managing the messages in your queue. The primary commands are postsuper and postqueue. You can perform the following tasks on messages in the queue:

- Listing messages
- Deleting messages
- Holding messages
- Requeuing messages
- Displaying messages
- Flushing messages

Each of the tasks, and the commands to accomplish them, are explained in the sections that follow.

Listing the Queue

The queue display contains an entry for each message that shows the message ID, size, arrival time, sender, and recipient addresses. Deferred messages also include the reason they could not be delivered. Messages in the active queue are marked with an asterisk after the Queue ID. Messages in the hold queue are marked with an exclamation point. Deferred messages have no mark.

You can list all the messages in your queue with the postqueue -p command. Postfix also provides the mailq command for compatibility with Sendmail. The Postfix replacement for mailq produces the same output as postqueue -p.

A typical queue entry looks like the following:

```
$ postqueue -p
-Queue ID- --Size-- ----Arrival Time---- -Sender/Recipient-------
DBA3F1A9       553 Mon May  5 14:42:15  kdent@example.com
        (connect to mail.ora.com[192.168.155.63]: Connection refused)
                             kdent@ora.com
```

Since this entry is not marked with either an asterisk or an exclamation point, it is in the deferred queue.

Deleting Messages

The postsuper command allows you to remove messages from the queue. To remove the message in the sample entry displayed above, execute postsuper with the -d option:

```
# postsuper -d DBA3F1A9
postsuper: DBA3F1A9: removed
postsuper: Deleted: 1 message
```

If you have a lot of messages to remove, you can clear out your entire queue with the ALL argument:

```
# postsuper -d ALL
postsuper: Deleted: 23 messages
```

The ALL argument must be capitalized. Be very careful when using the command, since it will delete all queued messages without asking any questions.

Rather than deleting all of the queued messages or just one at a time, frequently you want to delete messages with a specific email address. Example 5-1 is a Perl script that provides a convenient way to specify an email address to delete particular messages from the queue.

Example 5-1. Perl script to delete queued messages by email address

```perl
#!/usr/bin/perl -w
#
# pfdel - deletes message containing specified address from
# Postfix queue. Matches either sender or recipient address.
#
# Usage: pfdel <email_address>
#

use strict;

# Change these paths if necessary.
my $LISTQ = "/usr/sbin/postqueue -p";
my $POSTSUPER = "/usr/sbin/postsuper";

my $email_addr = "";
my $qid = "";
my $euid = $>;

if ( @ARGV != 1 ) {
        die "Usage: pfdel <email_address>\n";
} else {
        $email_addr = $ARGV[0];
}
```

```
if ( $euid != 0 ) {
        die "You must be root to delete queue files.\n";
}


open(QUEUE, "$LISTQ |") ||
  die "Can't get pipe to $LISTQ: $!\n";

my $entry = <QUEUE>;      # skip single header line
$/ = "";                  # Rest of queue entries print on
                          # multiple lines.
while ( $entry = <QUEUE> ) {
        if ( $entry =~ / $email_addr$/m ) {
                ($qid) = split(/\s+/, $entry, 2);
                $qid =~ s/[\*\!]//;
                next unless ($qid);

                #
                # Execute postsuper -d with the queue id.
                # postsuper provides feedback when it deletes
                # messages. Let its output go through.
                #
                if ( system($POSTSUPER, "-d", $qid) != 0 ) {
                        # If postsuper has a problem, bail.
                        die "Error executing $POSTSUPER: error " .
                            "code " . ($?/256) . "\n";
                }
        }
}
close(QUEUE);

if (! $qid ) {
        die "No messages with the address <$email_addr> " .
            "found in queue.\n";
}

exit 0;
```

Holding Messages

The hold queue is available for messages you would like to keep in your queue indefinitely. Figure 5-2 shows the hold queue and how you can move messages into the hold queue where they will not be delivered until you specifically remove them or move them back for normal queue processing. To place the example message into the hold queue, use the postsuper command with the -h option:

```
# postsuper -h DBA3F1A9
```

The queue entry now contains an exclamation point to show that the message is on hold:

```
-Queue ID- --Size-- ----Arrival Time---- -Sender/Recipient-------
DBA3F1A9  !     553 Mon May  5 14:42:15  kdent@example.com
         (connect to mail.ora.com[192.168.155.63]: Connection refused)
                                         kdent@ora.com
```

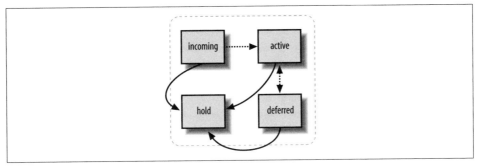

Figure 5-2. Putting messages on hold

To move the message back into the normal queue for regular processing, execute the command with a capital -H option instead:

```
# postsuper -H DBA3F1A9
```

After the message is moved back, the queue manager marks it for redelivery according to its normal scheduling, or you can flush the message to have it sent out immediately (see "Flushing Messages").

Requeuing Messages

If you have messages that were deferred because of a configuration problem that has been corrected, you may have to requeue the messages to have them delivered successfully. If the misconfiguration caused Postfix to store incorrect information about the next hop or transport method, or to rewrite the address incorrectly, requeuing causes Postfix to update the incorrect information based on your new configuration. The postsuper command uses the -r option to requeue messages. You can specify a queue ID for a single message, or the word ALL in capital letters to requeue everything:

```
# postsuper -r ALL
```

Requeued messages get a new queue ID and an additional Received: header.

Displaying Messages

The postcat command displays the contents of a queue file:

```
# postcat -q DBA3F1A9
```

Earlier versions of postcat did not support the -q option but required the full path to the queue file. Since a message can be in any of the queue compartments (maildrop, incoming, active, deferred, hold), and each of these has multiple subdirectories, the path to a particular queue file is not immediately apparent. If you are using an earlier version of postcat, which doesn't support the -q option, you can create a shell script like the one in Example 5-2 as a convenient way to view a queue file by specifying only the queue ID. The script accepts one queue ID as an argument, checks all of the queue directories to locate the queue file, and executes postcat with the full path as its argument. The contents are then displayed. This simple script displays only one queue file at a time.

Example 5-2. Shell script wrapper for postcat

```
#!/bin/sh

PATH=/usr/bin:/usr/sbin
QS="deferred active incoming maildrop hold"
QPATH=`postconf -h queue_directory`

if [ $# -ne 1 ]; then
        echo "Usage: pfcat <queue id>"
        exit 1
fi

if [ `whoami` != "root" ]; then
        echo "You must be root to view queue files."
        exit 1
fi

if [ ! -d $QPATH ]; then
        echo "Cannot locate queue directory $QPATH."
        exit 1
fi

for q in $QS
do
        FILE=`find $QPATH/$q -type f -name $1`
        if [ -n "$FILE" ]; then
                postcat $FILE
                exit 0
        fi
done

if [ -z $FILE ]; then
        echo "No such queue file $1"
        exit 1
fi
```

Flushing Messages

Flushing the queue causes Postfix to attempt to deliver messages in the queue immediately. You can flush queue messages with the `postqueue -f` command. However, unless you have a reason to expect successful deliveries, it's best to leave redelivery attempts to the Postfix queue manager. Repeated attempts to flush the queue can have a severe performance impact on your mail server.

You can flush messages destined for a particular site with the `-s` option. The site must be eligible for *fast flush* in order for this to work. To be eligible, the site must be listed in the `fast_flush_domains` parameter. By default, `fast_flush_domains` includes all of the hosts listed in `relay_domains`, but you can add additional sites if you want to flush them before the normally scheduled redelivery attempt.

```
fast_flush_domains = $relay_domains example.com
```

If you know that a previously unavailable, eligible site is ready to accept mail, execute `postqueue` with the `-s` option and name the site:

```
# postqueue -s example.com
```

See Chapter 9 for more information about fast flush and the SMTP command ETRN.

CHAPTER 6

Email and DNS

The *Domain Name System* (DNS) is a vast distributed database whose main job is to map hostnames to IP addresses. It also has an important role in email routing. In this chapter we'll look at how MTAs in general use DNS and some of the DNS issues that relate to Postfix and its configuration. Keep in mind that there are two important aspects to your mail servers and DNS:

- For sending mail, the system running your Postfix mail server must have access to a reliable DNS server to resolve hostnames and email-routing information.

- For receiving mail, your domains must be configured correctly to route messages to your mail server.

Misconfiguration of DNS servers is a common source of problems in setting up email servers.

DNS Overview

At one time, hostname to IP address mapping was handled by one large, centrally managed text file that contained an entry for every host accessible on the Internet. Each site downloaded a copy of the file periodically to get the latest hostname information. That scheme quickly became unwieldy, and the DNS service was conceived. It was defined in RFC 882 in 1983, and introduced two key ideas: the data is distributed and the naming of hosts is hierarchical. Making the data distributed means that every site updates its own information, and the updates become available almost immediately. Hierarchical naming prevents hostname conflicts and gives us the current domain-naming system that we are all very familiar with today. Each site obtains at least one domain name, and all of the hosts at that site are named by prefixing the simple hostname to the site's domain name. For example, a site that controls the domain name example.com might have any number of hosts with names like server1.example.com, hp4100.example.com, or www.example.com.

Each domain has at least two domain nameservers that are considered *authoritative* for the domain. Authoritative nameservers should have direct access to the database that contains all the information about a domain.

The data is comprised of different types of records called *resource records*. Different resource records provide different kinds of information, such as IP addresses, nameservers, hostname aliases, and mail routing. The resource records you need to know about for this discussion are the following:

A

> The mapping of names to IP addresses is handled by A records. These records contain a hostname and its IP address. The names that people use to refer to hosts have to be converted to IP addresses used for Internet routing. A records provide this name-to-address translation.

CNAME

> Some hostnames are aliases that point to other hostnames, rather than to IP addresses. This can be useful for directing requests to services (such as HTTP or POP) that might reside on systems generally known by a different name. The CNAME record provides the "real," or *canonical*, name that an alias hostname points to. For example, an administrator might publicize the hostname *www.example.com*, which is really a CNAME record pointing to *server1.example.com* most of the time. But during periods of maintenance on *server1.example.com*, for example, *www.example.com* could temporarily point to *server2.example.com*.

MX

> MX records provide mail-routing information. They specify *mail exchangers* for domains—that is, the names of the mail hubs that handle all the mail for a domain name. The MX records tell MTAs where to send messages. Since a domain can have multiple mail exchangers, MX records include a preference value to designate the order of priority when selecting a mail exchanger to deliver messages to.

PTR

> PTR records provide a reverse lookup of IP addresses to hostnames. These records normally match up with A records, so that forward lookups of hostnames return an IP address whose reverse lookup returns the hostname. However, many hostnames can point to the same IP address, so PTR records should map back to the canonical name associated with the IP address. Some applications use PTR records as a form of authentication to make sure that a connecting client's IP address maps to the expected hostname.

Email Routing

Let's consider for a moment one way that email routing might work. A user *horatio* in the domain example.com has a workstation named denmark. He could receive mail by using the email address *horatio@denmark.example.com*. An MTA with a message to deliver would simply look up the IP address for denmark.example.com and deliver it to that system for the user *horatio*. This scenario requires that Horatio's workstation is always turned on, that it has a functional MTA running at all times to receive messages, and that it is accessible by unknown MTAs from anywhere on the Internet. Rather than manage hundreds or thousands of MTAs on workstations and expose them to the Internet, nearly all sites make use of mail hubs that receive all the mail for a domain. MTAs such as Postfix need a way to determine which host or hosts are the mail hubs for a domain. DNS MX records provide this information.

A mail exchanger either delivers mail it receives or forwards it to another mail system. A domain may have multiple mail systems for reliability, and therefore multiple MX records. Generally, one host is the primary mail server and the others serve as backup or secondary mail servers. Each MX record in DNS contains a preference value that orders mail systems from most preferred to least preferred.

BIND is one of the most common DNS server applications. (O'Reilly's *DNS and BIND* by Paul Albitz and Cricket Liu fully explains the DNS system and documents the BIND software.) A simple BIND configuration file for the domain *example.com* looks like the following:

```
example.com. IN SOA ns.example.com. kdent.example.com. (
     1049310513
     10800
     3600
     604800
     900 )

;
; Nameservers
;
example.com.    IN NS ns.example.com.


;
; Host Addresses
;
example.com.           IN A 192.168.100.50
server1.example.com.   IN A 192.168.100.220
ns.example.com.        IN A 192.168.100.5
mail1.example.com.     IN A 192.168.100.50
mail2.example.com.     IN A 192.168.100.54
mail3.example.com.     IN A 192.168.100.123


;
; Mail Exchangers
;
example.com.    IN MX 10 mail1.example.com.
example.com.    IN MX 20 mail2.example.com.
example.com.    IN MX 30 mail3.example.com.


;
; CNAME Records
```

```
;
pop.example.com.        IN CNAME mail1.example.com.
www.example.com.        IN CNAME server1.example.com.
```

For this discussion, we're primarily interested in the mail exchanger records:

```
example.com.    IN MX 10 mail1.example.com.
example.com.    IN MX 20 mail2.example.com.
example.com.    IN MX 30 mail3.example.com.
```

The domain name is in the first column. The second column indicates that the entries are Internet class records, and the third indicates that they are mail exchanger resource records. The last column shows the mail exchanger host, and the second-to-last column shows its preference value. Preference values can be any number between 0 and 65,536, and a lower value indicates a more preferred host. The numbers are meaningful only in relation to each other and can be anything within the allowed range. By convention, most administrators create priority values in multiples of 10, which allows some flexibility for inserting or temporarily rearranging preferences.

In our simple example above, *mail1.example.com* receives all the mail for the domain *example.com*. In this case, all mail must eventually arrive at *mail1.example.com*. When an MTA has to deliver a message to a user at the domain example.com, it retrieves all of the MX records and sorts them in order of priority. It first attempts delivery to mail1.example.com. If mail1.example.com is available and accepts the message, the delivery is finished; however, if for some reason mail1.example.com is not available to accept the message, the MTA continues down the list until it finds a mail exchanger able to accept the message. If a secondary mail exchanger accepts a message, it takes the responsibility of delivering it to a more preferred mail server (possibly the primary) when the unavailable server comes back online.

If no MX records are found for a domain, an MTA checks to see if there is an A record associated with the domain name itself. If there is an A record, the MTA attempts delivery to the system at that IP address.

This mail-routing scheme seems simple enough, but it does get slightly more complicated. Consider an example where the MTA on mail2.example.com receives a message for *ophelia@example.com*. Presumably, mail1.example.com is offline, since mail2 received the message. The MTA running on *mail2.example.com* gets the list of mail exchangers for example.com, determines that the message should go to mail1.example.com, and discovers that mail1 is not available. The next mail exchanger on the list is itself. Delivery to itself doesn't really make sense. So, the next mail exchanger in line is mail3.example.com. The MTA could deliver the message there, but mail3 will go through the same process and immediately try to hand the message back to mail2, creating a mail loop. (MTAs actually resolve hostnames to IP addresses for comparisons, since MX hosts might have multiple A records. Postfix compares the IP address to its list of addresses in inet_interfaces and proxy_interfaces.)

The solution is that when an MTA gets the list of mail exchangers and discovers itself among them, it discards its own record plus all other mail exchangers with an equal or less preferred priority (higher number). For our example, the host mail2 eliminates itself and mail3, thus reducing the list of mail exchangers to only mail1. Since mail1 is not available and mail2 has no other options for delivery, it queues the message and makes the delivery when mail1 comes back online.

In order for mail routing to work successfully, you should be very careful when setting up MX records. In particular, you should observe the following rules for MX records in your DNS configuration:

Mail exchangers must have valid A records.   The mail exchanger pointed to by the MX record must be a hostname with a valid A record. Once an MTA has determined which host should receive the mail, it has to be able to find that host.

Mail exchangers cannot be aliases.   The host pointed to by an MX record should not be an alias (CNAME record). Under normal circumstances, an MTA knows itself by its canonical name and looks for that name when checking the list of mail exchangers to prevent mail loops. The server must be able to find itself, so make sure that you list the canonical name in the MX record, or you risk creating a mail loop. Even if an MTA accommodates CNAME records (by looking up and using the canonical name), using them causes inefficiencies in mail delivery.

Use hostnames and not IP addresses for mail exchangers.   List a hostname rather than an IP address for mail exchangers. While you may get by with a bare IP address, RFC 974 states that you must use a name of a host. Future changes (IPv6, for example) might cause bare IP addresses to break mail routing.

Make sure that you specify preference values.   Leaving out the preference value for MX records may have different effects, depending on your DNS server and MTA. At best, the problem creates ambiguity; at worst, it can prevent mail delivery.

Postfix and DNS

When sending mail, Postfix uses system *resolvers*, which are programs or libraries that make requests for DNS information. To receive mail, the DNS for your domain must be configured to route messages to your Postfix server. This section looks at DNS issues both for sending and receiving mail.

DNS and Sending Mail

The Postfix SMTP delivery agent must be able to obtain IP address and MX records for mail-routing information. Postfix must make at least two DNS lookups: one to get the MX hostname and one to get the IP address for that hostname. Since Postfix uses the normal operating system resolver libraries for its DNS queries, the system that runs Postfix must have access to a DNS server. The DNS server does not have to be on the same system, although for most circumstances it should be.

If your system does not seem to be resolving domain names correctly, there are three common command-line tools that you can use to troubleshoot the problem: nslookup, dig, and host. You should check your system documentation to see which of these tools is available on your server and how to use them. You can use these tools to query all types of resource records for a domain, including the MX record that Postfix needs in order to successfully deliver mail to a domain.

DNS problems might stem from your own system's configuration or a problem with the DNS server configuration for the domain Postfix is trying to send mail to. When you are troubleshooting a problem, it is very important to remember that Postfix first looks for MX records and not A records. Even if you can resolve a domain to an IP address, Postfix may not be able to deliver mail for that domain if there is a problem in retrieving MX information.

Configuration options

When delivering mail, Postfix performs a DNS lookup to retrieve all of the MX records for the destination domain. It sorts them in order of preference and tries each one in priority order. Once Postfix has established a connection with an SMTP server, the server replies to Postfix requests with a status code. Codes within the 2xx range indicate that everything is okay. Error codes in the 4xx range indicate a temporary problem, and those in the 5xx range indicate a permanent problem. See Chapter 2 for more information on SMTP reply codes.

To provide compatibility with Sendmail, Postfix, by default, treats SMTP servers that respond with 4xx or 5xx reply codes as if the servers had not responded at all. If you prefer that Postfix react to the error codes returned by the MX server rather than ignore them, set the smtp_skip_5xx_greeting and smtp_skip_4xx_greeting parameters:

```
smtp_skip_4xx_greeting = no
smtp_skip_5xx_greeting = no
```

If smtp_skip_4xx_greeting is set to no, and Postfix attempts delivery to a mail exchanger that responds with a 4xx code, it does not try any more mail exchangers for the destination domain. It queues the message and attempts delivery later.

If smtp_skip_5xx_greeting is set to no, and Postfix attempts delivery to a mail exchanger that responds with a 5xx code, it does not try any more mail exchangers for the destination domain. It bounces the message back to the sender.

Some domains have MX records set to equal preference values. By default, the Postfix SMTP client randomly shuffles MX addresses of equal preference. You can change the default behavior by setting the `smtp_randomize_addresses` parameter:

```
smtp_randomize_addresses = no
```

Setting this parameter causes Postfix to attempt delivery to the MX servers in the same order it retrieved them.

Reverse PTR records

Due to the prevalence of spam, many sites now require that connecting clients have valid PTR records associated with their IP addresses. Your Postfix system's IP address should have a reverse PTR mapping to a hostname that returns the same IP address to ensure that you can deliver to all mail servers.

DNS and Receiving Mail

For Postfix to accept email for a particular domain, the system must be specified as an MX host in the domain's DNS setup, and Postfix must be configured to accept mail for the domain. Postfix accepts mail for domains that are either local to the system, relay domains, or virtual domains. Virtual domains might use virtual aliases or virtual mailboxes (see Chapter 8). Each type of domain must be listed in a different Postfix parameter, as shown in Table 6-1.

Table 6-1. Domain types and their parameters

Domain type	Parameter
Local	`mydestination`
Relay	`relay_domains`
Virtual mailboxes	`virtual_mailbox_domains`
Virtual aliases	`virtual_alias_domains`

Do not list a domain in more than one of the parameters. Postfix issues a warning if it detects a domain listed in two of the parameters. The error message "mail for example.com loops back to myself" occurs when the DNS configuration points to your mail server, but Postfix has not been configured to accept mail for the domain.

If your Postfix server accepts mail for the two local domains example.com and porcupine.org, then the `mydestination` parameter should look like the following in your *main.cf* file:

```
mydestination = example.com, porcupine.org
```

Chapter 9 explains configuration of relay domains. Chapter 8 covers virtual mailbox and virtual alias domains.

Common Problems

The following error messages in the mail log files indicate host lookup problems:

mail for domain loops back to myself
> This is one of the most common errors related to DNS. It happens when you have configured your Postfix server as an MX host in your DNS server, but you have not told your Postfix server that it is the final destination for the domain. Add the domain in question to the mydestination parameter, or configure it as a virtual domain or a relay domain. If your Postfix server is behind a proxy or NAT device, it may not realize that it is an MX host for the domain. In that case, add the proxy device's IP address to proxy_interfaces. Log entries for this error resemble the following:
>
> ```
> postfix/qmgr[3981]: 2CC3B229: from=<heloise@ora.com>, \
>     size=306, nrcpt=1 (queue active)
> postfix/smtp[3983]: warning: mailer loop: best MX host for \
>     example.com is local
> postfix/smtp[3983]: 2CC3B229: to=<abelard@example.com>, \
>     relay=none, delay=0, status=bounced (mail for example.com \
>     loops back to myself)
> ```

Host found but no data record of requested type
> The domain's DNS configuration has no MX records and there is no A record for the domain itself. You will have to contact an administrator of the domain to fix the problem. For your own domains, be sure they all include MX records pointing to your mail server. Log entries for this error resemble the following:
>
> ```
> postfix/qmgr[3818]: D31CD20F: from=<heloise@ora.com>, \
>     size=312, nrcpt=1 (queue active)
> postfix/smtp[3824]: D31CD20F: to=<abelard@example.com>, \
>     relay=none, delay=1, status=bounced (Name service \
>     error forname=example.com type=A: Host found but \
>     no data record of requested type)
> ```

no MX host for domain has a valid A record
> The domain's DNS configuration has MX records, but lookups for the IP addresses fail. You will have to contact an administrator of the domain to fix the problem. For your own domains, be sure that any hosts you specify as MX hosts are valid and have correct A records. Log entries for this error resemble the following:
>
> ```
> postfix/qmgr[3818]: 068DB20F: from=<heloise@ora.com> \
>     size=306, nrcpt=1 (queue active)
> postfix/smtp[3846]: warning: no MX host for example.com has \
>     a valid A record
> postfix/smtp[3846]: 068DB20F: to=<abelard@example.com> \
>     relay=none, delay=1, status=deferred (Name service \
>     error for name=mail.seaglass.com type=A: Host not found)
> ```

Host not found, try again

The DNS query produced no answer. Either the DNS server is not reachable, or it is broken. Assuming the DNS server for this domain is up and working correctly, this error message could be due to a networking problem, or perhaps your system's resolver is misconfigured. Check over the documentation for the *nsswitch.conf* and *resolv.conf* files on your platform. Be sure that your system is resolving DNS queries correctly, using one of the tools mentioned earlier in the chapter, before trying to troubleshoot the problem with Postfix. Log entries for this error resemble the following:

```
postfix/qmgr[3818]: CCBED1E8: from=<heloise@ora.com> \
        size=306, nrcpt=1 (queue active)
postfix/smtp[3937]: CCBED1E8: to=<abelard@example.com> \
        relay=none, delay=1, status=deferred (Name service error \
        for name=example.com type=MX: Host not found, try again)
```

If you are running Postfix in a chrooted environment, there are several configuration files related to DNS that must be within the chrooted compartment. See Chapter 4 for more information on running Postfix within a chroot.

## CHAPTER 7

Local Delivery and POP/IMAP

Chapter 1 explained that POP and IMAP are protocols that deal with how users retrieve their email messages from message stores. Postfix is a mail transfer agent and does not implement POP or IMAP. This chapter looks at how Postfix delivers messages and how they are read by POP/IMAP servers. There are many POP/IMAP servers available, and the information presented here should be applicable to any standards-conforming server. The last part of this chapter deals with configuring Postfix to work with the Cyrus IMAP server. Before we look at local delivery, we'll first discuss more broadly the different delivery transports Postfix uses. Transports other than local are discussed in subsequent chapters.

Postfix Delivery Transports

Postfix offers delivery for four different classes of recipient addresses: local, relay, virtual alias, and virtual mailbox. How you configure the domains you accept mail for determines the delivery method used by Postfix. The following are the delivery transports used by Postfix:

local
> Delivers mail on the local system. Each address has an account on the system or comes from the local aliases file (historically */etc/aliases*). Delivered messages go to the system's mail spool or mail files in individual home directories. Deliveries are handled by the local delivery agent or passed to a custom delivery program. Lists local domains in the mydestination parameter.

relay
> Delivers mail to other systems, usually on the same network. Relay domains are generally configured on gateway systems when Postfix accepts mail for an entire network. The gateway system relays messages to the correct internal mail system. Deliveries are handled by the relay transport, which is simply a clone of the smtp agent, but it is optimized for making deliveries to internal systems on a local network. Lists relay domains in the relay_domains parameter. Mail relaying is discussed in Chapter 9.

virtual

Delivers mail for virtual mailbox domains. Virtual mailbox domains are used for hosting multiple domains using a separate mail spool that contains mailboxes for many separate domains. Email users typically do not have system accounts on the mail server. Lists virtual mailbox domains in the `virtual_mailbox_domains` parameter. Virtual hosting is discussed in Chapter 8.

Deliveries to nonlocal domains are handled by the `smtp` transport. It determines where to deliver messages for any nonlocal domain through DNS lookups. Virtual alias addresses are resubmitted to Postfix for delivery to the new address, at which point they'll be handled by one of the above transports.

The rest of the chapter discusses the details of local delivery.

Message Store Formats

When Postfix makes local deliveries it transfers the contents of messages to the local message store. The most common types of message stores are the traditional *mbox* format and the newer *maildir* style. Both use regular files to store messages, but they are structured in different ways. In Postfix, you specify maildir style by including a trailing slash when you configure any mail file or directory parameters (see configuration information later in this chapter).

The Mbox Format

Historically, Unix systems have used a single file to store each user's email messages. This type of message store format is commonly referred to as *mbox*. Each message within the file starts with a line that begins with the word *From*. It is important that the string start on the first character of the line, and that there is a space after the end of the word. The From line is commonly referred to as `From_` with an underscore character to indicate the space following the word. Don't confuse the `From_` line used for separating messages within an mbox file with the `From:` line included in email message headers. The last line of a message is always a blank line.

A complete `From_` line looks like the following:

```
From jmbrown@example.com Sun Feb  3 16:54:01 2002
```

As described, the line starts with the word *From* followed by a space. Following the space is an email address that is usually the envelope address of the message. Following the envelope address is the date of delivery in the common Unix date format occupying 24 characters. The mbox format allows for an optional comment string following the date, but it is generally not used.

When Postfix delivers a message to an mbox file, it first creates the `From_` line using the envelope sender and the current date. Postfix then copies the contents of the delivered message into the mbox file. If Postfix encounters any lines that begin with

From followed by a space, it has to quote them by adding a > to the beginning of the line, so that they won't be confused with the start of the next message.

When a POP/IMAP server reads messages from the mbox file, it scans the file, looking for `From_` lines, which mark the beginning of each message. It can read to the next `From_` line (or the end of the file) to know when a message is finished. The POP/IMAP server may unquote any of the ">From" quoted lines, or they may remain in the quoted form.

Since both Postfix and the POP/IMAP servers access the mailbox file, they must use file locking. Postfix must obtain an exclusive lock on the file when it is delivering a message, so that it can write the message to the file. Postfix offers a variety of locking mechanisms, depending on the platform. You can use the `postconf -l` command to see which mechanisms Postfix can use on your system:

```
$ postconf -l
flock
fcntl
dotlock
```

If you want more information about the locking types listed by Postfix on your system, check your system's man pages for the specific lock name:

```
$ man flock
```

The `dotlock` type, which should be available on all systems, is probably not documented on your system, because it is not a function of the operating system or supporting libraries as `flock` and `fcntl` are. The `dotlock` is simply a file. The lock file name is made up of the name of the file to be locked with a *.lock* extension appended to it. If such a lock file exists, then Postfix knows that another process is using the mail file. If the file does not exist, Postfix creates it to signal other processes that it is using the file. When Postfix is finished, it removes the lock file, making the mail file available again. The drawback of `dotlock` locking is that it is susceptible to stale locks, and it is not very efficient.

For the most part, you do not need to worry about locking, and the lock types available, because Postfix does a good job of figuring out the best option.

The Maildir Format

The maildir mailbox format differs from mbox in that it uses a structure of directories to store email messages. It was designed to solve some of the reliability and locking problems of the mbox format. For example, if a system crashes at the instant an email message is being delivered to an mbox file, it is possible that the message will be truncated at the point where the delivery was interrupted. When the system comes back online, the mail transport agent will attempt to deliver the message again. The partially written message at the bottom of the mbox file may cause problems when the next message is appended to the file.

Other problems can occur if a POP/IMAP server tries to access the mbox file at the same time as the SMTP server. If the programs do not use the same locking mechanism, the mail file will most likely be corrupted. There are several possible mail file locking mechanisms (see above), which are not necessarily used by all mail programs. With the maildir format, no locks are necessary because each message gets its own file. Different mail processes do not need access to the same files at the same time.

A maildir-style directory has three subdirectories, which must all be on the same filesystem: *tmp*, *new*, and *cur*. These subdirectories are usually below a mail directory in a user's home directory:

```
$ ll /home/kdent/maildir
total 12
drwxr-x---   2 kdent    kdent        4096 Mar 13 12:24 cur
drwxr-x---   2 kdent    kdent        4096 Mar 13 12:24 new
drwxr-x---   2 kdent    kdent        4096 Mar 13 12:24 tmp
```

Files in the *new* directory are messages that have been delivered but have not yet been read. The modification time of the file is the delivery date of the message. The file usually contains the message in RFC 2822 format, and no From_ line is needed.

Once a message has been viewed, it is moved to the *cur* directory. The *tmp* directory is used during message delivery to store the contents of a file before it can be confirmed to have been written to the *new* directory.

Mbox Versus Maildir

There is no simple answer to help you decide which type of mailbox format is best for you. The mbox format has the advantage of being almost universally supported, but has the file-locking problems that prompted the development of the maildir format. On the other hand, there are concerns about the ability of the maildir format to scale to handle large numbers of messages on some filesystems. There are performance arguments to support both formats: locating and accessing or deleting a particular message is probably quicker with maildir, but delivery by simply appending the text of a message to the end of a single file is probably quicker in the mbox format. Your choice will most likely be driven by your selection of a POP/IMAP server. If you settle on a POP/IMAP server that requires the maildir format, the choice is made for you. Postfix easily supports either format, so you can safely allow other considerations to drive your decision. If you think it will be significant in your environment, you should run tests of both formats, simulating your own mail tasks as closely as possible.

Local Delivery

All destination domains that should be handled by the local transport should be listed in the mydestination parameter. You can list as many domains as you like, but individual local users receive mail at all of the domains listed. For example, if both *ora.com* and *oreilly.com* are listed in mydestination, then messages to either *kdent@ora.com* or *kdent@oreilly.com* go to the same local mailbox.

All local recipients should be listed in tables configured in the local_recipient_ maps parameter to avoid accepting messages for unknown users. By default, local_recipient_maps is set to the system password file and alias maps, so you normally don't have to make any changes. Once Postfix has determined that it is the final destination for a message, and that the message should be delivered locally, it has to decide what to do with the message.

Before looking for a user account that matches the local part of the email address, Postfix consults its alias maps (see Chapter 4). If there is a forwarding alias that matches the recipient address, Postfix resubmits the message as a new delivery, based on the forwarding information from the alias lookup. Otherwise, it tries to deliver the message to a user on the system. Postfix first checks for the existence of a *.forward* file for the local user, and may resubmit the message based on information there. If no *.forward* exists for the user, Postfix delivers the message to the user's mailbox.

.forward Files

.forward files allow local users to set up their own aliases. The contents of the *.forward* file are the same as the righthand side of an alias entry. When an alias entry has multiple values on the righthand side, they are separated by commas; while *.forward* files use the same convention, they also allow multiple entries to be entered on multiple lines.

.forward files must be owned by the recipient, and are normally found in users' home directories. You can specify different locations with the forward_path parameter. When specifying a path for the parameter, there are eight variables whose values are expanded at delivery time:

$user
> Recipient username as specified in */etc/passwd*

$home
> Recipient home directory as specified in */etc/passwd*

$shell
> Recipient shell as specified in */etc/passwd*

$recipient
> The complete recipient email address

$extension
> An optional extension of a local part of the recipient address, separated by a delimiter such as the + character

$domain
> Domain from the recipient email address

```
$local
```
Complete local part of recipient email address (includes extensions if any)
```
$recipient_delimiter
```
Delimiter character from the recipient email address, if there is an extension

If you want to add support for a nonstandard *.forward* file, you could configure forward_path as follows:

```
forward_path = /home/$user/.forward /home/$user/other_forward
```

See the Postfix local manpage for more information on specifying paths with variable expansion.

Alias Deliveries

When Postfix delivers to a command or file specified in alias files, it makes the delivery or executes the command as the user who owns the alias file. The exception is when the file is owned by *root*, in which case Postfix uses the account specified in the default_privs parameter. By default it is set to the account *nobody*. Aliases are discussed in Chapter 4.

Mailbox Delivery

When Postfix delivers a message to a local user, it writes the message to the system's message store. By default Postfix uses the mbox format for deliveries. When you install Postfix, it can normally figure out the default location of the mail spool directory depending on the type of Unix system you have. The mail_spool_directory parameter can be used to specify a directory other than the default. To change the directory to something other than the default for your system, edit the *main.cf* file, and add or modify the mail_spool_directory parameter:

```
mail_spool_directory = /var/spool/mail
```

To cause Postfix to use the maildir format for delivery, append the directory with a trailing slash:

```
mail_spool_directory = /var/spool/mail/
```

Postfix can also be configured to deliver messages to mailboxes within users' home directories. Assign a relative path to the home_mailbox parameter to indicate which file should be used for mailboxes:

```
home_mailbox = mbox
```

Append the path with a trailing slash to indicate that Postfix should use the maildir-style delivery:

```
home_mailbox = maildir/
```

This causes Postfix to deliver messages into a directory called *maildir*, below users' home directories.

With maildir-style delivery, Postfix normally creates the necessary directories and files, if the user's credentials permit it; however, as a security precaution, if the parent directory is world-writable, Postfix delivery agents will not create any additional files or directories.

POP and IMAP

After Postfix has delivered a message, users need a way to read it. Many sites provide a POP/IMAP server for users to retrieve their email messages over the network. In most cases Postfix works seamlessly with POP/IMAP servers, so that no special configuration is required on either side.

POP Versus IMAP

The POP protocol works best when you have limited, or less than full-time, network access because it allows you to connect to your mail server, fetch all of your messages, and disconnect from the network. You now have local copies that you can read offline. Most POP clients have a configuration option to delete your messages from the server when you retrieve them, since you then have the local copies. If you don't delete them at some time, the messages accumulate, taking up more and more space on your mail server. POP was designed to be easy to implement, but the major problem with the POP protocol is that if you ever work from more than one computer, your messages may not be where you need them. It also does not handle multiple mailboxes very well, and it forces you to download complete messages. There is no option to retrieve just the subject, for example, to decide if you want the complete message.

The IMAP protocol was designed to overcome some of POP's shortcomings. It keeps all messages on the server. You have to be connected while working with your email messages, but you can manage them as if they were local. Since everything happens on the server, it doesn't matter if you work from your desktop computer at home, another machine at work, and even on a laptop while traveling. IMAP still allows for saving messages locally, if necessary, and it also provides much more flexibility than POP. You can download just the headers from your messages and then decide to retrieve the rest of a message if you want to read it. You don't have to be stuck downloading a huge message or attachment that you might not be interested in. You can maintain multiple mailboxes and folders on the IMAP server.

Postfix and POP/IMAP Servers

The cooperation between Postfix and POP/IMAP servers is simple. When Postfix accepts delivery of an email message, it places it in the message store. The POP/IMAP server simply retrieves messages from the same store when a user requests them.

Figure 7-1 shows how simple the cooperation is between Postfix and POP/IMAP servers. Postfix and the POP/IMAP server must agree on the type of mailbox format and the style of locking. Postfix should work with any standards-compliant POP/IMAP server that uses one of the traditional message stores. You may have to adjust the `mail_spool_directory` parameter, as described earlier in the chapter, but for most POP/IMAP servers, you can simply follow the standard installation instructions and start the server. For POP/IMAP servers that don't use a traditional message store, Postfix can still deliver messages using the Local Mail Transfer Protocol, which is discussed in the next section.

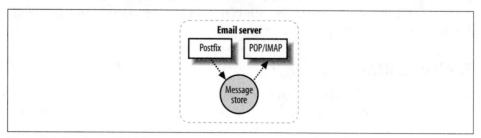

Figure 7-1. Postfix and POP/IMAP servers

Local Mail Transfer Protocol

Some POP/IMAP servers use nonstandard message stores. Since it would be unreasonable to expect MTAs such as Postfix to understand many different proprietary formats, the *Local Mail Transfer Protocol* (LMTP) provides a way to pass email messages from one local mail service to another without depending on a common message store. LMTP is based on, and is a simplified version of, SMTP. With LMTP, the server can either accept an email message immediately or it cannot accept it at all. There is no attempt by the LMTP server to queue or redeliver a message that cannot be delivered immediately.

When an MTA makes a delivery to an SMTP server, where the message is destined for multiple recipients, and one or more recipients cannot accept the message for some reason, the SMTP server takes the responsibility of queuing the message to deliver it later, and reports an overall successful delivery to the MTA. LMTP servers do not queue messages, so they must return an individual status reply for every recipient of a particular email message. For those recipients that could not be delivered, the MTA, and not the LMTP server, takes the responsibility of queuing the message and attempting redelivery.

LMTP conversations can occur between mail subsystems on the same machine or on different machines on a local area network. It is not recommended for wide area networks, since the protocol depends on a quick response to indicate whether the message was delivered. With SMTP there is a recognized synchronization problem between sending and receiving mail systems that sometimes causes duplicate messages to be delivered. It is believed that LMTP over wide area networks would make the problem worse.

 Apart from delivery to nonstandard message stores, a real benefit of the LMTP protocol is that it allows for a highly scalable and reliable mail system. One or more Postfix servers can receive mail from the public Internet and make deliveries to multiple LMTP backend systems. As the load increases, it is a simple matter to add more boxes to the front- or backend systems.

The most common implementation of LMTP delivery is the Cyrus IMAP server from Carnegie Mellon University. It is available from the Project Cyrus web page at *http:// asg.web.cmu.edu/cyrus/*. Cyrus IMAP uses its own message store, as shown in Figure 7-2. This section looks at how Postfix can use the LMTP protocol to hand off messages to Cyrus IMAP. For more information about configuring Cyrus IMAP, see *Managing IMAP* by Dianna Mullet and Kevin Mullet (O'Reilly).

Postfix and Cyrus IMAP

Cyrus IMAP is intended to run on servers that provide POP/IMAP access only, where users do not need a shell account. If you are creating a mail server for existing users on a system, you will probably want to use another simpler POP/IMAP solution, such as Qualcomm's Qpopper (POP access only) or the University of Washington's IMAP Toolkit, which doesn't require any special configuration to work with Postfix. This section deals with configuration issues for getting Postfix to work together with Cyrus IMAP.

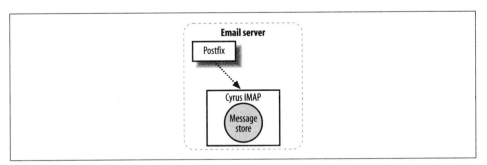

Figure 7-2. Postfix and Cyrus IMAP

Cyrus IMAP can listen for LMTP deliveries using either Unix-domain sockets or TCP sockets. You must know which method you are using so that you can configure Postfix appropriately. If you want to use Unix-domain sockets, both Postfix and the Cyrus IMAP server must be on the same machine. If you use TCP sockets, the Cyrus IMAP server could be on the same system or any other system on your network. LMTP delivery is configured in your *main.cf* file or in a transport map.

For Postfix to accept messages to be delivered locally to Cyrus IMAP, the destination domain name of the email address must be listed in the mydestination parameter. (You may also want to configure Cyrus deliveries via the virtual transport. See Chapter 8.) Then you must configure Postfix to pass messages to Cyrus IMAP. Use the mailbox_transport, local_transport, or fallback_transport parameter to tell Postfix how much local processing to do before handing off messages to Cyrus. If you are using local_transport or fallback_transport, make sure that Postfix knows about all of the Cyrus users, by including the usernames in a lookup table listed with the local_recipient_maps parameter.

mailbox_transport

> The mail message is given to the local delivery agent first. The local delivery agent checks for and expands any aliases or entries in *.forward* files. After expansion of the original address, the message is delegated to the Postfix LMTP client, which delivers it to the LMTP server.

local_transport

> When you specify that the local transport should be LMTP, Postfix transfers the message directly to the Postfix LMTP client. The normal local delivery agent does not process the message at all, so there is no expansion of aliases or *.forward* files.

fallback_transport

> When the fallback transport is LMTP, Postfix gives the message to its local delivery agent first. The normal aliases and *.forward* files are expanded, and if the recipient has a normal account on the system, delivery is made to the appropriate mail store on the system. If no such account exists, delivery is delegated to the Postfix LMTP client for delivery to the LMTP server. If you have actual accounts on the system that should receive email messages in the conventional message store, and the rest of your email users do not have system accounts but do receive mail through the Cyrus IMAP server, you should configure the fallback_transport to use LMTP delivery.

Specify your chosen transport type using the following format:

```
xxx_transport = service:socket_type[:/path/to/socket]
```

For LMTP delivery, service must be lmtp, which refers to the lmtp service in the */etc/postfix/master.cf* file. The socket_type is either unix or inet for Unix domain, or TCP sockets, respectively. The default is inet, which means that if your LMTP server uses an inet socket, you can simply specify the service as:

```
local_transport = lmtp
```

A typical LMTP transport configuration in */etc/postfix/main.cf* using local_transport and a Unix domain socket looks like the following:

```
local_transport = lmtp:unix:/var/imap/socket/lmtp
```

A Postfix and Cyrus IMAP Example

To build Cyrus IMAP, you need the Cyrus SASL library, which is used to authenticate users for the IMAP server.* You must first build and install the Cyrus SASL library, and then you can build the Cyrus IMAP server. The Cyrus software requires at least Version 3 of Berkeley DB. If you were using a version of Berkeley DB prior to Version 3, you may need to update your entire system. Having different versions of Berkeley DB intermixed on your system will likely lead to problems that can be difficult to track down. If you have to upgrade your libraries, consider rebuilding other packages that use Berkeley DB (such as Perl and Postfix), so that everything on your system uses the same version of the library.

Follow the instructions in the Cyrus SASL and IMAP distributions to compile and install them correctly on your system. There might be binary distributions available for your platform. Check your normal software sources to see if you can save yourself the trouble of building the Cyrus software.

For this example, assume that you have a Postfix server receiving mail for the domain example.com. All of the email accounts are set up within the Cyrus IMAP server running on the same system, so there are very few actual login accounts on the system. However, you want mail destined for the root account or postmaster alias to be sent to the correct person, which means that you need to expand local aliases before handing off messages to the Cyrus IMAP server. To achieve this, set the mailbox_transport parameter to point to the lmtp delivery agent, which will be configured to deliver mail to the Cyrus IMAP server:

1. Complete the installation and configuration of Cyrus IMAP on your system. Check the Cyrus configuration file (normally */etc/cyrus.conf*) to make sure that it is configured to use Unix-domain sockets, and note the location of the socket file. You should see an entry that resembles the following:

   ```
   SERVICES {
     # add or remove based on preferences
     imap        cmd="imapd" listen="imap" prefork=0
     pop3        cmd="pop3d" listen="pop3" prefork=0
     # LMTP is required for delivery
     lmtpunix    cmd="lmtpd" listen="/var/imap/socket/lmtp" prefork=0
   }
   ```

   The lmtpunix entry shows the correct path to the socket file.

2. Follow the documentation that came with your package to add users to your Cyrus IMAP server.

3. Check the */etc/postfix/master.cf* to make sure that the lmtp service is set up correctly. The line should look like the following:

   ```
   lmtp     unix -      -       n      -       -      lmtp
   ```

---

* It is the same library that is used to add authentication support for Postfix. See Chapter 12 for more information on adding SMTP authentication support to Postfix.

If you have a default Postfix installation, the lmtp line will already be in the file, as shown in the example. The fifth column indicates whether the LMTP delivery agent should run within a chrooted environment. In this example, the Postfix LMTP delivery agent must read the socket file created by the Cyrus IMAP server, so leave this column with the value n.[*]

4. Check the *main.cf* file to make sure that the domain you are receiving mail for is listed in the mydestination parameter. It might be listed explicitly:

   ```
   mydestination = $myhostname, localhost.$mydomain, $mydomain,
       example.com
   ```

   or it might come from the $mydomain variable:

   ```
   mydomain = example.com
   mydestination = $myhostname, localhost.$mydomain, $mydomain
   ```

5. Specify that the mailbox_transport parameter should use the lmtp service from the *master.cf* file, and point to the Cyrus IMAP socket file whose path you determined from the Cyrus configuration file (see item 1):

   ```
   mailbox_transport = lmtp:unix:/var/imap/socket/lmtp
   ```

6. Reload Postfix:

   ```
   # postfix reload
   ```

---

[*] It is possible to set up your system in such a way that allows the LMTP delivery agent to read the socket file even from within the Postfix chroot environment, but it is probably not necessary.

## CHAPTER 8

Hosting Multiple Domains

It is very common these days for a single system to host many domains. For instance, *oreillynet.com* and *onlamp.com* might run on a single host, but act as if they were two totally different hosts. A system usually has a *canonical* domain, which is considered its usual or common domain name. Additional domains are configured as *virtual* domains. Each virtual domain can host services such as web sites and email as if it were the only domain on a server. This chapter explains several different mechanisms for hosting multiple domains. The techniques are explained separately, but it is possible to mix techniques if you must handle different domains in different ways.

To determine which technique or techniques you need, you must decide how Postfix should deliver messages for virtual domains. There are two important considerations that influence how you should configure Postfix for hosting multiple domains:

- Should your domains have separate namespaces? For example, should mail for the two addresses *info@ora.com* and *info@oreilly.com* go to the same mailbox or separate ones? We'll refer to the same mailbox scenario as shared domains, and the other as separate domains.

- Does every user require a system account? We'll make the distinction between system accounts that are real Unix accounts on your system and virtual accounts. With virtual accounts, users can have mailboxes on your server, but don't otherwise log in to the system and don't require an entry in */etc/passwd*.

We'll consider four different ways Postfix can handle mail for virtual domains:

- Shared domains with system accounts
- Separate domains with system accounts
- Separate domains with virtual accounts
- Virtual domains with a proprietary message store not managed by Postfix

Your POP/IMAP server will be a major factor in deciding which technique you need. If your POP/IMAP server does not understand virtual domains, then it will most likely require that you have system accounts for all addresses. Some POP/IMAP servers inherently support multiple domains, and deliver messages into a particular directory structure on the local filesystem. Other POP/IMAP servers use their own proprietary message store. Postfix can hand off messages to them using LMTP.

Regardless of the technique you use, all of your virtual domains must be configured correctly in DNS. You should configure DNS for virtual domains the same way you do for your system's canonical domain. See Chapter 6 for information on Postfix and DNS.

Shared Domains with System Accounts

Accepting mail for multiple domains where every user can receive mail for every domain is the simplest configuration of virtual domains. Simply add your virtual domains to the mydestination parameter. Create user accounts as you normally would, and they can start receiving mail addressed to any of the domains. This technique uses the local delivery agent, providing all of the same features as your normal canonical domain hosting. Users can create their own *.forward* files, and local aliases are available. On a system whose canonical name is *oreillynet.com*, hosting two virtual domains, *ora.com* and *oreilly.com*, the mydomain parameter is set as if *oreillynet.com* were the only domain, and mydestination is set as follows:

```
mydomain = oreillynet.com
mydestination = $myhostname, $mydomain, ora.com, oreilly.com
```

Make sure you reload Postfix after making changes. Users can now receive mail at any of the domains you listed in mydestination:

```
# postfix reload
```

Messages addressed to either *info@ora.com* or *info@oreilly.com* all go to the same local user account.

Separate Domains with System Accounts

If you require separate namespaces for each of your virtual domains, the configuration is only slightly more complicated. With separate domains, mail to *info@ora.com* should go to a different mailbox than mail to *info@oreilly.com*. In this case, do not list the additional domains in the mydestination parameter. Instead, use virtual_alias_domains:

```
virtual_alias_domains = ora.com, oreilly.com
```

You must create a user account for every email address that will receive messages on your system. Your system accounts do not have to match the email addresses in any way, since you will be mapping the addresses to the accounts separately, but each account must be unique. If your platform supports long usernames, a good way to create unique account names, and to avoid confusion about which accounts are meant to receive mail at which domains, is to use the domain name itself as part of the account name. One possible naming convention is to create accounts such as *info.ora.com* and *info.oreilly.com*.

Once Postfix knows which domains to accept mail for, and you have accounts for each address, use `virtual_alias_maps` to map the email addresses to the accounts you create. In *main.cf*, point the `virtual_alias_maps` parameter to the virtual alias lookup file. In this example, the file */etc/postfix/virtual_alias* is used:

```
virtual_alias_maps = hash:/etc/postfix/virtual_alias
```

The */etc/postfix/virtual_alias* file contains entries with the email addresses pointing to the system accounts you created, plus any non-local forwarding you need:

```
info@ora.com        helene@localhost
info@oreilly.com    frank@localhost
kdent@oreilly.com   kyle.dent@onlamp.com
```

Whenever you create or update a virtual aliases file, don't forget to execute the postmap command on the file:

```
# postmap virtual_alias
```

If *helene* and *frank* plan to send messages from the system, you may also want to set up canonical maps so that their outbound messages show the correct sending addresses. Assign a lookup table like the following to `canonical_maps`:

```
helene    info@ora.com
frank     info@oreilly.com
```

And remember to execute postmap against the file:

```
# postmap canonical
```

Separate Domains with Virtual Accounts

The drawback for the techniques so far is that you must maintain system accounts for all email addresses on your server. As the number of domains you host increases, so does the effort to maintain all the accounts. In particular, if users only receive email at your server, and don't otherwise log in, you probably don't want to have to create system accounts for each one. Instead, configure Postfix to deliver to a local message store where each virtual email address can have its own mailbox file. Your users then retrieve their messages through a POP/IMAP server.

The local message store works much like normal local delivery, but it doesn't require a one-to-one correspondence between each mail file and a local user account. For this configuration, list each virtual domain in the `virtual_mailbox_domains` parameter:

```
virtual_mailbox_domains = ora.com, oreilly.com
```

If you have many domains, you can list them in a file and point `virtual_mailbox_domains` to the file:

```
virtual_mailbox_domains = /etc/postfix/virtual_domains
```

The file */etc/postfix/virtual_domains* then contains a line for each domain:

```
#
# /etc/postfix/virtual_domains
#
ora.com
oreilly.com
```

Virtual domains listed in `virtual_mailbox_domains` are delivered by the virtual delivery agent, which is actually a streamlined version of the local delivery agent. It makes deliveries in a highly secure and efficient manner, but local aliases, *.forward* files, and mailing list programs are not available. You can make use of the `virtual_alias_maps` parameter that you saw earlier in the chapter to accomplish aliasing, and we'll look at a technique to accomplish delivery to programs later in this chapter.

When setting up the virtual mailboxes, you should structure the directories to accommodate the expectations of your POP/IMAP server. Let's assume for this explanation that the virtual mailboxes are all located below the base directory */usr/local/vmail*. Each virtual domain has its own subdirectory below that, so that you have directories like the following:

```
/usr/local/vmail/ora.com
/usr/local/vmail/oreilly.com
```

This is a common configuration for POP/IMAP servers that support virtual hosting. Below each domain subdirectory are the mail files for each user. Indicate to Postfix the base directory of the mail store with the `virtual_mailbox_base` parameter:

```
virtual_mailbox_base = /usr/local/vmail
```

You must create a lookup file that maps email addresses to their mailbox files. Specify the lookup table with the `virtual_mailbox_maps` parameter:

```
virtual_mailbox_maps = hash:/etc/postfix/virtual
```

Every user receiving mail to a virtual mailbox file must have an entry in a Postfix lookup table. The mailbox file is specified relative to `virtual_mailbox_base`. Mail files can use either mbox or maildir format (see Chapter 7). To use maildir format, include a slash at the end of the filename. A virtual mailbox map file looks like the following:

```
info@ora.com        ora.com/info
info@oreilly.com    oreilly.com/info
```

The email address *info@ora.com* goes to a different mailbox from the address *info@oreilly.com*.

Mailbox File Ownership

The virtual mailbox files must be owned by a user account and associated with a group on your system. How your users retrieve their messages determines what the ownership of mailbox files should be. Often, your POP/IMAP server executes under its own account and expects all of the mailbox files to be owned by this user, but if necessary, Postfix lets you configure ownership for mailbox files in any way you need. Each can be owned by a separate user, or one user can own all of the mailboxes for one domain, while a different user owns the mailboxes of another.

The virtual_uid_maps and virtual_gid_maps parameters determine the owner and group Postfix uses when making deliveries to virtual mailbox files. You can specify that all of the virtual mailboxes should be owned by the same user account with the static map type. Assume, for this example, that you have created an account called *vmail* that has a UID of 1003, and a group called *vmail* that has a GID of 1005. You want all of the virtual mailbox files to be owned by this user and group.

Set the virtual_uid_maps and virtual_gid_maps parameters in *main.cf*:

```
virtual_uid_maps = static:1003
virtual_gid_maps = static:1005
```

If you want to use different UIDs for different mailbox files, you must create a lookup file that maps the addresses to the UIDs. Then point the mapping parameter to your lookup file:

```
virtual_uid_maps = hash:/etc/postfix/virtual_uids
```

If most of your virtual mailboxes should have the same fixed ownership but some require different UIDs, you can combine static and table lookups:

```
virtual_uid_maps = hash:/etc/postfix/virtual_uids static:1003
```

If you also need separate group mappings, they work exactly the same way.

The file */etc/postfix/virtual_uids* contains entries like the following, with each address mapped to the correct UID. In this case, the mailboxes for *ora.com* use one ID and those for *oreilly.com* use another:

```
#
# /etc/postfix/virtual_uids
#
info@ora.com          1004
kdent@ora.com         1004
info@oreilly.com      1007
service@oreilly.com   1007
```

Virtual Aliases

It is possible for a virtually hosted domain to have some addresses that are delivered to the local message store and some that are forwarded. Since all recipient addresses are checked for virtual aliasing regardless of their class, simply place the forwarded addresses in the virtual_alias_maps file instead of the virtual_mailbox_maps file. Make sure the virtual_alias_maps parameter points to a virtual alias lookup table:

```
virtual_alias_maps = hash:/etc/postfix/virtual_alias
```

The */etc/postfix/virtual_alias* file contains entries for addresses that should be forwarded elsewhere:

```
kdent@oreilly.com    kyle.dent@onlamp.com
```

Do not list a domain in both `virtual_mailbox_domains` and `virtual_alias_domains`. Use `virtual_mailbox_domains` for domains that have a mix of aliases and mailboxes and `virtual_alias_domains` only when all of the addresses are aliases.

Catchall Addresses

For either virtual mailboxes or virtual aliases, your lookup table can have a key value of the domain without a local part to catch any message destined for the domain addressed to a nonexistent address. Catchall addresses should be used advisedly, since they tend to receive a lot of spam. Spammers often send messages to nonexistent accounts at a domain, which are received by catchall addresses.

Virtual mailbox catchall

The first step is to identify a mailbox to receive messages sent to nonexistent addresses. You can use an existing mailbox or create a new one. Add a new `virtual_mailbox_maps` entry like the following to deliver any message with an unknown destination address to the *service* mailbox:

```
@ora.com        ora.com/service
```

Virtual alias catchall

Catchall addresses with virtual aliases work similarly to virtual mailboxes, but you should set up a catchall alias address only if all addresses in a domain are configured as aliases and not mailboxes. Since virtual aliases are checked before virtual mailboxes, a catchall alias intercepts all messages, including those otherwise destined for virtual mailbox addresses. Once you've identified the address that should receive messages sent to nonexistent addresses, add a new `virtual_alias_maps` entry like the following:

```
@ora.com        customer.service@onlamp.com
```

It's possible to have a virtual alias catchall address in conjunction with virtual mailbox addresses by creating entries for all of your virtual mailbox addresses in your virtual alias lookup maps. Assuming you have virtual mailboxes configured like the following:

```
info@ora.com       ora.com/info
info@oreilly.com   oreilly.com/info
```

your virtual alias lookup table that includes a catchall alias must also contain the mailbox entries:

```
@ora.com           customer.service@onlamp.com
kdent@oreilly.com  kyle.dent@onlamp.com
info@ora.com       info@ora.com
info@oreilly.com   info@oreilly.com
```

In this way, a message addressed to *info@oreilly.com* won't be intercepted by the *@ora.com* catchall alias.

Separate Message Store

The last configuration we'll consider is hosting virtual domains with a system using a proprietary message store. To work with these systems, Postfix hands off messages using a protocol like LMTP, letting the proprietary system handle delivery to the correct mail box.

Since Postfix must receive messages before handing them off to the LMTP server, it has to know that it should accept mail for each of the virtual domains. List them in virtual_mailbox_domains:

```
virtual_mailbox_domains = ora.com, oreilly.com
```

You also have to list each email address, so Postfix can accept messages for valid addresses and reject unknown users. Use the virtual_mailbox_maps parameter to point to a lookup file with valid addresses:

```
virtual_mailbox_maps = hash:/etc/postfix/virtual
```

In the */etc/postfix/virtual* file, the righthand value isn't used because all messages are passed along to the POP/IMAP server. You must still include a righthand value because lookup tables must have a key and a value, but the value you use doesn't matter:

```
info@ora.com        General Information Address
info@oreilly.com    General Information Address
```

In order to have Postfix pass mail for virtual domains through to your POP/IMAP server, specify the correct transport in the virtual_transport parameter in *main.cf*. You have to know how your LMTP server socket is set up. Assuming it's on the same host as Postfix and uses a socket file located at */var/imap/socket/lmtp*, the transport lookup table for the example domains looks like the following:

```
virtual_transport = lmtp:unix:/var/imap/socket/imap
```

This causes all of your virtual_mailbox_domains to be delivered to your POP/IMAP server over LMTP.

Delivery to Commands

As mentioned earlier in the chapter, you can't use local aliases, *.forward* files, and mailing-list programs with virtual domains delivered by the virtual delivery agent. You've seen that you can easily set up aliases through the virtual_alias_maps parameter, but you cannot deliver messages to a command. In this last section, we'll look at working around that issue by demonstrating how to deliver virtual addresses to external programs. The first example sets up delivery to an autoreply program, and the second to a mailing-list manager.

Auto-responders are scripts or programs that process incoming messages and return a reply to the sender of the message without any human intervention. The autoreply program used in this example, inforeply.pl, is listed in Example 8-1. This program is meant to handle mail for a dedicated information email address. Users or customers can send a message to the address to request special information. Note that this simple example is inadequate as a general autoreply program, such as the Unix vacation command. It does not cache addresses it has already replied to, and it does not do full checking for addresses that should not receive automatic replies (see the sidebar). You might also like to enhance the program to return different types of information, based on the subject or a keyword in the body of the request messages.

Example 8-1. Simple automatic reply program

```
#!/usr/bin/perl -w
#
# inforeply.pl - Automatic email reply.
#
# All messages are logged to your mail log. Check the
# log after executing the script to see the results.
#
# Set $UID to the uid of the process that runs the script.
# Check the entry in master.cf that calls this script. Use
# the uid of the account you assign to the user= attribute.
# If you want to test the script from the command line,
# set $UID to your own uid.
#
# Set $ENV_FROM to the envelope FROM address you want on
# outgoing replies. By default it's blank, which will
# use the NULL sender address <>. You can set it to an
# address to receive bounces, but make sure you don't set
# it to the same address that invokes the program, or
# you'll create a mail loop.
#
# Point $INFOFILE to a text file that contains the text of
# the outgoing reply. Include any headers you want in the
# message such as Subject: and From:. The To: header is
# set automatically based on the sender's address. Make
# sure you have an empty line between your headers and the
# body of the message.
#
# If necessary, change the path to sendmail in $MAILBIN.
#
# @MAILOPTS contains options to sendmail. Make changes if
# necessary. The default options should work in most
# situations.
#
# The calls to syslog require that your Perl installation
# converted the necessary header files. See h2ph in your
# Perl distribution.
#

require 5.004;  # for setlogsock in Sys::Syslog module
```

Example 8-1. Simple automatic reply program (continued)

```perl
use strict;
use Sys::Syslog qw(:DEFAULT setlogsock);

#
# Config options. Set these according to your needs.
#
my $UID = 500;
my $ENV_FROM = "";
my $INFOFILE = "/home/autoresp/inforeply.txt";
my $MAILBIN = "/usr/sbin/sendmail";
my @MAILOPTS = ("-oi", "-tr", "$ENV_FROM");
my $SELF = "inforeply.pl";
#
# end of config options

my $EX_TEMPFAIL = 75;
my $EX_UNAVAILABLE = 69;
my $EX_OK = 0;
my $sender;
my $euid = $>;

$SIG{PIPE} = \&PipeHandler;
$ENV{PATH} = "/bin:/usr/bin:/sbin:/usr/sbin";

setlogsock('unix');
openlog($SELF, 'ndelay,pid', 'user');

#
# Check our environment.
#
if ( $euid != $UID ) {
        syslog('mail|err',"error: invalid uid: $> (expecting: $UID)");
        exit($EX_TEMPFAIL);
}
if ( @ARGV != 1 ) {
        syslog('mail|err',"error: invalid invocation (expecting 1 argument)");
        exit($EX_TEMPFAIL);
} else {
        $sender = $ARGV[0];
        if ( $sender =~ /([\w\-.%]+\@[\w.-]+)/ ) {    # scrub address
                $sender = $1;
        } else {
                syslog('mail|err',"error: Illegal sender address");
                exit($EX_UNAVAILABLE);
        }
}
if (! -x $MAILBIN ) {
        syslog('mail|err', "error: $MAILBIN not found or not executable");
        exit($EX_TEMPFAIL);
}
if (! -f $INFOFILE ) {
        syslog('mail|err', "error: $INFOFILE not found");
        exit($EX_TEMPFAIL);
```

Example 8-1. Simple automatic reply program (continued)

```
}

#
# Check sender exceptions.
#
if ($sender eq ""
    || $sender =~ /^owner-|-(request|owner)\@|^(mailer-daemon|postmaster)\@/i) {
    exit($EX_OK);
}


#
# Check message contents for Precedence header.
#
while ( <STDIN> ) {
        last if (/^$/);
        exit($EX_OK) if (/^precedence:\s+(bulk|list|junk)/i);
}


#
# Open info file.
#
if (! open(INFO, "<$INFOFILE") ) {
        syslog('mail|err',"error: can't open $INFOFILE: %m");
        exit($EX_TEMPFAIL);
}


#
# Open pipe to mailer.
#
my $pid = open(MAIL, "|-") || exec("$MAILBIN", @MAILOPTS);


#
# Send reply.
#
print MAIL "To: $sender\n";
print MAIL while (<INFO>);

if (! close(MAIL) ) {
        syslog('mail|err',"error: failure invoking $MAILBIN: %m");
        exit($EX_UNAVAILABLE);
}

close(INFO);
syslog('mail|info',"sent reply to $sender");
exit($EX_OK);


sub PipeHandler {
        syslog('mail|err',"error: broken pipe to mailer");
}
```

Configuring a Virtual Auto-Responder

To configure an auto-responder to work with virtual domains, you must create a special transport type in *master.cf* for delivery to the specific command. In order to have messages delivered to your new component, you have to map an address to the transport you created using transport maps.

Many auto-responders can handle only a single message at a time with only one recipient. You can limit the number of recipients to any transport type by setting a parameter of the form `transport_destination_recipient_limit`, where the string `transport` is the name of the transport type. If a transport called `inforeply` should be limited to only one recipient at a time, set the following parameter:

```
inforeply_destination_recipient_limit = 1
```

Writing an Auto-Responder

If you are writing your own auto-responder, there are several considerations you should take into account. The first, and possibly most important, is that your program is receiving data from the network, which is an untrusted source. Don't make any assumptions about the supplied input you are processing, other than to assume that it's designed to compromise your system in some way. Under no circumstances should you invoke a shell where the untrusted input might be able to gain access to your system.

Other issues to think about have more to do with being polite than anything else. For example, you don't want your auto-responder to blast out a reply to a mailing list of hundreds or thousands of recipients. Never send replies to addresses that have the form `owner-list` or `list-request`. There are several other addresses you probably don't want to reply to, such as `postmaster`, `daemon`, and `majordomo`. Your program should set its own envelope address to the null string to prevent mailer loops.

Many mailing lists make use of a header field called `Precedence:`. They generally set the value to something like `bulk` to indicate its purpose. Your program should check the `Precedence:` field, and if it is set to `bulk`, `list`, or `junk`, do not send a reply.

Finally, make sure that your program has a way to log what happens to each message received. Once Postfix delivers a message to your program, the program has the responsibility of checking for errors and providing a way to communicate them to an administrator.

The following steps walk through setting up the email address *info@ora.com* to use `inforeply.pl`. The domain *ora.com* is configured as a virtual domain. The local domain on the host is *example.com*:

1. Create a local account under whose privileges the `inforeply.pl` program should execute. In this example, an account called *autoresp* is used. You should create a new pseudo-account for this purpose. Use the normal administrative tools on your system to make the account.

2. Create a transport type called `inforeply` by adding an entry to your *master.cf* file. The entry should look something like the following:

```
inforeply     unix -     n     n     -     -     pipe
    flags= user=autoresp argv=/usr/local/bin/inforeply.pl ${sender}
```

The pipe daemon is used to deliver messages to external commands. You can specify `flags` if your program requires any special options. (See the pipe(8) man page for information on the available options.) The `user` attribute is required for any pipe components in *master.cf*. The `argv` attribute must be specified last, and should start with the path to the autoreply command. There are several values that you can pass to your command when Postfix executes it. The values are supplied through special macros. In this example, the envelope sender address (`${sender}`) is passed. For the simple `inforeply.pl` responder, you need only the sender address, but you will often want the recipient (`${recipient}`) address, too, for auto-responders that can handle multiple recipient addresses. See the pipe(8) manpage for the list of available macros.

3. If you haven't already set up any transports on your system, set the `transport_maps` parameter in *main.cf* to point to the transport table:

```
transport_maps = hash:/etc/postfix/transport
```

4. Add an entry in your transport table that contains the address to direct messages to the `inforeply` transport. In this case, we'll use the address *autoresp@ora.com*:

```
autoresp@ora.com              inforeply
```

Now, all messages sent to *autoresp@ora.com* are delivered to the auto-responder.

5. Execute postmap against the transport lookup table:

 # postmap /etc/postfix/transport

6. Point `virtual_alias_maps` to your virtual alias lookup table:

```
virtual_alias_maps = hash:/etc/postfix/virtual_alias
```

7. Add an entry to the virtual_alias lookup table to map *info@ora.com* to both the new autoreply address and the actual recipient address that can receive the messages:

```
info@ora.com        autoresp@ora.com service@oreilly.com
```

8. Execute postmap against the virtual alias lookup table:

 # postmap /etc/postfix/virtual_alias

Now messages sent to *info@ora.com* will be delivered to *autoresp@ora.com* and *service@oreilly.com*.

9. Reload Postfix so that it recognizes the changes to its *main.cf* and *master.cf* files:

 # postfix reload

When a message is sent to *info@ora.com*, Postfix first finds the destination address in the virtual_alias lookup table. The address points both to *autoresp@ora.com* and *service@oreilly.com*. Postfix finds *autoresp@ora.com* in the transport lookup table, which points to the `inforeply` transport in the *master.cf* file. The entry in *master.cf* pipes the message to the `inforeply.pl` program, which sends the reply to the original sender. Finally, the message is also resubmitted for delivery to *service@oreilly.com*.

Configuring a Virtual Mailing List Manager

In the next example, you'll set up a mailing list for a virtual domain. Mailing-list managers are discussed in Chapter 10. You may want to review that chapter before setting up your virtual mailing lists. This example creates a mailing list for Majordomo. You should first install and configure Majordomo according to the directions in Chapter 10.

Virtual mailing lists work by creating a parallel version of the list under a local domain. The local version is only used internally on your system. External users can use the virtual addresses and never know that the local version exists. When naming the local version, you may want to include the virtual domain name in some way to distinguish the list from lists for other virtual domains hosted on your system. The following procedure creates a mailing list at the virtual address *astronomy@ora.com* that is handled by the local version *astronomy-ora@example.com*:

1. Set up the local version of the mailing list just as you would a normal mailing list, as described in Chapter 10, by adding the following entries to */usr/local/majordomo/aliases*:

   ```
   # astronomy@ora.com list
   astronomy-ora:      :include:/usr/local/majordomo/lists/astronomy
   owner-astronomy-ora:     kdent@ora.com
   astronomy-ora-request: "|/usr/local/majordomo/wrapper request-answer \
       astronomy-ora"
   astronomy-ora-approval:      kdent@ora.com
   ```

2. Rebuild the Majordomo aliases table:

   ```
   # postaliases /usr/local/majordomo/aliases
   ```

3. Create the file to hold the email addresses for list subscribers, and set its ownership to the *majordom* account:

   ```
   # touch /usr/local/majordomo/lists/astronomy
   # chown majordom /usr/local/majordomo/lists/astronomy
   ```

4. If desired, create an *info* file for the list at */usr/local/majordomo/lists/astronomy-ora.info*.

5. Create the necessary addresses for the list at the virtual domain. Add the following entries to the virtual alias map file *virtual_alias*:

   ```
   # astronomy@ora.com list
   astronomy@ora.com           astronomy-ora@localhost
   owner-astronomy@ora.com     owner-astronomy-ora@localhost
   astronomy-request@ora.com   astronomy-ora-request@localhost
   astronomy-approval@ora.com  astronomy-ora-approval@localhost
   ```

6. Rebuild the virtual alias map file:

```
# postmap virtual_alias
```

7. Add addresses to the */usr/local/majordomo/lists/astronomy* list file.

You should now be able to send messages to *astronomy@ora.com* for distribution to all of the addresses in your list file.

## CHAPTER 9

Mail Relaying

Up until now, we've mostly considered Postfix in its role as the end node for email messages. That is, messages that arrive at the Postfix system are, for the most part, delivered to the local system. But it's also common to find Postfix serving as an intermediate node on the path a message follows to its ultimate destination. In this chapter we'll look at some of the configuration options for Postfix as a client in MTA-to-MTA communications.

Backup MX

In DNS, MX records refer to *mail exchangers* (see Chapter 6). MX records contain both host and priority (or preference) information for sending mail to a domain. A backup MX server is one that receives mail for a particular domain, but is not the preferred server to receive the mail. If the preferred server or servers are down, the backup MX server receives the mail and queues it until one of the more preferred servers comes back online. Figure 9-1 illustrates delivery to a backup host when the primary host is not available. The backup queues messages until the primary is back online, whereupon the backup can deliver messages to it.

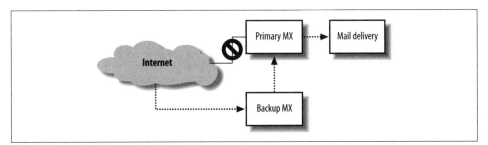

Figure 9-1. Delivery to backup MX host

When your system is configured in DNS as a backup MX host, you don't have to configure any special transport from your system to the primary system. Postfix uses the DNS records to determine how to route mail to the primary MX host. The only configuration required in Postfix is to indicate that it should receive mail for the domain by adding the domain name to the relay_domains parameter. When a sending MTA discovers that the primary mail system for a domain is down, it tries the next preferred one until it finds one that accepts delivery. If your system is a backup MX host, and the destination domain is listed in your relay_domains parameter, Postfix accepts the mail and queues it. Postfix periodically scans its queue and checks for a more preferred system to see if any are able to accept the message. Once a higher priority mail exchanger is back online, Postfix can deliver the message to it.

Postfix continues trying to deliver queued messages for the amount of time specified in the maximal_queue_lifetime parameter, which determines how long deferred messages stay in the queue before they are bounced back to the sender. The default value is five days. If you provide secondary mail service for primary servers that you know will be down longer than the default, you can extend the time.

Relay Recipients

It is highly recommended that you maintain a list of valid recipients for domains you provide backup MX services to. You should develop a regular process for obtaining an updated user list from your primary MX servers. If your system does not know all of the available mailboxes on the primary mail server, it must accept all messages. It's only when your backup MX server tries to deliver them to the primary server that it discovers that a message cannot be delivered. At that point, your server must bounce the message back to the original sender.

Since spammers often send messages to made-up addresses, if your server does not know all the valid email addresses on the primary server, your server will unnecessarily accept a lot of mail that must be bounced. The bounce problem is exacerbated by the spammer tactic of forging sender addresses by using the real email addresses of innocent bystanders. The forged addresses receive all of the error notices for messages they never sent (see Chapter 11). The relay_recipient_maps parameter specifies lookup tables that should contain all of the addresses for domains listed in your relay_domains parameter:

```
relay_recipient_maps = hash:/etc/postfix/relay_recipients
```

The *relay_recipients* file should contain entries with the recipient address on the lefthand side. The righthand side is not used by Postfix, but you must specify a value:

```
#
# relay_recipients
#
user1@example.com       any_value
user2@example.com       any_value
user3@example.com       any_value
```

If your system is on the same network as the primary, and the user accounts are stored in some kind of database, you may be able to perform real-time lookups using MySQL or LDAP (see Chapter 15).

A potential problem is that once you set relay_recipient_maps, you must include email addresses for all domains you provide backup service to. If not, Postfix will reject messages that don't appear in the lookup table. If you don't know the valid addresses for some domains, you can specify a wildcard entry for that domain:

```
#
# relay_recipients
#
user1@example.com       any_value
user2@example.com       any_value
user3@example.com       any_value
@oreillynet.com         any_value
```

The final entry is a wildcard entry that allows messages for any address at the domain. Obviously, it's better to obtain the list of valid addresses for the reasons mentioned earlier.

Fast Flushing

Networks that receive mail for many sites, such as ISP networks, typically have some customers whose systems aren't always connected to the network. When the customer network is offline, the ISP queues its messages. When the site comes online, it can request immediate delivery of all its queued mail with the ETRN SMTP command:

```
220 mail.ora.com ESMTP Postfix
EHLO mail.example.com
250-auger.seaglass.com
250-PIPELINING
250-SIZE 10240000
250-VRFY
250-ETRN
250-STARTTLS
250 8BITMIME
ETRN example.com
250 Queuing started
```

If there are a lot of messages queued when a domain is ready to accept mail, searching every queue file would be time-consuming. Postfix provides a capability called *fast flush* to speed up queue processing for a particular domain. Fast flush is handled by the flush daemon, which maintains lists of messages that are queued for specific domains so that Postfix knows which messages to deliver when it receives an ETRN command.

By default, all of the sites listed in relay_domains are eligible for the fast flush service. You can include domains in addition to your relay domains by adding them to the fast_flush_domains parameter. Add a domain name as follows:

```
fast_flush_domains = $relay_domains, example.com
```

In this case *example.com* is a domain not already listed in `relay_domains`.

You can manually notify Postfix that a fast flush domain is ready to accept messages by issuing the `postqueue -s` command (or its equivalent, `sendmail -qR`) with the site name:

```
$ postqueue -s example.com
```

Transport Maps

Postfix can be configured to relay to any other host, regardless of how DNS MX records are set up. This section discusses the `transport_maps` parameter in general. Later sections and other chapters in the book present specific configurations that use it.

Conceptually, transport maps override default transport types for delivery of messages. The `transport_maps` parameter points to one or more transport lookup tables. The following entry sets up */etc/postfix/transport* as a transport map lookup table:

```
transport_maps = hash:/etc/postfix/transport
```

The keys in a transport lookup table are either complete email addresses or domains and subdomains. (Email addresses as lookup keys for transport maps require Postfix 2.0 or later.) When a destination address or domain matches a lefthand key it uses the righthand value to determine the delivery method and destination. Example 9-1 lists some possible transport map entries.

Example 9-1. Transport map entries

```
example.com       smtp:[192.168.23.56]:20025
oreilly.com       relay:[gateway.oreilly.com]
oreillynet.com    smtp
ora.com           maildrop
kdent@ora.com     error:no mail accepted for kdent
```

The format of righthand values can differ depending on the transport type, but generally has the form *transport:nexthop*, where *nexthop* often indicates a host and port for delivery. Each of the possible portions of the righthand value are described here:

transport

> Refers to an entry from *master.cf*. If you are adding a new transport type, first create an entry for it in *master.cf*.

host

> The destination host for delivery of messages. The host is used only with `inet` transports such as SMTP and LMTP. Postfix treats the hostname like any destination domain. It performs an MX lookup to determine where to deliver messages. If there are no MX records, Postfix delivers to the A record IP address. If you know that Postfix should deliver directly to the IP in the A record for the specified host, you can have Postfix skip the check for MX records by enclosing the name in brackets. If you use an IP address, the brackets are required.

---

port

The destination port for message delivery. The port is used only with inet transports such as SMTP and LMTP. The port can be specified using the actual number or its symbolic name from the /etc/services file.

Each of the sample entries from Example 9-1 uses a different format in their righthand values, which are explained below:

example.com smtp:[192.168.23.56]:20025

All messages destined for *example.com* are relayed using the smtp transport to the host at IP address 192.168.23.56. Messages are delivered over port 20025 instead of the default SMTP port 25. Notice that the IP address is in brackets, as required for IP addresses.

oreilly.com relay:[gateway.oreilly.com]

All messages destined for *oreilly.com* are relayed using the relay transport to the host *gateway.oreilly.com*. Since no port is specified, Postfix uses the default port 25. The hostname is in brackets to prevent Postfix from looking up MX records. Instead, it looks up the A record and delivers to the IP address that the hostname resolves to.

The relay transport was introduced in Version 2 of Postfix to fix a potential performance bottleneck with queue scheduling. You should direct inbound messages relayed to internal systems over the relay transport, so that they don't compete with messages destined for many different systems on the Internet.

oreillynet.com smtp

All messages destined for *oreillynet.com* are relayed using the smtp transport. Since both the next hop and port are left off, Postfix uses the default port 25 and determines the next hop based on the destination address. Most often, the next hop is determined by performing a DNS lookup, which determines the MX host for the domain. This example is a bit contrived, since simply listing *oreillynet.com* with relay_hosts achieves the same thing in this case.

ora.com maildrop

All messages destined for *ora.com* are delivered to the maildrop service. maildrop must be an entry in *master.cf*. Since delivery occurs over a pipe rather than an inet socket, no host and port are specified.

kdent@ora.com error:no mail accepted for kdent

The special error transport causes all mail to be rejected. After the colon, specify a message to report when email is rejected.

Transport maps can also be used for special handling of certain messages on the local system. (Chapter 14 discusses content filters, which provide a good example of configuring special local transports.) Another local use of transport maps is to temporarily defer all of a domain's messages. To demonstrate a simple use of transport maps, the next section describes a procedure to defer all of the messages for a domain.

Postponing Mail Delivery

Under some circumstances you want Postfix to postpone delivery of messages until it has received an explicit command to deliver them. Deferred messages are delivered when you issue the postqueue -f *domain* command or Postfix receives an ETRN SMTP command from a fastflush–eligible domain.

A common scenario for deferring messages is when an ISP receives mail for a customer network that is not always online. The ISP must queue messages until the network is online and can receive them. Similarly, users on the customer network should send messages through a local gateway that queues them until they can be delivered once the network is online. This section presents configurations for both situations.

Deferring mail relay

This procedure sets up a new transport type called "ondemand," and configures a transport map to defer all messages for the *example.com* domain:

1. Create a new transport in your *master.cf* file called ondemand. It should be identical to your smtp transport except for the name:

   ```
   ondemand      unix -    -    n    -    -    smtp
   ```

2. Tell Postfix that delivery of all messages over your new transport should be deferred automatically. Edit the defer_transports parameter in *main.cf* to include your ondemand transport:

   ```
   defer_transports = ondemand
   ```

3. Make sure that the transport_maps parameter points to your transport lookup table:

   ```
   transport_maps = hash:/etc/postfix/transport
   ```

4. Add an entry to your *transport* file for *example.com* that points it to the ondemand transport:

   ```
   example.com       ondemand
   ```

5. Execute *postmap* on the file.

   ```
   # postmap /etc/postfix/transport
   ```

6. Reload Postfix so that it recognizes the changes in its configuration files:

   ```
   # postfix reload
   ```

Now any message destined for *example.com* is deferred until there is an explicit command to deliver it.

When you are ready to release the deferred messages, issue the postqueue -f command:

```
$ postqueue -f example.com
```

Deferring delivery

A home network or small office network that wants to trigger delivery manually should defer all SMTP deliveries, so that delivery attempts only occur when a connection to the Internet has been established:

1. In *main.cf*, assign the smtp transport to the defer_transports parameter:

    ```
    defer_transports = smtp
    ```

2. Reload Postfix so that it recognizes the changes in its configuration file:

    ```
    # postfix reload
    ```

Once a connection is established, all of the messages can be delivered using postqueue -f.

The rest of this chapter describes various scenarios where Postfix must relay mail to other systems. In many cases, transport maps are necessary for configuring the next-hop delivery details.

Inbound Mail Gateway

A mail gateway is an email system that accepts messages and relays them to another system. Gateways might provide a path from one network to another, or from one protocol to another. A common use of a mail gateway is a server that accepts all the mail for a network from the Internet and relays it to internal mail systems. Mail gateways are commonly set up in conjunction with firewall systems to limit the number of servers that need direct access to the Internet.

Imagine a company network such as the one depicted in Figure 9-2. There are subdomains for different workgroups at the company, and each workgroup has its own internal mail server. The gateway system *gw.example.com* receives all the mail for the network. The human resources department gets email addressed as *user@hr.example.com*, and their mail should go to the server *mail1.example.com*. The sales department uses *user@sales.example.com*, and their mail should go to *mail2.example.com*. The client hosts in each subnet retrieve mail from their respective mail servers. Transport maps are required to set up the mail gateway *gw.example.com* to relay messages to the correct internal mail servers.

The following procedure demonstrates how to configure *gw.example.com* to relay messages to the correct internal systems:

1. Make sure that the DNS has been configured correctly with MX records for *hr.example.com* and *sales.example.com* pointing to the gateway *gw.example.com*.

2. In your *main.cf* file, set relay_domains to include the two internal domains:

    ```
    relay_domains = hr.example.com, sales.example.com
    ```

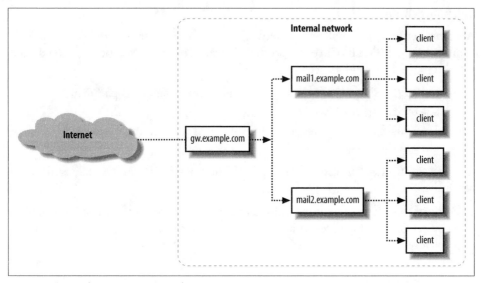

Figure 9-2. Email gateway to internal systems

3. Make sure that the transport_maps parameter points to your transport lookup table:

```
transport_maps = hash:/etc/postfix/transport
```

4. Add entries to your *transport* file for each domain pointing to the correct internal mail systems:

```
#
# transport maps
#
hr.example.com          relay:[mail1.example.com]
sales.example.com       relay:[mail2.example.com]
```

We've used brackets around the internal mail system host names to disable MX lookups for those systems.

5. Reload Postfix so that it recognizes the changes in its configuration files:

```
# postfix reload
```

It is highly recommended that you maintain a list of valid recipients for all of your internal users with the relay_recipient_maps parameter. See "Relay Recipients" earlier in the chapter.

Outbound Mail Relay

When a mail system does not have adequate connectivity or all of the information it needs to relay messages, it can forward them to another system that is in a better position for relaying. Consider the network in Figure 9-2 again. If the internal mail systems don't have direct access to the Internet, they can't deliver messages sent by the users in their subnets. They can, however, pass along all messages to the gateway mail system, which can make the deliveries for them. The following procedure demonstrates setting up Postfix on *mail1.example.com* to relay all messages it receives to *gw.example.com*, which can then make the outbound deliveries.

Before configuring the internal mail systems, make sure that the mail gateway is set up to permit relaying from the internal mail systems. The mynetworks parameter (see Chapter 4) should encompass the IP addresses of the internal mail systems, and if you use SMTP UBE restrictions (see Chapter 11), be sure to include permit_ mynetworks among the rules to allow relaying:

1. Check the mynetworks (or mynetworks_style) parameter to make sure it includes the client systems.
2. Have the users in the workgroup configure their various mail clients to use *mail1.example.com* as their SMTP server.
3. In *main.cf*, set the parameter relayhost to point to the gateway system:

   ```
   relayhost = [gw.example.com]
   ```
4. Reload Postfix so that it recognizes the changes in its configuration file:

   ```
   # postfix reload
   ```

Now all messages delivered to *mail1.example.com* are relayed through *gw.example.com*.

UUCP, Fax, and Other Deliveries

The Postfix online documentation describes configuring Postfix for delivery to a FAX system and setting up a gateway for UUCP. These provide good examples for configuring Postfix to work with all kinds of special devices. If you need to create a gateway between different types of systems or different networks, transport maps provide the mechanism for directing mail to the other systems or devices.

CHAPTER 10
Mailing Lists

Mailing lists provide a convenient way to send a single email message to many recipients. They allow a nearly unlimited number of correspondents to carry on conversations through email. A server-based, centrally managed mailing list has many advantages over other mechanisms to send messages to multiple recipients. If you regularly send email to the same group of people, typing in lists of recipients is too tedious and prone to error to be practical. MUAs usually have a facility that lets you create personal aliases that associate an easily remembered name with a list of email addresses. Personal aliases are fine for an individual, but as soon as the list has to be shared with others, it is no longer a practical solution. Major advantages of centrally managed mailing lists are that changes are made in a single place, and the new information is immediately available to anyone sending messages to the list. Other advantages become evident when you use Mailing List Managers (MLMs) to administer the list, relieving administrators from manually updating addresses.

In this chapter we look at creating simple mailing lists within Postfix itself, and then configuring Postfix to deliver messages to MLMs for more sophisticated list management. In deciding whether or not to create your mailing list within Postfix or to use an MLM, consider how often the list has to be changed, who will make the changes, and whether you need some of the other features of an MLM, such as moderated lists and digest versions. MLMs allow users to subscribe and unsubscribe themselves and to make changes to their addresses, if necessary. If you have relatively static lists or users who come to you for subscribing and unsubscribing anyway, you probably don't need the overhead of an MLM. You can always run both flavors of lists, if that fits your environment.

There are many aspects and nuances to managing a mailing list. If you will be taking on the task, you should consult a text that deals specifically with mailing-list management such as *Managing Mailing Lists* by Alan Schwartz (O'Reilly).

Simple Mailing Lists

Postfix provides the means to create simple mailing lists through the normal alias facility (see Chapter 4). Because aliases can point to lists of addresses or files that contain lists of addresses, it is easy to create an alias that points to multiple names. You can create list aliases in the system *aliases* file, or in any other file that you specify in the alias_maps parameter. See more about the alias_maps parameter later in the chapter. The default alias file when you install Postfix is */etc/aliases*.

Let's suppose that you administer mail for the domain *example.com*, and you want to create a new mailing list for people to discuss needlepoint. You decide to create a mailing list alias *needlepoint@example.com* to be used for online discussions. Edit your alias file, and add the following line with the email addresses of people who want to subscribe to the list:

```
needlepoint:        rgrier@oreilly.com, gmhopper@onlamp.com,
    grayburn@oreilly.com
```

After making changes to the file, rebuild the alias lookup table by executing:

```
# postalias /etc/aliases
```

Now any messages sent to *needlepoint@example.com* will be forwarded to each of the email addresses listed in the example.

Mailing-List Owners

If any messages cannot be delivered to one of the addresses listed, the original sender of the message receives an error message explaining that there was a delivery problem. For small or internal lists this may be perfectly acceptable; however, if you are creating a large list, or the members of the list do not necessarily know each other, it is probably more appropriate to have error messages sent to the administrator of the list. The convention is to create an additional alias for lists using a format like *owner-<list_alias>@example.com*, where *owner-* is prepended to the name of the list alias. For the previous example, we would create the alias *owner-needlepoint*.* This *owner-* alias should point to an administrator, who is generally in a better position than the original sender to deal with bounced messages:

```
owner-needlepoint: kdent@example.com
```

Sending error notifications to the *owner-* alias is achieved by setting the envelope sender to the *owner-needlepoint@example.com* alias instead of the original sender's email address. Example 10-1 shows typical headers from a mailing-list message.

Example 10-1. Sample headers from mailing-list message

```
Return-Path: <owner-needlepoint@example.com>
Delivered-To: rgrier@oreilly.com
```

---

* Some MLM systems have adopted the convention of placing *-owner* after the alias instead of before.

Example 10-1. Sample headers from mailing-list message (continued)

```
Received: from cowrie.example.com (cowrie.example.com[192.168.100.7])
    by mail.oreilly.com (Postfix) with ESMTP id B712120DD5B
    for <needlepoint@example.com> Mon, 13 May 2002 11:55:40 -0400 (EDT)
Date: Mon, 13 May 2002 12:00:43 -0400 (EDT)
From: G.M. Hopper <gmhopper@onlamp.com>
X-Sender: gmhopper@cowrie
To: needlepoint@example.com
Subject: Just finished latest project
Message-ID: <Pine.GSO.4.10.10205131200230.692-100000@cowrie>
```

When the *owner-* alias exists, Postfix automatically uses it as the envelope sender address when sending out messages to list members. If, for some reason, you don't want Postfix to use the *owner-* alias but rather to keep the originator's address, you can set the parameter owner_request_special to no:

```
owner_request_special = no
```

You can also cause Postfix to use the actual administrator's email address instead of the *owner-* alias by setting expand_owner_alias to yes:

```
expand_owner_alias = yes
```

If this parameter is set, the address *kdent@example.com* is used instead of *owner-needlepoint@example.com*.

Although users do not generally need to send mail directly to the list owner, you should create owner aliases even for simple lists so other postmasters can contact the correct person in case they run into any problems with your list.

Another list convention is to provide a *request* alias for your lists. Request aliases use the format *<list_alias>-request@example.com*. The request alias for the needlepoint alias looks like *needlepoint-request@example.com*. Request aliases are used for requests to subscribe and unsubscribe from lists or to get nontechnical information about a list.

Separate List Files

If you have more than just a few names on a list, it is more convenient to create a text file that lists all of the email addresses for the list. The format of the alias entry that points to a file is as follows:

```
email_alias: :include:/path/to/file.
```

Let's take the needlepoint alias from earlier in the chapter and move the list addresses into a separate file. Your alias entry should be revised to point to the text file that contains the list of addresses:

```
needlepoint:        :include:/etc/postfix/needlepoint
```

The file */etc/postfix/needlepoint* contains the email address of each member of the group. Put one address on each line. When you need to make changes to the list, simply edit the file:

```
rgrier@oreilly.com
gmhopper@onlamp.com
grayburn@oreilly.com
bogus@example.com
```

I'm adding an invalid address, *bogus@example.com*, for testing later in the chapter.

Additional Alias Files

Recall from Chapter 4 that the alias_maps parameter allows you to specify any number of alias files to use with Postfix. For example, you might want to use a separate alias file to store your mailing lists. Simply include the separate alias filename along with the system alias to set the alias_maps parameter. You should also set the alias_database parameter, so that you can run the command newaliases to update all of your alias-mapping files:

```
alias_maps = hash:/etc/postfix/aliases, hash:/etc/postfix/mail_lists
alias_database = hash:/etc/postfix/aliases, hash:/etc/postfix/mail_lists
```

It may be more convenient to assign all of your alias files to alias_database and then assign alias_database to alias_maps. If you use other map types for aliases, simply assign them to alias_maps as well:

```
alias_database = hash:/etc/postfix/aliases, hash:/etc/postfix/mail_lists
alias_maps = $alias_database, nis:mail.aliases
```

Remember to reload Postfix when you make changes to *main.cf*.

Creating a Simple Mailing List

Let's review everything discussed so far and consider all the pieces of our needlepoint mailing list. The alias file contains the following lines:

```
needlepoint:           :include:/etc/postfix/needlepoint
owner-needlepoint:     kdent@example.com
needlepoint-request:   kdent@example.com
```

The first line in the example causes messages sent to *needlepoint@example.com* to be delivered to every address listed in the */etc/postfix/needlepoint* file. This file should contain a list of email addresses of all members of the list. Bounce messages and requests are forwarded to the real address *kdent@example.com*. If necessary, users or other postmasters can send messages to the list owner, and users can send messages to the request alias for subscription or other information.

When a message is sent to the list, the To: header contains just the address of the mail list alias and not an expansion of all the names on the list (which could be hundreds or even thousands of names). Each member of the list receives a copy of the message with headers that resemble those shown in Example 10-1. In this example, *gmhopper@onlamp.com* has sent a message to the list. Notice that the Return-Path: contains the owner alias rather than the actual originator of the message (*gmhopper@onlamp.com*).

Testing Your List

You can test your list by sending a message to the alias you created for it. In this example, we'll use the list alias *needlepoint@example.com*. Example 10-2 shows the log entries for a sample test message. Imagine that the address *bogus@example.com* is invalid.

Example 10-2. Log entries for message to astronomy mailing list

```
postfix/local[7411]: 6C2CE20DD5B: to=<needlepoint@example.com>,
    relay=local, delay=1, status=sent (forwarded as ACDC120DD70)
postfix/qmgr[8163]: ACDC120DD70: from=<owner-needlepoint@example.com>,
    size=1121, nrcpt=8 (queue active)
postfix/local[0835]: ACDC120DD70: to=<bogus@example.com> relay=local,
    delay=1, status=bounced (unknown user: "bogus")
postfix/smtp[6556]: ACDC120DD70: to=<grayburn@oreilly.com>
    relay=mail.oreilly.com[10.82.6.11], delay=1,
    status=sent (250 Mail accepted)
postfix/smtp[6556]: ACDC120DD70: to=<rgrier@oreilly.com>
    relay=mail.oreilly.com[10.82.6.11], delay=1,
    status=sent (250 Mail accepted)
postfix/smtp[5954]: ACDC120DD70: to=<gmhopper@onlamp.com>
    relay=mail.onlamp.com[10.171.8.111], delay=1,
    status=sent (250 Message received: GZCLUC00.E8F)
```

Some of the information, such as the timestamp and hostname, has been removed for clarity. Notice that at the end of the first line there is a comment saying (forwarded as ACDC120DD70) and the rest of the log entries use the new queue ID. Also notice in the first line of the example that the message enters the system addressed to *needlepoint@example.com*. The second line shows that Postfix uses the owner alias as the envelop sender address (from=<owner-needlepoint@example.com>) while delivering the message to all members of the list. The bogus address shows a status of "bounced." The address *kdent@example.com* pointed to by the owner alias receives the bounce notification, which looks like Example 10-3. Notice in the example that the bounce notification message is delivered to *owner-needlepoint@example.com*. The sender of the message does not receive a notification.

Example 10-3. Bounce notification for invalid address

```
From MAILER-DAEMON@mail.example.com Tue Jul 16 12:03:49 2002
Date: Tue, 16 Jul 2002 11:25:27 -0400 (EDT)
From: Mail Delivery System <MAILER-DAEMON@mail.example.com>
To: owner-needlepoint@example.com
Subject: Undelivered Mail Returned to Sender

...

<bogus@example.com>: unknown user: "bogus"

...
```

Mailing-List Managers

Running mailing lists within Postfix is fine for static lists. But lists that change frequently are better handled by a mailing-list manager (MLM). With an MLM, the administrator of the list doesn't have to manually edit the list file to add, delete, or change addresses because list members can subscribe and unsubscribe themselves. MLMs also support other features such as archiving of messages, digests of discussions, and the ability to moderate a list by allowing an administrator to review messages before they are posted to all members.

MLMs work by pointing normal Postfix aliases to commands that handle the distribution of messages and management of lists. MLMs use administrative aliases that point to programs to handle list functions such as subscribing and unsubscribing members from the list, handling bounced messages, and possibly filtering messages sent to the list. The lists themselves actually work the same way as the simple aliases from the last section. Each list has its own file to store list members, but rather than editing the file yourself, you can have the MLM automatically add and remove addresses.

The next two sections look at two popular MLMs: Majordomo and Mailman.

Majordomo

Majordomo is one of the more popular MLMs and has been available since the early 1990's. It offers a complete set of MLM features, and nearly all administration takes place by sending commands through email messages. Little to no intervention is required by a postmaster once a list has been created. There are also web-based administration packages available to work with Majordomo, allowing much of the list administration to take place from a web site.

Majordomo is available at the Majordomo home page (*http://www.greatcircle.com/majordomo/*.) It requires Perl and works with Perl4 Version 4.036 or Perl5 Version 5.002 or better. Future releases will probably require Perl5. Majordomo also makes use of a small wrapper program written in C. If you are planning to build the package from scratch, you must have an ANSI C compiler.

If you configure Majordomo for moderated lists, where a list administrator approves posts using the Majordomo-supplied approve, you have to make an adjustment for Postfix and Majordomo to work together correctly. Postfix prepends a Delivered-To: header to messages it handles. It then uses the header to detect mailer loops. When a Majordomo message is delivered to a moderator for approval who then pipes the message through the approve command, it is sent back to the list with all of its original headers intact. When Postfix receives the message again, it recognizes that it has already seen the message and reports a mail delivery loop.

The easiest way to fix this issue is to make a small change to the Majordomo approve script (which is written in Perl). You'll have to edit the file, normally located in the */bin* directory located below the main Majordomo installation directory. If you follow the steps in the procedure below, your file will be located at */usr/local/majordomo/bin/approve*. Edit the file and find the subroutine called process_bounce. Within that routine, there is a while loop, as shown below. Insert the emphasized line as shown, save the file, and you're done:

```
while (<$FILE>) {
        if (/^>?From / && ! defined($from_skipped)) {
                # Skip any initial "From " or ">From " line
                $from_skipped = 1;
                next;
        }
        next if ( /^delivered-to:/i );  # Added for Postfix
        s/^^/~~/;
        print MAIL $_;
}
```

Creating a Majordomo list

The following steps walk you through setting up the astronomy list alias using Majordomo and Postfix. These instructions assume that you will create a user called *majordom* and install the package at */usr/local/majordomo*. If you create a different username or install to a different location, keep that in mind as you read through this example.

1. Make sure that you have Perl installed on your system and that it is at least Version 5.002 or better. You can check your Perl installation by typing perl -v at a command prompt. This will display license and other information about your installation of Perl, including the version number:

   ```
   $ perl -v
   This is perl, version 5.005_03 built for i386-freebsd
   Copyright 1987-1999, Larry Wall
   ...
   ```

2. Obtain a copy of Majordomo either in source form from the Majordomo home page or find a prepackaged version from your normal software sources. Follow the instructions that come with your bundle to install Majordomo on your system. If you are installing from source, you will need an ANSI C compiler to build it.

   If you build Majordomo yourself, when you modify the *Makefile* and *majordomo.cf* file, you should be able to follow the instructions as if you were installing Majordomo to work with Sendmail as the MTA. If the location for $sendmail_command in *majordomo.cf* is correct, the rest of the mailer variables with the default options will be correct.

3. Create and edit a file called */usr/local/majordomo/aliases* to store the Majordomo aliases. Add the aliases for the Majordomo commands as specified in the Majordomo instructions. Then add the aliases for your list. The file should look like the following:

```
majordomo:              "| /usr/local/majordomo/wrapper majordomo"
owner-majordomo:        kdent@example.com
majordomo-owner:        kdent@example.com
# astronomy list
astronomy:              :include:/usr/local/majordomo/lists/astronomy
owner-astronomy:        csagan@example.com
astronomy-request:      "|/usr/local/majordomo/wrapper request-answer astronomy"
astronomy-approval:     csagan@example.com
```

4. Edit */etc/postfix/main.cf* to add the Majordomo alias file to the alias_maps parameter:

```
alias_maps = hash:/etc/aliases, hash:/usr/local/majordomo/aliases
```

5. You can also add the new alias file to the alias_database parameter to automatically rebuild the datafile when you run the newaliases command:

```
alias_database = hash:/etc/aliases, hash:/usr/local/majordomo/aliases
```

6. Reload Postfix so that it recognizes the changes in its *main.cf* configuration file:

```
# postfix reload
```

7. Create the file to hold the email addresses for the astronomy list. Set its ownership to the majordom account:

```
# touch /usr/local/majordomo/lists/astronomy
# chown majordom /usr/local/majordomo/lists/astronomy
```

8. Create the *info* file that contains the message sent to new members of the list and anyone who sends the info command. Create the file as */usr/local/majordomo/lists/astronomy.info* and include any text that is appropriate for your list:

```
Welcome to the astronomy discussion list at example.com. The
purpose of this list is to discuss new astronomical phenomena.
To send a message to all the members of the list, address your
email to <astronomy@example.com>.
The basic rules and etiquette for the list are as follows:
1. ...
```

9. Make sure that the *info* file is accessible by the *majordom* account:

```
# chown majordom /usr/local/majordomo/lists/astronomy.info
```

10. Build the alias database:

```
# postalias /usr/local/majordomo/aliases
```

Or, if you added the Majordomo alias file to alias_database, just type newaliases.

You can test your Majordomo installation by running the following command:

```
$ echo 'lists' | mail majordomo
```

Executing the above sends an email message to Majordomo containing the command 'lists', telling Majordomo to send you information about all of the lists it maintains. On our example system, the reply from Majordomo looks like the following:

```
Date: Tue, 16 Jul 2002 18:14:59 -0400 (EDT)
From: Majordomo@example.com
To: kdent@example.com
Subject: Majordomo results


--

>>>> lists
Majordomo@example.com serves the following lists:

  astronomy

Use the 'info <list>' command to get more information
about a specific list.
>>>>
>>>>
```

You or your users can now send Majordomo commands at the address *majordomo@example.com* to get help and be added to lists. To add yourself to the new mailing list, send a message to `majordomo` with the `subscribe` command in the body of the message:

```
To: majordomo@example.com
From: tbrahe@porcupine.org
Subject:

subscribe astronomy
```

If you send a subscription request, you should receive a confirmation message from Majordomo. You must reply to the message with the authentication code provided to complete your subscription to the list (see the Majordomo documentation).

Potential problems

If you had no problems during the Majordomo installation, everything should work as expected. The main issue that you may run into has to do with file permissions. If you send a message to the list and receive a bounce notification like the following, then you know you have a permissions problem:

```
   ...

                   The Postfix program

<astronomy@example.com>: cannot open include file
        /usr/local/majordomo/lists/astronomy: Permission denied

   ...
```

Majordomo needs read access to the list file (*/usr/local/majordomo/astronomy*) and the list configuration file (*/usr/local/majordomo/astronomy.config*) when Postfix invokes it for deliveries to the list. Postfix delivers the message to Majordomo running with the privileges of the user that owns the alias map file containing the majordomo alias, */usr/local/majordomo/aliases.db*. The normal mechanism used to ensure that Majordomo has access to the necessary files is to set the Majordomo wrapper program to *set user ID* (suid) with *root* as the owner. This means that regardless of the user executing the command, the process runs with *root* privileges. The Majordomo installation takes care of setting the permissions properly, but if for some reason they are not correct, you will see an error message like the one described above. You can correct the problem by setting the permissions yourself:

```
# chmod 4755 /usr/local/majordomo/wrapper
```

A better solution than setting the wrapper program suid is to make sure that the alias file and all of the list files are owned by the *majordom* user.

Mailman

Mailman is another full-featured MLM. It is available at the Mailman home page at *http://www.gnu.org/software/mailman/*. It includes web-based administration and creates a home page for each list where list administrators and members can perform administrative functions. It also accepts administrative commands via email much like Majordomo does.

Mailman requires at least Version 1.5.2 of Python. It includes some security wrapper programs that are written in C, so you must have an ANSI C compiler if you are planning to build the package from scratch.

There is one slightly tricky aspect to get Postfix and Mailman working together correctly. Mailman expects to be invoked by a process running with a particular group ID (GID). The GID it expects is specified at the time the Mailman package is built. If you are building the package yourself, make sure that you first create an account and a group called mailman. You should be able to use the normal administrative tools on your system to create both the account and the group. When you are finished, you should have an entry in */etc/passwd* that resembles the following:

```
mailman:*:26413:60003:Mailman List Manager:/home/mailman:/bin/sh
```

and an entry in */etc/group* like the following:

```
mailman:*:60003:
```

Make sure that the account mailman has the group mailman as its primary group. In the examples above, 60003 specifies the mailman group and the mailman account has that as its primary group.

When you run configure for Mailman, be sure that you include the option --with-mail-gid=*xxx*, where *xxx* is the actual GID for the mailman group that you created. According to the examples above, you should execute configure using 60003 for the GID option:

```
$ ./configure --with-mail-gid=60003
```

You may have additional options for configure according to your environment. Be sure to read the Mailman documentation for building the package. If you have already built your Mailman package and you did not specify the group, build it again. If you didn't build your Mailman package, see the sidebar below.

WANTED gid 12 GOT gid 99?

If you didn't build the Mailman package yourself (and don't have the option of rebuilding it), there is no good way to find out which GID it is expecting other than by looking at what is reported in an error message. If you have a mismatch between the group of the Postfix process and the group that Mailman expects, you will receive a bounce error message after you send an email message to a Mailman list. Mailman also logs the error, which will look something like the following:

```
Failure to exec script. WANTED gid 12 GOT gid 99 (Reconfigure
to take 99?)
```

In order to get Postfix to deliver the message to Mailman using the correct GID, you have to set the permissions correctly on the Mailman alias file. When Postfix makes a normal local delivery, it assumes the identity of the recipient of the message. In the case of an alias, Postfix assumes the identity of the owner of the alias file, unless the owner is *root*, in which case Postfix uses the identity specified in its default_privs parameter. Make sure that the alias file is owned by the mailman user and that the mailman user has the mailman GID as its primary group. Postfix will then use the mailman group when it delivers a message to the Mailman system.

If you did not build your own Mailman package and therefore cannot control the GID that it expects, you will have to accommodate Mailman by getting Postfix to use the GID Mailman expects. Generate an error message like the one above by first creating a list (see the steps in this chapter) and then by sending a message to it. You should receive a bounce error email message (or you can check for the error in the Mailman log). Note the GID Mailman reports that it wants (WANTED gid 12). Change the primary group of the mailman account to that group. Make sure that the Mailman alias file is owned by the mailman account.

Creating a Mailman list

The following steps walk you through setting up the astronomy list alias using Mailman and Postfix. They assume that you create an account and a group called mailman and install the package in */home/mailman*.

1. Make sure that you have Python installed on your system and that you have at least Version 1.5.2. Test this by executing the python command, which will display version information and a Python prompt. You can exit the Python shell by typing Ctrl-D:

```
$ python
Python 1.5.2 (#1, Jul  5 2001, 03:02:19) [GCC...
Copyright 1991-1995 Stichting Mathematisch Centrum, Amsterdam
>>> ^D
$
```

If the version number following "Python" on the first line of output is not at least 1.5.2, you will have to upgrade your copy of Python.

2. Obtain a copy of Mailman either in source form from the Mailman home page or find a prepackaged version from your normal software sources. Follow the instructions that come with your bundle to install Mailman on your system. If you are installing from source, you will need an ANSI C compiler to build it. Be sure to specify the correct GID when you build Mailman. (See the discussion earlier in this chapter.)

3. You should create a separate alias file to store all of your Mailman aliases and set the owner and group correctly. Become the *mailman* user and execute the following commands. This example assumes that you want the alias file in the *mailman* home directory located at */home/mailman*:

```
$ cd /home/mailman
$ touch aliases
$ postalias aliases
```

These commands create both the alias file and the necessary map files that Postfix uses for lookups. Since you perform these steps as the *mailman* user, the group and ownership of the files will automatically be correct, assuming your account is set up as it should be.

4. Edit */etc/postfix/main.cf* to add the new alias file for storing Mailman mailing lists. Simply add the Mailman alias file to the existing list of files for the alias_maps parameter:

```
alias_maps = hash:/etc/aliases, hash:/home/mailman/aliases
```

5. You can also add the new alias file to the alias_database parameter to automatically rebuild the datafile when you run the newaliases command:

```
alias_database = hash:/etc/aliases, hash:/home/mailman/aliases
```

6. Reload Postfix so that it recognizes the changes in its main.cf configuration file:

```
# postfix reload
```

7. Execute the Mailman command newlist to initialize your new mailing list. The output of newlist includes lines of text that must be inserted into the */home/mailman/aliases* file. Copy the lines from the newlist output into */home/mailman/aliases*. Save and exit the file. The emphasized lines in Example 10-4 are the lines that must be added to */home/mailman/aliases*.

8. Build the new alias datafile:

```
# postalias /home/mailman/aliases
```

Or, if you added the Mailman alias file to alias_database, just run the newaliases command.

Example 10-4. Executing the Mailman newlist command

```
# bin/newlist
Enter the name of the list: astronomy
Enter the email of the person running the list: kdent@example.com
Initial astronomy password:
Entry for aliases file:

## astronomy mailing list
## created: 08-Mar-2002 root
astronomy:          "|/home/mailman/mail/wrapper post astronomy"
astronomy-admin:    "|/home/mailman/mail/wrapper mailowner astronomy"
astronomy-request:  "|/home/mailman/mail/wrapper mailcmd astronomy"
astronomy-owner:    astronomy-admin

Hit enter to continue with astronomy owner notification...
```

You or your users can now send requests to *astronomy-request@example.com* to get help and be added to the list. You can now use Mailman's web- or email-based command interface to specify options for your new list. See the Mailman documentation to learn its options and other ways to work with the package.

## CHAPTER 11

Blocking Unsolicited Bulk Email

Unsolicited Bulk Email (UBE), also referred to as Unsolicited Commercial Email (UCE), is commonly called spam. Spamming is the practice of sending mass mailings to large numbers of people who have had no prior relationship with the sender and who didn't ask to receive such mail. Spam exists because it's so cheap to send. The incremental cost of adding even hundreds of thousands of recipients to a mailing is relatively small, so spammers target as many email addresses as they possibly can. This chapter looks at the problem of spam and the tools Postfix provides to help limit the consequences.

The Nature of Spam

There is a decidedly dishonest component to most spam. Spammers make no effort to match message content with a recipient's interests, and their messages frequently lie, claiming that the recipient has an association with the company or its partners or in some way requested information. Messages are sometimes designed to look like an actual exchange between two people that was mistakenly misdelivered in the hopes of sparking interest in some product or service.

Spam frequently offers instructions to *opt out* from receiving more messages; however, in many cases this is simply a subterfuge on the part of the spammer to confirm that your email address is good. By replying to such messages, you confirm that your address is a legitimate one. Following the directions provided will more than likely cause your address to be added to more spammer lists.

Spammers often try to hide their trail so their messages cannot be traced back to them. They purposely use false return addresses and forge header information. They seek out misconfigured systems that allow them to relay anonymously. More recently spammers have broken into systems and installed their own secret relay servers. Spammers commonly encode their messages or insert random letters to circumvent spam filters.

Some of the techniques employed by spammers have sideeffects that make the problem much worse than the act of spamming itself. In their scatter-shot approach, spammers send messages to email addresses they think are likely to exist whether they actually do or not. Some launch dictionary assaults on mail servers where they run through preassembled lists of names hoping to find a match with a user on the mail server.

The Problem of Spam

While spam may seem like a minor issue on a small scale, it is a significant problem on the Internet. A system hosting hundreds or thousands of users each receiving dozens or hundreds of unwanted messages every day can have substantial difficulties dealing with the onslaught. There is a real cost to the victims of spam. It unfairly uses the bandwidth and disk space of its recipients and their providers.

Other costs brought on by spam include technical support personnel time, when technicians or administrators must help users clean up flooded mailboxes. Sometimes the volume of spam can even make a system unusable for its intended purpose (clogging bandwidth or filling disk space). In such a case the effects of spam are no different from those of a denial-of-service attack. Even in less drastic circumstances, spam interferes with legitimate uses of email. Important messages can easily be overlooked in a flood of spam or mistakenly deleted when littered mailboxes are cleaned up.

A significant issue with spam is dealing with messages addressed to nonexistent users. Some mail systems recognize that a destination address is bogus and can reject mail before it is accepted; other systems must receive the mail first and then bounce it as undeliverable. The volume of bounces can easily clog a queue and interfere with the delivery of legitimate messages. Since the return addresses often don't really exist, the bounces cannot be delivered and sit in the queue undergoing many redelivery attempts until they expire.

Another spamming trick is to use a legitimate return address that belongs to an innocent third party. The target or relay systems that receive the spam send bounce messages to the supposed sender, helpfully letting that person know that the recipient does not exist. In this case, thousands or millions of bounce messages will be delivered to the unfortunate victim in a phenomenon referred to as *backscatter*. This victim isn't involved in any way in the original delivery of the spam. In most cases, the only solution for these completely innocent bystanders is to abandon the victimized address and start using a new one.

Open Relays

If you operate an email server on the Internet, you have a responsibility to make sure that you do not create an *open relay* that spammers can use as a launching point for their activities. An open relay is a mail system that permits outside systems to send mail to other outside systems, passing the messages along so that the originating system does not have to deliver directly to its target. Spammers constantly scan for misconfigured systems that permit them to relay mail. Before spam became such a problem on the Internet, mail administrators often operated open relays because it made their systems convenient for their users. Now nearly all SMTP software systems are configured by default not to be open relays. Postfix is no exception.

If your system is abused as an open relay, it will most likely be so bogged down with sending spam that its performance will be hindered for your legitimate users. If you choose to accept spam into your own system that is, of course, up to you, but you must take steps to ensure that your system is not used to abuse other systems. There is a good possibility that if spammers use your system to relay mail, your network will end up on a blacklist. Once your site is blacklisted, many sites will reject all messages from your network, both relayed spam and legitimate messages from your users. Chapter 4 discusses safely configuring Postfix to prevent your system from being abused.

Spam Detection

As long as you're not operating an open relay, you can be confident that your systems are not being used to harm other systems. Your next consideration is to protect yourself and your users by limiting the spam your network receives. Ideally, your mail server could simply reject any message that looks like spam. Unfortunately, whereas humans can look at a message and know instantly that it's spam, computers have a tougher time detecting it without making mistakes. The ugly truth is that once you start to reject spam, there is always a risk that you will block legitimate correspondence.

Misidentifying a legitimate message as spam is referred to as a *false-positive* identification. Your anti-spam efforts are an attempt to detect as much spam as you can with the fewest possible false-positives. You have to weigh the size of your spam problem against the possibility of rejecting real email when deciding how aggressive to be in implementing your anti-spam measures. The extremes range from permitting all spam to accepting mail only from preapproved individuals. Preapproval may seem severe, but the problem is getting bad enough for some people that *whitelist* applications, where any correspondent you receive mail from must be identified ahead of time, are becoming more common.

There are two primary ways of detecting spam: identifying a known spamming client and inspecting the contents of a message for tell-tale phrases or other clues that reveal the true nature of a spam message. Despite the difficulties, postmasters can achieve some success with minimal false-positives by implementing various spam-detection measures.

Client-Based Spam Detection

Client-blocking techniques use IP addresses, hostnames, or email addresses supplied by clients when they connect to deliver a message. Each piece of information supplied can be compared to lists of items from known spamming systems. Spamming systems might be owned by actual spammers, but they might also be unintentionally open relays managed by hapless, (almost) innocent mail administrators. In either case, if a system is regularly sending you spam, you will probably decide to block messages from it. One problem with identifying spam by IP address, hostname, or email address is that these items are easily forged. While the IP address of the connecting system requires some sophistication to spoof, envelope email addresses are trivial to fake.

DNS-based blacklists

In a grass-roots effort to stem the tide of spam on the Internet, various anti-spam services, generally called DNS-based Blacklists (DNSBL) or Realtime Blacklists, have developed. These services maintain large databases of systems that are known to be open relays or that have been used for spam. A newer, increasingly more common problem is with systems that have been hijacked by spammers who install their own proxy software that allows them to relay messages. These hijacked systems can also be used in distributed denial-of-service attacks. There are DNSBL lists that are dedicated to listing these unwitting spam relays. The idea is that by pooling the information from hundreds or thousands of postmasters, legitimate sites can try to stay ahead of spammers.

Usually, these systems work by adding a DNS entry to their domain space for each of the IP addresses in their database that have been identified as spam-friendly open relays. For example, if the host at IP address 192.168.254.31 has been identified as an open relay, the (fictitious) DNSBL service No Spam Unlimited using a domain name of *nospam.example.com* creates a DNS entry like 31.254.168.192.nospam.example.com. When a client connects to your Postfix system, Postfix can check the No Spam DNS server to see if there is an entry for the client's IP address. If the IP address has been identified as an open relay system, Postfix can reject the message.

Consider very carefully before you decide to make use of a DNSBL service. Many open relays used to forward spam also operate mail services for nonspamming users. You are very likely to block legitimate mail in addition to the spam. Also keep in mind that you are offloading to a third party the responsibility of making important decisions about who can and cannot send mail to your users. On the other hand, if you're buried in spam, DNSBL services can definitely help. If you decide to use one, review their service options and policies very carefully. Again, you have to balance your aggressiveness and the likelihood of losing legitimate mail against the magnitude of your spam problem.

Content-Based Spam Detection

In addition to identifying clients, you can often recognize spam by its contents. Certain strings within email messages mark them as likely to be spam ("Our Rates Have Never Been Lower!!"). But trying to distinguish spam by the contents of the message can be problematic. Imagine that you receive lots of spam offering new house mortgages. You figure you can eliminate most of it by blocking messages that contain words like "really low interest rate on a new mortgage." This may indeed block many spam messages, but you might also block a message from your friend (or one of your user's friends) who just got a great deal on a new house and wrote to tell you about it.

Detection Difficulties

The problem with both client- and content-based techniques to identify spam is that spammers are constantly finding ways to get around them. There is a sort of arms race going on between legitimate users of email and spammers. You can compile lists of open relays, but spammers expend a great deal of effort seeking out new open relays or proxy servers to abuse (and there always seem to be more of them).

You may discover that you receive a lot of spam with the same return address. You can block messages that use that return address, but spammers use hit-and-run tactics. They obtain an email address from one of the free email sites and use that address to send thousands or millions of spam messages, and then discard it for another. Within a couple of days, you'll never see the address you listed again.

Even content filters have to adjust for spammers escalating tactics. Some spammers embed HTML codes within the words of their messages to break up phrases you might filter against. Or they encode the entire message so that when Postfix scans it for recognized spam phrases, there are no intelligible phrases. Most email clients oblige users by automatically rendering such messages—decoding or ignoring extraneous HTML codes. Recipients often don't even notice that the message had originally been encoded.

Anti-Spam Actions

Broadly speaking you have a few choices once you have detected spam:

- Reject spam immediately during the SMTP conversation. Rejecting spam outright is an attractive idea because you never have to store a copy of the message and worry about what to do with it. The sender of the message is responsible for handling the error. If your site has a low tolerance for rejecting legitimate messages, you might prefer to accept suspect messages and develop a process to review them periodically to make sure that there are no good messages in with the bad.

- Save spam into a suspected spam repository. If you save the suspect messages and review them periodically, you can be sure that you don't miss any legitimate mail. The task is cumbersome and usually requires frequent reviews, so you may not gain much over allowing suspect messages into users' mail boxes.

- Label spam and deliver it with some kind of spam tag. This option provides users with flexibility in determining their own tolerance for spam versus their sensitivity to missing real messages. Postfix doesn't currently have a built-in mechanism for labeling spam. You can easily have Postfix work with an external content filter to handle the labeling (see Chapter 14). If the content filter delivers tagged messages to individual users, they can configure their email software to deal with it according to their own preferences.

When using an MTA for spam detection, the rejection option is usually best. If you want more flexibility, consider using options that filter spam at the MDA or MUA level. A combination of spam filtering is also a good alternative. You can configure Postfix to reject the obvious spam, allowing suspicious messages through to the next level where another agent can perform the most appropriate action.

Postfix really excels in its tools to help you identify spam clients and reject them. Rejecting messages with Postfix requires fewer system resources than invoking external filters after the message has been accepted. If you are concerned about losing legitimate mail, there are still a couple of safety measures available that we'll look at when configuring Postfix.

Postfix Configuration

The rest of this chapter discusses the various types of UBE checks Postfix provides. It considers four different categories of spam detection which are listed below.

Client-detection rules.
> Four parameter rules that work with pieces of the client identity. Each rule is assigned a list of one or more restrictions that can explicitly reject or accept a message or take no position one way or the other (commonly indicated as DUNNO). For example, you can configure a rule that includes a restriction to reject a particular client IP address.

Syntax-checking parameters.
> Parameters that check for strict adherence to the standards. Since spammers often don't follow the published standards, you can reject messages that come from misconfigured or poorly implemented systems. Some of the client restrictions also fall under this category.

Content checks.

You can check the headers and the body of each message for tell-tale regular expressions that indicate probable spam.

Restriction classes

You can define complex client-detection rules with restriction classes. These allow you to combine restrictions into groups to form new restrictions.

When configuring Postfix to detect spam, you also specify what to do with messages identified as spam. In general, Postfix can reject them outright, separate them into a different queue, or pass them along to an external filter.

Client-Detection Rules

Postfix provides the following rules that are assigned restrictions based on client information:

- smtpd_client_restrictions
- smtpd_helo_restrictions
- smtpd_sender_restrictions
- smtpd_recipient_restrictions
- smtpd_data_restrictions

Each one corresponds to a step of the SMTP transaction. At each step, the client provides a piece of information. Using the client-supplied information, Postfix considers one or more restrictions that you assign to each rule. Figure 11-1 shows an SMTP conversation along with the client rule applied at each step. The header_checks and body_checks are discussed later in the chapter.

Let's review the SMTP conversation to see where each of the parameters fits in.

The SMTP Conversation (Briefly)

The SMTP conversation in Figure 11-1 should be familiar to you from Chapter 2. Example 11-1 shows the log entries for the transaction. First, an SMTP client connects to Postfix over a socket. Because of the way sockets function, Postfix learns the IP address of the client when it establishes the connection. You don't see the client IP address in the figure, but it is logged by Postfix. You can accept or reject a message based on the client hostname or IP address, thus blocking specific hostnames or IP and network addresses.

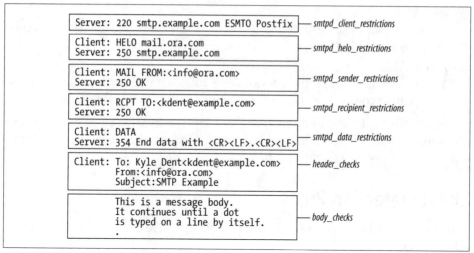

Figure 11-1. SMTP conversation with client rules

Example 11-1. SMTP logging

```
1. postfix/smtpd[866062]: connect from mail.ora.com[10.143.23.45]
2. postfix/smtpd[866062]: D694B20DD5B: client=[10.143.23.45]
3. postfix/cleanup[864868]: D694B20DD5B: \
   message-id=<20030106185403.D694B20DD5B@smtp.example.com>
4. postfix/qmgr[861396]: D694B20DD5B: from=<info@ora.com>, \
   size=486, nrcpt=1 (queue active)
5. postfix/local[864857]: D694B20DD5B: to=<kdent@smtp.example.com>, \
   relay=local, delay=98, status=sent (mailbox)
6. postfix/smtpd[866062]: disconnect from mail.ora.com[10.143.23.45]
```

Once connected, the client sends a HELO command with an identifying host-name. The hostname provided can be used to accept or reject a message using smtpd_helo_restrictions.

In the next step, the client issues a MAIL FROM command to indicate the sender's email address, followed by a RCPT TO command to indicate the recipient's email address.

If everything is acceptable up to the point of the DATA command, the client is permitted to send the contents of the message, which consist of message headers followed by the message body. Postfix provides another opportunity to reject the message based on its contents (see "Content-Checking" later in this chapter). If the final header and body checks are acceptable, the message is delivered.

Postfix indicates to the client that it has rejected a message by sending reply codes. Standard reply codes are described in Chapter 2. In this chapter, we consider codes in the 4xx and 5xx range. More information appears in a sidebar later in this chapter.

Listing Restrictions

When you assign restrictions to Postfix UBE rules, it is not necessary to use all of the rules. You can define restrictions for the ones you need and leave out the others. The default setting if no rules are set in *main.cf* looks like the following:

```
smtpd_client_restrictions =
smtpd_helo_restrictions =
smtpd_sender_restrictions =
smtpd_recipient_restrictions =
        permit_mynetworks, reject_unauth_destination
```

This prevents your system from being an open relay by allowing any computer on your network to relay while rejecting all others unless they are sending messages destined for one of your users.

There are many restrictions available. Table 11-1 lists each one along with the client information it operates on. One important concept that confuses many people at first is that any of these restrictions can be used in any rule. While it may seem logical that check_helo_access should be assigned to smtpd_helo_restrictions, it could equally be assigned to smtpd_sender_restrictions or any of the others. This gives you a lot of flexibility in ordering your restrictions when deciding what to accept and what to block.

Table 11-1. SMTP rules and restrictions

Restrictions	Client-supplied information
check_client_access *maptype:mapname*	Client IP address or hostname
reject_rbl_client	
reject_rhsbl_client	
reject_unknown_client	
check_helo_access *maptype:mapname*	HELO hostname
permit_naked_ip_address	
reject_invalid_hostname	
reject_non_fqdn_hostname	
reject_unknown_hostname	
check_sender_access *maptype:mapname*	MAIL FROM address
reject_non_fqdn_sender	
reject_rhsbl_sender	
reject_unknown_sender_domain	
check_recipient_access *maptype:mapname*	RCPT TO address
permit_auth_destination	

Table 11-1. SMTP rules and restrictions (continued)

Restrictions	Client-supplied information
permit_mx_backup	
reject_non_fqdn_recipient	
reject_unauth_destination	
reject_unknown_recipient_domain	
reject_unauth_pipelining	DATA command

You'll notice from Table 11-1 that some rules take an argument of the form *maptype*: *mapname*. The *mapname* refers to a normal Postfix lookup table whose lefthand key is matched against the piece of client information, and the righthand value is the action to perform. Access maps are discussed in Restriction Definitions following.

How restrictions work

Each of the nonaccess map restrictions *evaluates* to or returns one of three possible values that determine what action Postfix takes with the message: OK, REJECT, and DUNNO. (Access maps can also return the same values, but they allow additional actions as well.) The restrictions are evaluated in the order you list them. During processing, if a rule returns an explicit REJECT, the message is immediately rejected. If a rule returns an explicit OK, the processing stops *for that parameter* but continues on to the next until all of the assigned rules have been evaluated or Postfix encounters a rejection. It's important to note that a rule might explicitly accept a message, but it can still be rejected by another rule's restrictions. If the set of rules comes to no definite conclusion (all DUNNOs), the default action is to accept the message. Any single parameter can reject a message, but all of them must accept it in order for it not to be rejected. There are generic restrictions such as permit and reject that return explicit OK or REJECT values without considering any of the client information.

When a rule evaluates to REJECT, by default Postfix does not actually reject the message until after the client has sent the RCPT TO command. Even though it may know at the HELO command that it's going to reject this client, it waits until after it receives the RCPT TO command before returning the reject code. The reason for this default is that some SMTP clients do not check that they have been rejected during the transaction and continue trying to deliver the message. In such a case, you end up with connections that last longer than they should and several warning messages in your log file. Another advantage to the default is that you get more complete information in your log. If you want to change the default to have a rejection take effect as soon as possible, set the parameter smtpd_delay_reject in *main.cf*:

```
smtpd_delay_reject = no
```

You might want to do this in a controlled environment where you know all of the connecting SMTP clients are well-behaved; otherwise, the default makes sense for most situations.

Testing new restrictions

A useful parameter for testing new restrictions is soft_bounce:

```
soft_bounce = yes
```

When it is set, hard reject responses (5xx) are converted to soft reject responses (4xx). When you add a new restriction that you're not sure about, you might want to turn soft_bounce on and then watch your logs for what's rejected so that you can fine-tune your settings by the time another delivery attempt is made.

Another useful option for testing restrictions is the warn_if_reject qualifier. Simply precede any restriction with it to have that restriction log a warning instead of rejecting a message. If you're not sure what effect a new restriction will have in your environment, you can try it out with warn_if_reject, and then implement it completely only if it works as you expect:

```
smtpd_recipient_restrictions =
        permit_mynetworks
        reject_unauth_destination
        warn_if_reject reject_invalid_hostname
        reject_unknown_recipient_domain
        reject_non_fqdn_recipient
```

In this example, if a client uses an invalid HELO hostname when delivering a message, Postfix logs a warning but still delivers the message (assuming it's not blocked for other reasons).

A simple example

Before moving on to the restriction definitions, let's consider a simple example:

```
smtpd_recipient_restrictions =
     permit_mynetworks
     reject_unauth_destination
     reject_invalid_hostname
     reject_unknown_sender_domain
```

This example expands on the default configuration with two additional restrictions. When a client connects, if it's from your own network, permit_mynetworks returns OK, so it is allowed to send mail. The other restrictions are not checked. If the client is from outside your network, permit_mynetworks does not return OK and does not return REJECT, so it returns DUNNO. Postfix then checks reject_unauth_destination.

If the message is not addressed to somebody at one of your destination domains, it returns REJECT; otherwise, it returns DUNNO. Assuming it returns DUNNO, Postfix then checks reject_invalid_hostname, which says to return REJECT if the hostname supplied with the HELO command is not valid. Otherwise, it returns DUNNO. Finally, Postfix checks reject_unknown_sender_domain, which returns REJECT if the domain name of the address supplied with the MAIL FROM command does not have a valid DNS entry. If none of the restrictions has rejected the message, Postfix accepts it for delivery.

Restriction Definitions

There are six types of restrictions introduced below. Each of the restrictions are defined in the sections that follow.

Access maps for client checking
> Restrictions of the form check_*_access point to lookup tables that might list IP addresses, hostnames, or email addresses (depending on the parameter) that should be accepted or rejected by Postfix.

Other client checks
> Other client restrictions compare the client information to general configuration information instead of access tables. An example is permit_mynetworks, which you saw earlier.

Strict syntax checking
> Some restrictions tell Postfix to enforce SMTP standards very strictly. Since spammers often misconfigure or use poorly implemented software, you can stop a lot of spam by making sure that connecting clients follow the rules.

DNS checking
> DNS-checking rules ensure that DNS information is correct. Spammers often work from networks that do not configure DNS correctly. Unfortunately, rules of this type are appropriate only for a very aggressive anti-spam stance because of the number of legitimate sites that also do not configure their DNS correctly.

Real-time blacklist checking
> Real-time blacklists are services listing suspected spamming clients. Postfix can check with real-time blacklist services and reject clients based on their listing.

Generic
> Generic rules explicitly reject or accept a message. They usually specify your default stance if a message isn't explicitly accepted or rejected elsewhere. Since these rules will always accept or reject a message, they should come last in your list of rules.

Access maps

Restrictions in the client-checking category all point to *access map* files. Access maps are simply a type of Postfix lookup table (see Chapter 4 for more information about lookup tables). In the lookup table, you specify the client information as a key and the action to take (accept or reject) as the value:

check_client_access *maptype:mapname*

> The check_client_access restriction points to an access table containing entries with IP addresses, network addresses, hostnames, and parent domains to match against the client IP address. (Postfix performs a reverse lookup on the IP address to obtain a hostname to compare host and parent domain name information.) Each entry includes an action to take when the IP address matches a key.

check_helo_access *maptype:mapname*

> The check_helo_access restriction points to an access table containing hostnames and parent domains to match against the host information supplied with the HELO command. Each entry includes an action to take when the supplied host information matches a key.

check_recipient_access *maptype:mapname*

> The check_recipient_access restriction points to an access table containing entries with email addresses, domains, and local parts to match against the address specified with the RCPT TO command. Each entry includes an action to take when the supplied address matches a key.

check_sender_access *maptype:mapname*

> The check_sender_access restriction points to an access table containing entries with email addresses, domains, and local parts to match against the address specified with the MAIL FROM command. Each entry includes an action to take when the supplied address matches a key.

The restrictions check_sender_access and check_recipient_access both check a supplied email address. For them, the key in your index file can be an email address (*user@example.com*) to match a specific address, a domain name (*example.com*) to match the domain name portion or subdomains of the address, or the local part of an email address (*user@*) to match all addresses using the specified local part.

The rules check_client_access and check_helo_access compare the key to a supplied hostname or IP address. The index file pattern can be a hostname, an IP address (192.168.143.23), or a network address specified by the initial octets of the address (10 or 10.12 or 10.12.154).

Actions can be indicated as follows:

OK

> Accept the item. Processing for the current rule stops. Postfix moves on to the next restriction rule.

REJECT

> Reject the item. You can optionally specify a short string of text to be used in the reply and with logging for this message; otherwise, Postfix uses the general reply code and text configured for the restriction. The parameter access_map_reject_

code contains the default reply code for the check_*_access rules and maps_rbl_reject_code contains the default reply code for reject_maps_rbl. If you don't specify a value, they both default to 554.

DUNNO

Stop checking entries for the lookup table. Postfix moves on to the next restriction for the current rule.

FILTER

Redirect the message to a content filter. You must specify a transport and next hop as you would in a transport table.

HOLD

Place the message in the hold queue. You can optionally specify a short string of text to be logged; otherwise, Postfix logs a generic message.

DISCARD

Report a successful delivery to the client, but drop the message. You can optionally specify a short string of text to be logged; otherwise, Postfix logs a generic message. Don't use this action unless you have carefully considered the ramifications. Silently dropping messages runs counter to the expected behavior of email systems. When dealing with spam, dropping messages might be the best course of action, but discarding any legitimate mail can affect the overall perceived reliability of Internet email.

4xx message text

Reject the message. The response sent to the client is the numerical code you specify. A response in the 4xx range tells the client there is a temporary problem; queue the message and try delivery later. (See sidebar.)

5xx message text

Reject the message. The response sent to the client is the numerical code you specify. A response in the 5xx range tells the client there is a permanent problem; send a bounce notification to the original sender. (See sidebar.)

You can also set up regular expression tables for access maps. In most cases, it probably doesn't make sense to use a regular expression table for your access lists. Postfix already breaks up email addresses, domains, and IP addresses into the individual pieces to make its comparisons, so you really don't gain much through regular expressions here. On the other hand, regular expression tables work very well for header and body checks, which are discussed later in this chapter.

Let's expand the configuration example with some access maps:

```
smtpd_client_restrictions =
    check_client_access hash:/etc/postfix/client_access
smtpd_sender_restrictions =
    check_sender_access hash:/etc/postfix/sender_access
smtpd_recipient_restrictions =
```

```
permit_mynetworks
reject_unauth_destination
reject_invalid_hostname
reject_unknown_sender
```

We've now added restrictions to consult the lookup tables *client_access* and *sender_access*.

The *client_access* file can have entries like the following:

```
10.157                    REJECT
192.168.76.23             REJECT
currentmail.com           REJECT
```

and the *sender_access* file can have entries like the following:

```
hardsell@example.com           REJECT
marketing@                     REJECT
specials.digital-letter.com    REJECT
```

Other client-checking restrictions

The following client restrictions make their decisions by comparing client-supplied information to the local Postfix configuration. The default rules fall under this category.

permit_auth_destination

Permits a request if the resolved destination address matches a hostname or subdomain where the Postfix system is the final destination for the message or a relay for the final destination. Final destinations are listed in mydestination, inet_interfaces, virtual_alias_maps, or virtual_mailbox_maps, and relays are listed in relay_domains. Furthermore, the address must not contain any sender-specified routing (e.g., *user@example.com@example.net*). If permit_auth_destination does not find a match, it returns DUNNO rather than REJECT. Postfix continues to check all subsequent restriction rules.

permit_mynetworks

Allows a request if the client IP address matches any of the addresses listed in the mynetworks parameter. You normally use this restriction to exclude local clients from other UBE restrictions and to allow them to relay through your SMTP server.

reject_unauth_destination

Rejects a request if the Postfix system is not the final resolved destination email address or a relay for the final destination. Final destinations are listed in mydestination, inet_interfaces, virtual_alias_maps, or virtual_mailbox_maps, and relays are listed in relay_domains. Addresses must not contain any sender-specified routing (e.g., *user@example.com@example.net*). The relay_domains_reject_code parameter specifies the response code for rejected requests. The default is 554.

Strict syntax restrictions

Restrictions in the strict syntax category check for misconfigured clients and reject mail when they don't comply with the standards. These rules can detect a lot of spam, but they might also reject legitimate clients. You should study the nature of your spam and real messages to see which rules will benefit you most without rejecting real messages. You can use access maps with OK actions to whitelist known senders that would otherwise be rejected.

reject_invalid_hostname
> Rejects a request if the hostname supplied with the HELO command is not a valid hostname. The invalid_hostname_reject_code parameter specifies the response code for rejected requests. The default is 501. Most legitimate senders use valid hostnames.

reject_non_fqdn_hostname
> Rejects a request if the hostname supplied with the HELO command is not in the fully qualified form, as required by the RFC. The non_fqdn_reject_code parameter specifies the response code for rejected requests. The default is 504.

reject_non_fqdn_recipient
> Rejects a request if the address supplied with the RCPT TO command is not in the fully qualified form, as required by the RFC. The non_fqdn_reject_code parameter specifies the response code for rejected requests. The default is 504. Most legitimate senders use fully qualified domain names.

reject_non_fqdn_sender
> Rejects a request if the address supplied with the MAIL FROM command is not in the fully qualified form, as required by the RFC. The non_fqdn_reject_code parameter specifies the response code for rejected requests. The default is 504.

reject_unauth_pipelining
> Pipelining is a technique supported by Postfix to speed up bulk mail deliveries by sending multiple SMTP commands at once. The protocol requires that clients first check that the server supports pipelining. Some clients incorrectly begin pipelining before they confirm that Postfix actually supports it. The rule reject_unauth_pipelining immediately rejects such requests. There is no more processing, and the message is rejected.

DNS restrictions

The DNS checking rules make sure that clients and email envelope addresses are sent from domains that have valid DNS information. It would be a great improvement to email in general if postmasters could always require valid DNS information because it would be harder for spammers to hide. Unfortunately, there are too many legitimate domains that do not configure their DNS correctly for such strictness to be practical. You should study the nature of your spam and real messages to see which will benefit you most without rejecting false-positives. You can use access maps with OK actions to whitelist known senders that would otherwise be rejected.

`reject_unknown_client`

> Rejects a request if the client IP address has no DNS PTR record or if a follow-up lookup on the hostname listed in the PTR record does not match the connecting IP address. The `unknown_client_reject_code` parameter specifies the response code for rejected requests. The default is 450. If you change the default, the reply code you specify is returned except when there is a temporary DNS error. In this case, your change is overridden and Postfix returns 450. This rule tends to find many false-positives for spam because it seems to be very common to have PTR records misconfigured or not configured at all.

`reject_unknown_hostname`

> Rejects a request if the hostname supplied with the HELO command doesn't have either a DNS A or MX record. The `unknown_hostname_reject_code` parameter specifies the response code for rejected requests. The default is 450. If you change the default, the reply code you specify is returned except when there is a temporary DNS error. In this case, your change is overridden and Postfix returns 450. Many clients do not use a fully qualified hostname and would be rejected by this restriction.

`reject_unknown_recipient_domain`

> Rejects a request if the domain name of the address supplied with the RCPT TO command doesn't have either a DNS A or an MX record. The `unknown_address_reject_code` parameter specifies the response code for rejected requests. The default is 450. If you change the default, the reply code you specify is returned except when there is a temporary DNS error. In this case, your change is overridden and Postfix returns 450.

`reject_unknown_sender_domain`

> Rejects a request if the domain name of the address supplied with the MAIL FROM command has neither an A nor an MX record in DNS. The `unknown_address_reject_code` parameter specifies the response code for rejected requests. The default is 450. If you change the default, the reply code you specify is returned except when there is a temporary DNS error. In this case, your change is overridden and Postfix returns 450.
>
> Since the MAIL FROM address is the address that bounce notifications must be sent to, it makes sense to require a known domain name. It is highly recommended that you include this rule in your restrictions.

Real-time blacklists

Restrictions for real-time blacklists cause Postfix to perform DNS lookups using client information with domains you specify to determine if a client is listed with one of the DNSBL services:

`reject_rbl_client domain name`
> Rejects a request if a DNS lookup of a hostname composed of the octets of the client IP address in reverse in the specified domain lists an A record.

`reject_rhsbl_client domain name`
> Rejects a request if the client hostname has an A record under the specified domain.

`reject_rhsbl_sender domain name`
> Rejects a request if the domain of the sender address has an A record under the specified domain.

Generic restrictions

There are two generic restriction rules that explicitly accept or reject a message:

`permit`
> Immediately permits a message. Processing for the current restriction parameter stops, but Postfix continues checking the other restriction parameters.

`reject`
> Immediately rejects a request. There is no more processing, and the message is rejected.

Tracing a Restriction List

With what we know so far, let's trace what happens with some simple HELO restrictions. Consider that `smtpd_helo_restrictions` is assigned the following rules:

```
smtpd_helo_restrictions =
    check_helo_access hash:/etc/postfix/helo_access
    reject_invalid_hostname
```

and *helo_access* contains the following entries:

```
greatdeals.example.com      REJECT
oreillynet.com              OK
```

Let's follow four different scenarios when clients connect with different HELO commands:

HELO *example*
> Postfix first encounters the `check_helo_access` rule pointing to the *helo_access* lookup table. In checking the lookup table, it does not find the specified hostname *example*, so it moves on to the `reject_invalid_hostname` rule. Since *example* is not a complete hostname as required by the standard, Postfix rejects the message.

HELO *greatdeals.example.com*
> Postfix first encounters the `check_helo_access` rule pointing to the *helo_access* lookup table. In checking the lookup table, it finds an entry for *greatdeals.example.com* with an action of REJECT. Postfix, therefore, rejects the message.

Reject Spam with 4xx or 5xx?

There are two classes of reply codes you can use when rejecting spam. Reply codes in the 4xx range normally indicate a temporary problem. Given a 4xx reply, a client will queue a message and attempt delivery later. A 5xx code indicates a permanent error and tells the client to stop trying to send the message.

At first glance the 5xx code seems like the obvious choice for rejecting spam, because the spammer is told to stop attempting to deliver the message; however, there may be benefits to replying with a 4xx code. In case you reject legitimate mail, the client should attempt to deliver it again. Assuming that you check your logs for such things, you could tweak your anti-spam settings to allow the message the next time delivery is attempted. On the other hand, if you reject real spam with a 4xx code, and you have any secondary mail exchangers for your domain that do not also reject the message, you may be filling up their queues with your temporary rejections. As you populate your access tables, you can fine-tune your replies by choosing a code based on who you are blocking and the reason for it. Keep in mind, however, that spammers don't have to respect any reply you send, so you may not have much success in controlling what happens.

You can specify the reply code with any short text message for the action side of an access table. Postfix provides parameters to control the default reply code given for most of the restriction rules. The restriction definitions mention the relevant reject code parameter when it is available.

HELO *oreillynet.com*

> Postfix first encounters the check_helo_access rule pointing to the *helo_access* lookup table. In checking the lookup table, it finds an entry for *oreillynet.com* with an action of OK. Postfix stops processing for the smtpd_helo_restrictions parameter without considering any of the other restrictions and moves on to smtpd_sender_restrictions if specified.

HELO *mail.ora.com*

> Postfix first encounters the check_helo_access rule pointing to the *helo_access* lookup table. In checking the lookup table, it does not find the specified host *mail.ora.com*, so it moves on to the reject_invalid_hostname rule. Since *mail.ora.com* conforms to the format required by the standard, Postfix continues to the smtpd_sender_restrictions if specified.

Strict Syntax Parameters

There are two parameters configured in *main.cf* that require strict adherence to Internet email standards. Enable the smtpd_helo_required parameter to require that SMTP clients start the conversation with the HELO/EHLO verb, as described in the SMTP RFC.

By default Postfix is rather lenient with clients that do not follow the protocol exactly. If you specify smtpd_helo_required = yes, and a client skips this step, Postfix rejects the message. The RFC also specifies exactly how envelope addresses should be formatted. Normally, Postfix accepts nearly any envelope address that it can make sense of, but if you specify strict_rfc821_envelopes = yes, Postfix rejects messages from clients that do not send correctly formatted addresses.

In actual practice, it's probably a good idea to require HELO because most clients at least follow the basic steps of the protocol. On the other hand, there are a number of clients that don't get address formatting correct. Being too strict here might lose legitimate messages.

Content-Checking

The last chance you have to reject a message from Postfix directly is by checking the contents of the message itself. Postfix offers simple content checking through the parameters:

- header_checks for message headers
- mime_header_checks for MIME headers
- nested_header_checks for attached message headers
- body_checks for the body of a message

These checks are an all-or-nothing feature with Postfix. There is no way to bypass checks for certain senders or recipients. For more sophisticated analysis, you should use a separate content filter specifically designed to detect spam. See Chapter 14 for more information on using filters with Postfix.

Each parameter points to a lookup table containing regular expression patterns and actions. The patterns are compared to strings within email messages. If Postfix finds a match, the specified action is executed. By default regular expression checking is not case-sensitive. See Chapter 4 for information on using regular expressions with Postfix lookup tables.

Content Checking Configuration

By default mime_header_checks and nested_header_checks use the same lookup tables as header_checks. If you want to distinguish checks for each one, you can configure them separately; otherwise, configuring header_checks causes mime_header_checks and nested_header_checks to use the same patterns as header_checks. When you assign the checking parameters, indicate both the lookup table and which type of regular expression you are using (see Chapter 4):

```
header_checks = regexp:/etc/postfix/header_checks
body_checks = regexp:/etc/postfix/body_checks
```

In a pattern-checking lookup table, the lefthand key is a regular expression enclosed by two delimiters (usually forward slashes):

```
/match string/          REJECT
```

A typical *header_checks* file contains lines like the following:

```
/free mortgage quote/   REJECT
/repair your credit/    REJECT
/take advantage now/    REJECT
```

If any of the strings shown appear in any of the headers of a message (these would most likely show up in the Subject: header), the message is rejected. Postfix logs the rejection along with the offending line, and if you specified a message, it is also logged and sent to the client.

Content Checking Actions

The right hand action can be one of the following values. The values that allow an optional text message are indicated. The specified message is sent to the client and logged with the rejection. If you don't supply a message, Postfix uses the default.

REJECT *message*

Rejects the message when a line from the message matches the regular expression.

WARN *message*

Logs a rejection without actually rejecting the message. This action is useful for testing a regular expression to see what happens in the log before using a REJECT to actually reject the message.

IGNORE

Provides a way to delete headers or lines from the body of a message. If the regular expression matches, the line is dropped from the message. This can be useful to strip out internal network information before sending a message outside your network. Be careful about what you delete since most headers are required by the standards and can be very useful in tracking down email problems.

HOLD *message*

Causes the message to be placed in the HOLD queue. See Chapter 5 for information about the HOLD queue.

DISCARD *message*

Causes Postfix to claim successful delivery and silently discard the message. Sometimes spammer software won't take no for an answer. Even if you reject the message with a 5xx error, the client continues to try to deliver it. DISCARD makes it look as if the message was delivered even though it was simply thrown away. DISCARD can also be useful to minimize the backscatter problem mentioned earlier in the chapter. If an innocent user's email address is used as the sender address, you can claim successful delivery, so that the innocent user does not receive bounce messages.

FILTER transport:nexthop
> After queuing the message, Postfix sends it through a separate content filter. See Chapter 14 for more information about setting up separate content filters.

Actions cannot include specific error reply codes or customized restrictions as with access maps.

Comparing Patterns

Header checks compare each header against every pattern in the listed lookup files. Multiline headers are combined into a single line before making comparisons. Each pattern is checked in the order you list them, and checking stops as soon as Postfix finds a match, at which point the message is handled according to the action you specified.

The patterns indicated by the body_checks parameter are checked against each line of the body of the message. Lines are compared one at a time, and each one is checked against every pattern in the order you list them. Checking stops as soon as Postfix finds a match, at which point the message is handled according to the action you specified.

Very long body lines are compared in chunks that are at most as long as the value of the parameter line_length_limit. The default is 2048. Also, by default, Postfix checks the contents of the body only up to the value of body_checks_size_limit. The default is 50 KB. Message headers are compared in chunks that are limited by header_size_limit. These limits are useful in preventing Postfix from scanning the entire file when messages contain large attachments.

Some administrators use header checks for simple virus scanning. You can reject all messages that include attachments with file extensions that might be dangerous to your users:

```
/name ?="?.*\.(bat|com|dll|exe|hta|pif|vbs)"?/      REJECT
```

You should include any other extensions that you know might pose a problem for your users. Be aware, however, that this pattern is not really sufficient for true virus scanning since you are certain to miss some extensions, and many PC clients may execute files regardless of their extension.

A typical *body_checks* file contains lines like the following:

```
/increase your sales by/        REJECT
/lowest rates.*\!/              REJECT
/in compliance (with|of) strict/  REJECT
/[:alpha:]<!--.*-->[:alpha:]/   REJECT Suspicious embedded HTML comments
```

The second line matches any string that starts with "lowest rates" followed by any text leading to an exclamation point ("We have our lowest rates in 40 years!"). The fourth line checks for HTML comments that are embedded in the middle of words.

Remember that this is a common spammer trick to defeat your content filters, but it's also a dead giveaway that the message contains spam.

You can test your regular expressions with the postmap command. Place the contents of a message into a file, then redirect the file to postmap:

```
$ postmap -q - regexp:/etc/postfix/body_checks < msg.txt
opportunity. increase your sales by 500%. Consider      REJECT
```

postmap prints any lines that match any of the regular expressions along with the action specified.

Study the spam you receive to refine and add to your patterns. However, be aware of potential performance problems with poorly written regular expressions. Another potential issue with content checking is that there is no way to whitelist individual messages that you might want to receive despite their containing phrases that trigger a rejection. In particular, if a message is whitelisted during the restriction parameter checking (described earlier in this chapter), it might still be rejected by header and body checks.

As you create rules for detecting spam, keep in mind that your users may differ in what balance they'll accept between some spam and the possibility of blocking some real messages. If you must create different rules for different users, it's probably best not to try to accomplish this with an MTA. Instead consider a specialized delivery agent such as procmail, maildrop, or sieve to set up per-user UBE rules. You can use Postfix to set up broad per-user class restrictions, as you'll see in the next section.

Customized Restriction Classes

Restriction classes provide the last wrinkle in the Postfix anti-spam parameters. They allow you to define a set of restrictions that you can assign to the righthand side of an access table. They cannot be used in header and body checks—only in access tables. Restriction classes let you set up different restrictions for different clients, senders, and recipients. Restriction classes are a powerful tool that can provide great flexibility in Postfix UBE restrictions. If you require any sort of complicated rules to block spam, it is well worth your while to invest the time to understand restriction classes.

Restriction classes are particularly useful when you need to create exceptions to your normal restrictions. To illustrate with an example, let's create two classes of users. One group wants to receive all messages addressed to them whether or not the messages are spam. The other group prefers particularly stringent checks against spam even at the risk of losing some legitimate mail.

Sample Restriction Classes

We'll call the two classes "spamlover" and "spamhater." You must list all of the restriction classes you plan to define in the smtpd_restriction_classes parameter:

```
smtpd_restriction_classes = spamlover, spamhater
```

We've invented the names of the classes, but once listed with smtpd_restriction_classes, they can be treated like any other restriction rule. You can assign a list of restrictions to be considered for the class. Once defined, the restriction class can be used as an action in an access table. When Postfix encounters the class, it steps through the assigned restrictions.

We'll define "spamhater" with several restrictions:

```
spamhater =
        reject_invalid_hostname
        reject_non_fqdn_hostname
        reject_unknown_sender_domain
        reject_rbl_client nospam.example.com
```

and "spamlover" with a simple "permit":

```
spamlover = permit
```

You could, of course, refine these with restrictions that make sense for your own configuration.

Now that the restriction classes have been declared and defined, you can put them to use by assigning the appropriate class to each of our recipients in a lookup table. We'll call the table *per_user_ube*.

```
#
# per_user_ube
#
abelard@example.com    spamhater
heloise@example.com    spamlover
```

Next, tell Postfix that it should check your recipient lookup table when checking restrictions:

```
smtpd_recipient_restrictions =
    permit_mynetworks
    reject_unauth_destination
    check_recipient_access hash:/etc/postfix/per_user_ube
```

When a message comes in addressed to *abelard@example.com*, Postfix goes through the normal default restrictions and then encounters check_recipient_access pointing to the recipient lookup table. Postfix finds the recipient address in the file, reads the action spamhater, and then invokes the restrictions defined for spamhater. If any of the "spamhater" restrictions returns REJECT, Postfix rejects the message; otherwise, it is delivered. Messages for *heloise@example.com* go through the same process, but when Postfix checks the "spamlover" restrictions, it finds permit and immediately accepts the message.

Postfix Anti-Spam Example

Now that we've covered the many aspects of Postfix's anti-spam arsenal, we'll finish with an example configuration. Requirements vary considerably from site to site, so it's impossible to make actual recommendations apart from the considerations that have been discussed in this chapter. Example 11-2 can provide a starting point, but you must decide for yourself which restrictions fit your own circumstances.

Example 11-2. Sample restrictions to block UBE

```
smtpd_restriction_classes =
        spamlover
        spamhater

spamhater =
        reject_invalid_hostname
        reject_non_fqdn_hostname
        reject_unknown_sender_domain
        reject_rbl_client nospam.example.com

spamlover = permit

smtpd_helo_required = yes
smtpd_client_restrictions =
                check_client_access hash:/etc/postfix/client_access
smtpd_helo_restrictions =
        reject_invalid_hostname
        check_helo_access hash:/etc/postfix/helo_access
smtpd_sender_restrictions =
        reject_non_fqdn_sender
        reject_unknown_sender_domain
        check_sender_access hash:/etc/postfix/sender_access
smtpd_recipient_restrictions =
        permit_mynetworks
        reject_unauth_destination
        reject_non_fqdn_recipient
        reject_unknown_recipient_domain
smtpd_data_restrictions =
        reject_unauth_pipelining
header_checks = /etc/postfix/header_checks
body_checks = /etc/postfix/body_checks
```

You should enter IP and email addresses into the access tables from messages you receive that you have identified as spam. It's very difficult to block a lot of spam with the check_helo_access and check_sender_access restrictions because it's so easy for spammers to fake that information. There is effectively an unlimited number of addresses and hostnames spammers might use. This makes it nearly impossible to keep up with them. Since it's so easy to fake this information, you might be blocking legitimate hosts and addresses that just have the bad luck of having their information used by spammers.

But these checks can be useful against messages that repeatedly use the same forged information and spammers that don't attempt to cover their tracks. Some online marketing services use their real information when sending spam. These sites might even honor removal requests, but if you object to having to request a removal from companies you've never heard of, you can block them based on the HELO or MAIL FROM information.

You can also block sites that you don't want to hear from whether they're real or fake. Mail from a site you consider objectionable is one example. Also, if you believe it's impossible that you would be receiving messages from the Republic of Maldives, you could block addresses and hostnames using the Republic of Maldive's top-level domain. Keep in mind, however, if you run a mail system for many users, you probably shouldn't force your own moral attitude on everyone, or assume your users don't have Maldivian relatives or a special interest in the cuisine.

## CHAPTER 12

SASL Authentication

The basic SMTP protocol does not provide a mechanism to authenticate users. Since email envelope addresses are so easy to fake, you can't know who is sending mail to your server unless you have a reliable means to authenticate clients. To allow mail relay privileges on your server, you need assurance that senders are who they claim to be, and you cannot rely on the senders' email addresses as identification. In this chapter, we look at using the *Simple Authentication and Security Layer* (SASL) as a means to control mail relaying and generally to identify who is using your mail server.

You might want to provide access to individuals using your mail server as their SMTP server, or to other MTAs that relay through your system. We'll also look at configuring Postfix to provide its own credentials to other MTAs that may require authentication before permitting email delivery or relaying. Chapter 4 discusses the mail relay problem in general, and some other solutions to consider.

Because you lock down your mail servers to prevent unauthorized relaying, some of your users might have trouble sending email when they are not on your network. If you have users that travel with laptops, for example, they will likely connect through a nearby ISP and get an IP address from its dial-up pool. Or perhaps you have users that work from home. In any case, whenever you don't know what users' IP addresses will be, SASL can provide the means to reliably identify them.

RFC 2554, "SMTP Service Extension for Authentication," provides an extension to the basic SMTP protocol that allows clients to authenticate to an SMTP server using the SASL protocol. We'll show how to use the Cyrus SASL libraries from Carnegie Mellon to add SASL to Postfix. You may optionally also want to add support for TLS (see Chapter 13). TLS (formerly SSL) is most commonly used to encrypt conversations between web browsers and servers, but works equally well for mail servers and clients. Since some of the SASL password mechanisms transmit passwords as plaintext, you can use TLS to make sure your passwords are not sent in the clear.

Adding SASL to Postfix requires that you have the Cyrus libraries on your system and that your Postfix system be compiled with them. Remote users must configure their email clients to send a login and password when they want to relay mail through your system. Most modern email clients make this a fairly easy configuration option.

SASL Overview

SASL is a general method to add or enhance authentication in client/server protocols. Its primary purpose is to authenticate clients to servers. When you configure SASL, you must decide on both an *authentication mechanism*, for the exchange of authentication information (commonly referred to as user *credentials*), and an *authentication framework* for how user information is stored. The SASL authentication mechanism governs the challenges and responses between the client and server and how they should be encoded for transmission. The authentication framework refers to how the server itself stores and verifies password information. Figure 12-1 illustrates these two processes. Once an authentication is successful, the server knows the user's identity and can determine which privileges the identified user should have. In the case of Postfix, it is the privilege to relay mail. You can also optionally limit identified users to using a particular sender address when they relay mail.

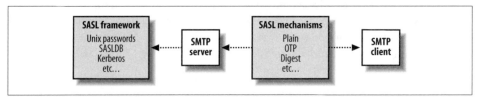

Figure 12-1. SASL authentication frameworks and mechanisms

Choosing an Authentication Mechanism

The client and server must agree on the authentication mechanism they'll use. (See the Cyrus documentation for currently supported mechanisms.) Some of the more common mechanisms are listed below:

PLAIN
> The PLAIN mechanism is the simplest to use, but it does not include any encryption of authentication credentials. You may want to use TLS (see TLS information in Chapter 13) in conjunction with the PLAIN mechanism. The login and password are passed to the mail server as a base64 encoded string.

LOGIN
> The LOGIN mechanism is not an officially registered or supported mechanism. Certain older email clients were developed using LOGIN as their authentication mechanism. The SASL libraries support it in case you have to support such clients.

If you need it, you must specify support for it when you compile the libraries and Postfix. See Appendix C if you are building your own Postfix. If you are using a packaged distribution and you need LOGIN support, check the documentation with your distribution to make sure it includes it. If it is used, the authentication exchange works the same as the PLAIN mechanism.

OTP

OTP is an authentication mechanism using *one-time passwords* (formerly S/Key). The mechanism does not provide for any encryption, but that may not be necessary since any captured password is good for only a single session. SMTP clients must be able to generate OTP authentication credentials.

DIGEST-MD5

With the DIGEST-MD5 mechanism, both the client and server share a secret password, but it's never sent over the network. The authentication exchange starts with a challenge from the server. The client uses the challenge and the secret password to generate a unique response that could be created only by somebody who has the secret password. The server uses the same two pieces, the challenge and secret password, to generate its own copy, and compares the two. Since the actual secret password is never sent across the network, it's not vulnerable to network eavesdropping.

KERBEROS

Kerberos is a network-wide authentication protocol. Unless you are already using Kerberos on your network, you probably don't need to support the KERBEROS mechanism. If you are using Kerberos, using SASL is a nice way to fit SMTP authentication into your existing infrastructure.

ANONYMOUS

SASL includes an ANONYMOUS mechanism, which might make sense for some protocols, but has no benefit for SMTP. An open relay is essentially using an anonymous mechanism, and the purpose of SMTP authentication is to eliminate open relays.

When a client connects to a mail server, the server typically lists all of the password mechanisms it supports, in order of preference. The client tries the first one it supports. If that fails, it may be configured to try additional mechanisms until it can authenticate successfully. If the client and server cannot successfully negotiate over a common mechanism, authentication fails.

Once the server and client agree on a mechanism, they begin the authentication process, consisting of one or more challenges and responses that are governed by the agreed-upon mechanism. The protocol also specifies how these exchanges should be encoded.[*]

---

[*] Note: that's encoded, not encrypted. A particular mechanism may or may not include encryption of the client's credentials.

Choosing an Authentication Framework

The SASL authentication framework can use your existing Unix system passwords (for example, *passwd*, *shadow*, or PAM) or a separate password file just for authenticating SMTP users. Other options include Kerberos or even a new scheme of your own.

Ultimately, your choice comes down to where and how you want to store your authentication information. Consider your network and how your users currently authenticate to decide which framework works best for you. If your mail users already authenticate on your network through PAM, for example, then you probably want to configure SASL to use your existing system. If, on the other hand, most of your SMTP users are virtual accounts (without system logins), you should opt for a separate password database for SMTP users. Often your POP/IMAP server can share the same user database, making this a convenient option for virtual mail accounts.

Postfix and SASL

Before getting started with SASL, you should decide which framework and mechanism you will use because it affects your installation and configuration. In order to enable SASL authentication in Postfix, you must have the Cyrus SASL library and a copy of Postfix with SASL support compiled in. Some platforms have precompiled packages available with support for SASL. If you want to use a precompiled Postfix package make sure that it specifically includes support for SASL and has the necessary SASL libraries. Furthermore, make sure that the SASL libraries were compiled with the options you need for your situation. The relevant options are described throughout the rest of this section.

Cyrus SASL library development is currently following two tracks: SASL and SASLv2. The SASL track is being phased out in favor of SASLv2. In the future, you can expect Postfix to include support for SASLv2 only. This chapter discusses SASLv2. You must have the correct combination of versions of both Postfix and the SASL libraries.

You should be able to use the latest stable version of the SASLv2 track of the Cyrus libraries. Postfix support for SASLv2 first appeared in the experimental release Version 1.1.7-20020331 and was included in the official release 2.0. It is very important that you use a version of Postfix that supports SASLv2 to follow the directions in this chapter. When the text mentions SASL, it refers to Version 2 of the library.

Configuring Postfix for SASL

Before you get started, decide on the authentication mechanisms you plan to support and the authentication framework you want SASL to use with Postfix.

Specifying a Framework

The SASL library uses a separate configuration file for each application it works with. Postfix uses a file named *smtpd.conf* for SASL purposes. This file is usually located at */usr/local/lib/sasl2/smtpd.conf*. At a minimum, *smtpd.conf* contains a line indicating the framework to use. We are going to look at specifying either Unix passwords or separate SASL passwords for Postfix authentication. See the Cyrus documentation to see other options you might include in *smtpd.conf*.

Unix passwords

Often, it's most convenient for SASL to use the existing system database to authenticate users. Historically, this meant using the */etc/passwd* file. Today, it's more likely that you use */etc/shadow*, PAM, or some related authentication database. Since these passwords are not available to unprivileged processes, and Postfix purposely runs with limited privileges, it cannot normally authenticate users.

The Cyrus libraries deal with the problem by providing a special authentication server called saslauthd. It handles requests on behalf of Postfix. The saslauthd daemon requires superuser privileges; however, since it runs as a process distinct from Postfix and does not have to communicate outside of your network, the security impact is minimized. If you are going to use Unix passwords with SASL, you must run the saslauthd daemon that ships with the Cyrus distribution. Note that using Unix passwords with saslauthd limits you to plaintext passwords because the daemon needs the actual passwords to verify them. See Chapter 13 for using encryption between Postfix and email clients.

To specify that you want Postfix to use the saslauthd daemon for authentication, create the *smtpd.conf* with a line like the following:

```
pwcheck_method: saslauthd
```

saslauthd comes with the Cyrus SASL distribution and should be installed in a convenient location. The daemon must be running in the background for Postfix to use it to authenticate clients. When you start saslauthd, you tell it what type of password system you are using with the -a option. The most common options are pam, shadow, or getpwent (for the conventional */etc/passwd*). For example, to start the daemon on a system that uses PAM for authentication, type the command:

```
# saslauthd -a pam
```

Consult the Cyrus documentation for other options when using saslauthd. Also, you probably want this daemon to start automatically at system initialization so that it is always available for your Postfix server. You can add saslauthd to your system's startup processes in the same way you add other daemons such as Postfix.

SASL passwords

If you don't want your mail server to use existing system accounts, you can create a separate database of users and passwords that is independent of the system password mechanism. You can create accounts for email users who have mail access only and will not be able to log into the host itself. Include the following line in your *smtpd.conf* file:

```
pwcheck_method: auxprop
```

The term auxprop comes from the Cyrus notion of auxiliary property plug-ins. Plug-ins allow you to insert external programs for authentication. The Cyrus SASL distribution ships with sasldb as the default auxiliary property plug-in and that should be all you need to work with Postfix. The keyword auxprop simply says to use an external SASL password file.

You do not have to run the saslauthd daemon when using SASL passwords, but you must create the external password file containing credentials for all of your email accounts. By default, the SASL username/password file is kept at */etc/sasldb2*. The Postfix SMTP server needs at least read access to the file, and if you use the auto_transition feature of Cyrus SASL (see the Cyrus documentation), Postfix will also require write access to the file. If you don't need the auto_transition feature, it's best not to give Postfix write access to the password file.

If you have other processes that also need access to the file (such as a POP/IMAP server), you may have to adjust the ownership and permissions so all the processes that need it can access it. For example, you might want to create an *sasl* group on your system. Make sure that the *postfix* user and other accounts that need access to the file are all in that group. If any of the other processes need to update the file, then read-only is too restrictive and you'll have to provide write access for the processes that need it. To set the permissions to 440, so that it is read-only and not generally readable by users on the system, type the following commands:

```
# chown postfix:sasl /etc/sasldb2
# chmod 440 /etc/sasldb2
```

To create accounts for your SMTP server, use the saslpasswd2 command included with the Cyrus SASL distribution. It stores accounts in */etc/sasldb2*. You must specify both a username and an SASL domain. For Postfix the domain should be the value specified in the myhostname parameter. If you use the command postconf -h myhostname to determine your hostname, you can be sure you have the correct one. The following command creates an account for the user *kdent*:

```
# saslpasswd2 -c -u `postconf -h myhostname` kdent
Password:
Again (for verification):
```

Enter the password twice, as prompted. The -c option tells saslpasswd2 to create the user account, and -u is used to specify the domain for this account, which you take directly from the Postfix configuration.

Configuring Postfix

All of the relevant Postfix parameters for SASL password authentication start with `smtpd_sasl*` for the SMTP server or `smtp_sasl*` for the SMTP client. For server configuration you need at a minimum the `smtpd_sasl_auth_enable` parameter and the `permit_sasl_authenticated` restriction, which must be assigned to one of the smtpd restriction parameters. See Chapter 11 for more information on UBE restrictions.

Enabling SASL

In order to turn on authentication in the Postfix SMTP server, add the enable parameter to your *main.cf* file:

```
smtpd_sasl_auth_enable = yes
```

In addition, some older email clients* don't follow the SMTP authentication protocol correctly. The specification calls for the server to list its supported mechanisms after the keyword AUTH followed by a space. These clients expect to receive AUTH followed by an equals sign. Postfix allows you to accommodate them by setting the following parameter:

```
broken_sasl_auth_clients = yes
```

By setting this parameter, you tell Postfix to advertise its SMTP authentication support in the nonstandard way as well as the standard way. This option is perfectly safe to use since it doesn't interfere with other mail clients, and the nonstandard ones will now work as well.

Preventing sender spoofing

To make sure that clients use correct sender addresses when relaying, Postfix allows you to map sender addresses to SASL logins. For example, if you have an address *kdent@example.com* that should be used only by the SASL user *kdent*, you can create a file requiring the correct user for that address:

```
kdent@example.com        kdent
```

The file is a normal Postfix lookup table and allows regular expressions as well as local parts and domains (see Chapter 4 for information on Postfix lookup tables). Use the parameter `smtpd_sender_login_maps` in *main.cf* to indicate the table you create:

```
smtpd_sender_login_maps = hash:/etc/postfix/sasl_senders
```

You can list as many addresses as you need in the table. To reject messages from users attempting to use incorrect sender addresses or users who are not authenticated at all who attempt to use a specified address, include the restriction `reject_sender_login_mismatch` with your restriction parameters (see Chapter 11 for information on UBE restrictions).

---

* Reportedly, Microsoft Outlook and Outlook Express before Version 5, but you may have to experiment to determine if your clients are culprits.

Permitting authenticated users

If you are already using the smtpd_recipient_restrictions parameter as part of your UBE blocking, you have to tell Postfix to allow authenticated users to relay by adding permit_sasl_authenticated to the list of restrictions. If you were previously using the default and didn't need a smtpd_recipient_restrictions parameter, just add the following line:

```
smtpd_recipient_restrictions = permit_mynetworks,
        permit_sasl_authenticated, reject_unauth_destination
```

If you are already using the smtpd_recipient_restrictions parameter, just add permit_sasl_authenticated to the list of restrictions. Be sure to include some kind of rejection restriction in your list (see Chapter 11).

Specifying mechanisms

The smtpd_sasl_security_options parameter lets you control which password mechanisms are listed when clients connect to your SMTP server. The complete list of available mechanisms depends on your system and the mechanisms that were available when your SASL libraries were built. If you don't specify any options, the default is to accept all available mechanisms including plaintext passwords, but not anonymous logins. If you are using the saslauthd daemon, you must accept plaintext passwords, so the default configuration probably makes the most sense. If you specify any of the options, you override the default, so make sure that you include noanonymous among your options. If you set this parameter, you can specify any combination of the following values. For example:

```
smtpd_sasl_security_options = noanonymous, noplaintext
```

Common mechanisms include:

noplaintext

If your security policy does not permit passwords to be sent as plaintext, specify noplaintext. This causes SASL to use one of the challenge/response techniques that authenticate without transmitting actual passwords.

noactive

In active attacks, attackers manage to insert themselves between the client and server. Some types of active attacks are commonly referred to as man-in-the-middle attacks. Attackers may be able to read or alter data as it is transmitted or pretend to be the client or server. Specify noactive to limit supported password mechanisms to those that are not known to be vulnerable to active attacks.

nodictionary

In dictionary attacks, attackers run through a preassembled database of possible passwords trying each one in turn to see if it allows access. Databases are typically made up of lists of cities, teams, proper names, and all dictionary words plus obvious variations on the words. Specify `nodictionary` to limit supported password mechanisms to those that are not known to be vulnerable to dictionary attacks.

noanonymous

Anonymous logins have no useful purpose for SMTP servers. By default Postfix does not allow anonymous logins. If you specify any other options, be sure to also specify noanonymous since you will be overriding the default.

mutual_auth

You can require mechanisms that provide mutual authentication where both the client and server provide credentials proving their identities. Specify `mutual_auth` to limit advertised mechanisms to those that provide for mutual authentication.

Configuration Summary

Following are step-by-step instructions summarizing the configuration described in this chapter. This is a broad overview of what's required to set up your Postfix system with SASL:

1. Determine the authentication mechanisms and framework you plan to support.

2. Install the SASL libraries and recompile Postfix with SASL support. Or obtain a Postfix distribution with SASL, including support for the authentication mechanisms and SASL options you need.

3. Reinstall Postfix.

4. Create the file */usr/local/lib/sasl2/smtpd.conf*. Enter either `saslauthd` or `auxprop` for `pwcheck_method`.

5. If you are using Unix passwords for authentication, start the `saslauthd` daemon, specifying the type of authentication in use on your system. Otherwise, use the `saslpasswd2` command to create email accounts on your system.

6. Edit *main.cf* to turn on authentication. This requires that you enable SASL and that you specify that authenticated clients should be allowed to relay mail. A basic setup requires at least the following parameters:

   ```
   smtpd_sasl_auth_enable = yes
   smtpd_recipient_restrictions = permit_mynetworks,
           permit_sasl_authenticated, reject_unauth_destination
   ```

7. Reload Postfix so that it recognizes the changes in its *main.cf* configuration file:

   ```
   # postfix reload
   ```

Testing Your Authentication Configuration

It's probably best to try authenticating to your SMTP server manually before having your users attempt it with their email clients. By connecting to your SMTP server and manually authenticating, you can see exactly what response you get, and you can immediately check your log file for any other important information.

The easiest way to connect to your SMTP server is to use a Telnet client and then start speaking SMTP to your server. (Chapter 2 shows a sample SMTP session.) The PLAIN mechanism is the easiest to test, so if you have disabled it, you may want to enable it just to confirm that authentication works. You can disable it after you are finished testing.

To authenticate using the PLAIN mechanism, you must send the command AUTH followed by your credentials encoded using base64. Your credentials are a combination of the authorization identity (identity to login as), followed by a null character, followed by the authentication identity (identity whose password will be used), followed by a null character, followed by the password. Usually, the authorization identity is the same as the authentication identity, and we'll assume as much here. Using the credentials for the user *kdent*, you need to encode the string 'kdent\ 0kdent\0Rumpelstiltskin'.

The tricky part is to encode your credentials in base64 without including a carriage return character. If your system has the mmencode and printf commands, it should be simple. The printf command prints formatted strings, and does not automatically include a linefeed like the more common echo command. The mmencode command simply converts strings into various MIME formats and uses base64 by default, which is exactly what we need.

You can get the encoded string you need by executing the following:

```
$ printf 'kdent\0kdent\0Rumpelstiltskin' | mmencode
a2RlbnQAa2RlbnQAcnVtcGxlc3RpbHRza2lu
```

On some platforms printf might not handle the null characters embedded in the middle of the string correctly. You'll know that you have this problem if the encoded string is shorter than your original string. You can try using the echo command with the -n switch instead of printf if it's available on your system. The -n tells echo not to include a trailing newline character. If you cannot get echo or printf to cooperate, or if you do not have the mmencode command, you can find a simple Perl solution in the sidebar in this chapter to get the string you need.

Once you have the string you need, cut and paste it into your Telnet session. In the example below, you type the telnet command to get things started, and then all of the bold lines. Here you are testing authentication on the host *mail.example.com*. You should specify your own system's name:

```
$ telnet mail.example.com 25
Trying 192.168.100.5...
Connected to mail.example.com.
Escape character is '^]'.

Server: 220 mail.example.com ESMTP Postfix
EHLO test.ora.com
```

---

encode_sasl_plain.pl

If you don't have the `mmencode` (or `mimeencode`) command, here's a simple Perl script to create the encoded string you need for testing. This script requires the MIME::Base64 module, which may not be installed on your system. You can easily retrieve it from your favorite CPAN mirror:

```perl
#!/usr/bin/perl

use strict;
use MIME::Base64;

if ( $#ARGV != 1 ) {
        die "Usage: encode_sasl_plain.pl <username> <password>\n";
}

print encode_base64("$ARGV[0]\0$ARGV[0]\0$ARGV[1]");
exit 0;
```

To get the required base64 authentication string for the user kdent using the password Rumpelstiltskin, execute the command as follows:

```
$ encode_sasl_plain.pl kdent Rumpelstiltskin
a2RlbnQAa2RlbnQAcnVtcGxlc3RpbHRza2lu
```

This produces the required string, which you can then cut and paste into your Telnet session.

```
250-mail.example.com
250-PIPELINING
250-SIZE 10240000
250-VRFY
250-ETRN
250-AUTH LOGIN PLAIN DIGEST-MD5 CRAM-MD5
250-XVERP
250 8BITMIME
AUTH PLAIN a2RlbnQAa2RlbnQAcnVtcGxlc3RpbHRza2lu
Server: 235 Authentication successful
quit
Server: 221 Bye

Connection closed by foreign host.
```

If you do not see a message that the authentication was successful, check your mail log to see what Postfix has reported. Problems can be tricky to track down because there are many pieces involved.

When you test authentication using Telnet, if you don't see the line:

```
250-AUTH LOGIN PLAIN DIGEST-MD5 CRAM-MD5
```

listed among the server's extensions, make sure that you didn't forget `smtpd_sasl_auth_enable` in your *main.cf* file. If the parameter is there (without typos), then you'd better look at how you compiled Postfix and make sure that it was built with support for SASL.

If the log tells you that it cannot open the db file, make sure that the password file exists in the */etc* directory and that the permissions are set so the *postfix* account has access to it. The Cyrus distribution comes with some utilities that might help you diagnose problems. Check the documentation for the `sasldblistusers2` and the `saslpasswd2` commands.

SMTP Client Authentication

You may want your Postfix server to relay through other servers that require SMTP authentication. In addition to requiring passwords on your own server, you can configure Postfix to provide login names and passwords when relaying mail through other SMTP servers.

You have to provide Postfix with a password file that contains the credentials it should use when authenticating to other servers. Entries in the password file contain a domain or hostname, username, and password in the form: *domain username:password*. For the domain or hostname, Postfix first checks for the destination domain from the recipient address. If it doesn't find the domain, it then checks for the hostname it is connecting to. This allows Postfix to work easily with sites that have multiple MX hosts that share the same user database. Use `smtp_sasl_password_maps` parameter to specify where your password file is.

The client `smtp_sasl_security_options` parameter works just like server `smtpd_sasl_security_options` (discussed earlier in the chapter) for the SMTP servers. If you don't specify any options, the default allows all available mechanisms including plaintext but not anonymous logins.

Procedure to Enable SMTP Client Authentication

Use the following steps to configure Postfix to provide a login and password when relaying mail. In this example, you'll set up two different passwords for Postfix to authenticate when relaying through any server for the domain *ora.com* and through a host called *mail.postfix.org*:

1. Create a file called */etc/postfix/sasl_passwd* with entries for each host, login, and password combination you need. Your file should resemble the following:

        ora.com   kdent:Rumpelstiltskin
        mail.postfix.org   kyle:quixote

2. Execute `postmap` on the file:

        # postmap /etc/postfix/sasl_passwd

3. Edit *main.cf* to turn on client authentication. Notice that you are now setting `smtp_sasl_auth_enable` instead of `smtpd_sasl_auth_enable` as you did to turn on

authentication at the server. You must also set `smtp_sasl_password_maps` to point to the password file you created:

```
smtp_sasl_auth_enable = yes
smtp_sasl_password_maps = hash:/etc/postfix/sasl_passwd
```

4. Reload Postfix so that it recognizes the changes in its *main.cf* configuration file:

```
# postfix reload
```

Now, when the Postfix SMTP client attempts to relay messages through any of the domains or hosts listed in */etc/postfix/sasl_passwd*, it will offer the corresponding authentication credentials. For example, if your Postfix smtp client connects to the server *mail.ora.com*, it authenticates with the username kdent and the password Rumpelstiltskin.

CHAPTER 13
Transport Layer Security

Transport Layer Security, or TLS (formerly known as SSL), enhances TCP communications by adding encryption for privacy and message integrity. RFC 3207 defines an extension to SMTP known as STARTTLS. Its primary purpose is to provide privacy in peer-to-peer communications. It can also give you assurances that your mail is not being delivered to a rogue system posing as the server you think you're sending mail to. Another useful application is in combination with SASL, to protect plaintext passwords that would otherwise be sent in the clear.

One nice benefit of TLS is that you can obtain the privacy and assurances of reliable server identification without a previous arrangement between systems. Strong authentication is also possible if your users' email clients support it. By using client certificates, which are cryptographically signed identifiers (see sidebar), your mail server can be sure that connecting clients are indeed who they claim to be. You can use client certificates in place of or in conjunction with SASL authentication discussed in Chapter 12. There is administrative overhead in managing client certificates and assisting users in configuring their email clients to use them, while using TLS just to encrypt authentication credentials is fairly easy to set up.

It is important to note, however, that TLS is not meant to protect the contents of email messages. When you encrypt the transmission between a client and server, everything (including the message) is encrypted. However, TLS protects only the transmission between the two systems. After the server receives a message, it is probably stored as plaintext. You can't be sure if the message will be encrypted or not when the server forwards it to the next destination, or when the final recipient downloads the message to read it. Unless you can control and encrypt the path all the way from the originating client to the ultimate recipient of the message, it will most likely pass in the clear at some point on its way to delivery. To achieve end-to-end privacy you need a client solution such as PGP or S/MIME.

Postfix and TLS

Support for TLS in Postfix is provided by a set of patches written by Lutz Jänicke. You can follow the link for Add-on Software from the Postfix home page to download the patches. (See Appendix C for information on building Postfix with the TLS patches.) If you are using a prebuilt Postfix package for your platform, make sure that it has the TLS patches built in.

In addition to compiling Postfix to support TLS, you must also create and configure TLS certificates. You need both a private key and a public key. The public key is a signed certificate identifying your server. It is validated and digitally signed by a certificate authority (CA), which attests that your certificate does, in fact, identify your system (see sidebar in Chapter 13). In addition to your own certificates, you must also have the public key of the CA that signed your certificate.

You can register with any of the many CAs to obtain a signed certificate, or you can act as your own CA. The clients connecting to your TLS-enabled server must recognize and acknowledge the CA you use and agree to accept it as an authority to attest to your identity. Generally, it is a fairly simple configuration option in email clients to accept a certificate and have the CA public key added to its list of trusted authorities if it isn't listed already.

TLS Certificates

The TLS patches for Postfix were written using the OpenSSL libraries. The libraries come with command-line tools for managing certificates, which you will need to generate certificates. For Postfix purposes, all of your certificates must be in the PEM format, which is base64 encoded data with some additional header lines. The default output for the OpenSSL tools is PEM, so you won't have to convert any certificates you generate to use with Postfix. By default, the OpenSSL tools are installed below */usr/local/ssl*. The openssl command is the utility you'll use most often in managing your certificates.

Becoming a CA

Your server certificates have to be signed by a CA. You can easily set yourself up as a CA to sign your own certificates. The OpenSSL distribution includes a script to configure yourself as a CA. From the SSL home directory, type the following:

```
# misc/CA.pl -newca
```

Answer all of the prompts as requested. This sets up all of the necessary CA files below *./demoCA*. Later, when you issue the command to sign a certificate, the openssl command will refer to these root certificates.

TLS Certificates Brief Overview

TLS uses public-key cryptography to allow a client and a server to communicate privately. It also provides assurance that no one has tampered with transmitted information and that the information is not forged because the protocol allows for both the client and server to authenticate each other. Always keep in mind, however, that the benefits of TLS are limited to just the end points of a given TLS connection. What happens to any data before or after it passes between the client and server is not protected by TLS.

Public-key cryptography uses a pair of complementary keys. One can be widely distributed and the other is a secret key. Data encrypted with one key can be decrypted with the other key and vice versa. Others can send you data encrypted with your public key that only you can decrypt with your private one. In most implementations, the private key can be used to create a digital signature of a block of data. The public key can then be used to verify that a particular private key created a given signature.

Moreover, your public key is associated with an identifier, referred to as its *common name* (often the hostname of your server). Others can be sure your server is what it claims to be by comparing the common name associated with its public key against its DNS hostname or a name supplied during connection handshaking. In general, you want everyone to have your public key, but your private key must be guarded at all costs.

Public keys are digitally signed by CAs to create certificates. CAs are usually third-party organizations that are *trusted* by both sides of the exchange. In theory, the CA's digital signature indicates that it has verified the identity of the public-key holder and attests that this public key belongs to this server.[a] A public key validated by a CA is often referred to as a signed certificate. Your trust in a certificate should extend only as far as your faith in the CA that signed it. The only assurance that exists with certificates comes from the CA that attests to a certificate holder's identity.

The public/private keys are actually used only at the beginning of a connection to determine identities and to encrypt a randomly chosen session key. This single key is used by both sides to encrypt and sign the rest of the exchange. A session key can be used only for a single session, and then it is discarded.

Let's take a look at the exchange between a client and server. The client contacts a server and requests an encrypted connection. On the Web, the client uses https; with email, the client issues the STARTTLS command to indicate that it wants an encrypted connection.

—continued—

---

a. In practice, this has turned out to be a very difficult aspect of public-key cryptography systems. There have been a number of high-profile failures revealing that trust in a trusted certificate authority might be misplaced.

The server obliges by sending back its signed certificate, which indicates its common name and the CA that has validated it. The client verifies the server's identity. It checks to see if the signing CA is listed among those it trusts and that the common name on the certificate is what it expects. If the certificate checks out, the client and server determine a *key agreement* to generate a session key to be used for this exchange and then discarded. The key agreement determination differs depending on the type of cypher in use. The conversation continues with both sides now using the private session key to encrypt and verify all transmissions.

Generating Server Certificates

You can use the openssl command to generate the public and private keys for your server. From the public key, you create a certificate signing request (CSR) to send to a CA for validation. Once signed, your public certificate can be widely distributed, but your private keys must be carefully guarded. In fact, many applications store encrypted private keys and require a pass phrase to access them. You cannot use encrypted keys with Postfix, however, because different components need read access to the keys as they are started by the master daemon.

The OpenSSL distribution includes scripts to help you generate keys and certificate-signing requests, but the scripts encrypt the keys by default. Since you want to leave the keys unencrypted, it's just as easy to use the openssl command directly. Execute the following command to create a public and private key to be used with Postfix:

```
$ openssl req -new -nodes -keyout mailkey.pem \
    -out mailreq.pem -days 365
```

The openssl command with the -new option creates both a private key and a CSR. The -nodes option tells openssl not to encrypt the key. -keyout and -out indicate the names of the files where the private key and the CSR should be created. Finally, -days 365 says to make the certificate valid for one year.

If you are using a third-party CA, follow its directions for getting your certificate request signed. You will be sending in the *mailreq.pem* file created above. If you are acting as your own CA, you can sign the file yourself with the following command:

```
# openssl ca -out mail_signed_cert.pem -infiles mailreq.pem
```

This produces the file *mail_signed_cert.pem*, which will serve as your signed certificate.

You probably want to copy all of your Postfix/TLS-related certificate files to a convenient location. If you used all of the defaults, execute the following commands to move the certificate files into the Postfix configuration directory:

```
# cp /usr/local/ssl/mailkey.pem /etc/postfix
# cp /usr/local/ssl/mail_signed_cert.pem /etc/postfix
```

These files represent your server private key and public certificate. Because you created the private key without encrypting it, you must protect it by using permissions that are as restrictive as possible. Use the following commands to make sure it is owned and readable only by the *root* account.

```
# chown root /etc/postfix/mailkey.pem
# chmod 400 /etc/postfix/mailkey.pem
```

Installing CA Certificates

Your Postfix/TLS server must have access to the public certificate of the CA that signed your server certificate and any CAs that signed certificates for your users. If a single CA signed both, you need only one CA certificate. If you are acting as your own CA, copy the *cacert.pem* file that was created after you ran the CA.pl script:

```
# cp /usr/local/ssl/demoCA/cacert.pem /etc/postfix
```

If you used a third-party CA to sign your public certificate, place that organization's PEM-format public certificate in the file */etc/postfix/cacert.pem*. You will also need public certificates from any CA that signed client certificates you intend to trust.

There are two different ways to add CA certificates to Postfix/TLS. The first keeps all of the certificates together in a single file defined by the smtpd_tls_CAfile parameter. You simply append new certificates to the existing file. If, for example, your CA certificates are stored in */etc/postfix/cacert.pem*, and you have a new certificate stored in a file called *newCA.pem*, use the following commands to add your new CA certificate:

```
# cp /etc/postfix/cacert.pem /etc/postfix/cacert.pem.old
# cat newCA.pem >> /etc/postfix/cacert.pem
```

(Be sure to type *two* angle brackets so that you don't overwrite the file.)

The other option is to keep all of your CA certificates in separate files. This option makes maintenance of CA certificates a little easier, but the certificates will not be automatically available to a chrooted Postfix. Most likely you would choose this option if you have a lot of CA certificates to deal with. The parameter smtpd_tls_CApath points to a directory where the CA certificates are stored. To add additional certificates, simply copy a new certificate file into the directory and execute the c_rehash utility that comes with OpenSSL. For example, if you have a new certificate stored in a file called *newCA.pem* and you store all of your certificate files in */etc/postfix/certs*, use the following commands to add it to your Postfix installation:

```
# cp newCA.pem /etc/postfix/certs
# c_rehash /etc/postfix/certs
```

Postfix/TLS Configuration

The TLS patches for Postfix introduce additional parameters for dealing with TLS within the SMTP server. Following are some of the critical TLS parameters that you'll need for the basic configuration. See the sample configuration file that comes with the patch distribution for additional TLS parameters.

smtpd_use_tls

> Turns on server TLS support. Otherwise, Postfix operates as it would without the TLS patch. For example: smtp_use_tls = yes

smtpd_tls_key_file

> Points to the file containing your server's private key. For example: smtpd_tls_key_file = /etc/postfix/mailkey.pem

smtpd_tls_cert_file

> Points to the file containing your server's signed certificate. For example: smtpd_tls_cert_file = /etc/postfix/mail_signed_cert.pem

smtpd_tls_CAfile

> Points to the file containing the public certificates identifying Certificate Authorities you trust. For example: smtpd_tls_CAfile = /etc/postfix/cacert.pem

smtpd_tls_CApath

> Points to a directory of files each containing a public certificate for a Certificate Authority you trust. For example: smtpd_tls_CApath = /etc/postfix/certs

Once you set these parameters in your *main.cf* file and reload Postfix, your server will be ready to handle encrypted connections.

Postfix/TLS Configuration Summary

Following is a summary of the steps to follow in order to set up Postfix to use TLS:

1. If it's not already installed on your system, install the OpenSSL distribution that you'll need to generate TLS certificates.

2. Recompile and reinstall Postfix with the TLS patch (see Appendix C) or obtain a Postfix distribution that includes the TLS code.

3. Generate server certificates including a certificate-signing request. You can validate the signing request yourself if you're acting as your own CA or send it to a third-party CA for validation.

4. Install your certificates (server secret key, signed public certificate, and your CA's public certificate) into the Postfix directory.

5. Edit *main.cf* and set the following parameters for TLS:

   ```
   smtpd_use_tls = yes
   smtpd_tls_key_file = /etc/postfix/mailkey.pem
   smtpd_tls_cert_file = /etc/postfix/mail_signed_cert.pem
   smtpd_tls_CAfile = /etc/postfix/cacert.pem
   ```

   If there are other TLS parameters that you want to set, do so here (see the TLS patches documentation).

6. Reload Postfix so that it recognizes the changes in its *main.cf* configuration file:

   ```
   # postfix reload
   ```

Now, when a client requests an encrypted session, your server should be able to respond appropriately.

Requiring Client-Side Certificates

You may want to use client-side certificates instead of, or in addition to, other SMTP authentication techniques. Client-side certificates provide an excellent method of authentication that can be very difficult to fake.

Client-side certificates must be signed by a CA. If you plan to have your users' certificates signed by a third-party CA, you should follow the directions from your CA for creating client-side certificates. You can also create client certificates and sign them yourself using tools from the OpenSSL package.

Creating client certificates

Creating client certificates is just like creating the server certificate we saw earlier in the chapter with the added step of converting the signed certificate into a format that email clients can import. Most popular mail clients expect certificates in the PKCS12 format, which packages together the signed certificate and private key and protects them with a password. If you use a third-party CA, the company will most likely provide you or your users with the correct format needed for your particular email client. If you are signing certificates yourself, you have to create a PKCS12-formatted file to give to your users. The file is created with the user's signed certificate, the private key corresponding to that certificate, and your own CA public certificate.

You have to create a separate certificate/key pair for each user you plan to authenticate with certificates. You should decide on a policy for choosing a distinguished name. Generally, you would use the individual's email address or the client machine's hostname when generating the certificates. The steps below walk through creating a certificate for a user with the email address *kdent@ora.com*:

1. Using the openssl command, generate a private and public key for your user. Remember that your public key also has to be signed by a CA (possibly yourself):

   ```
   $ openssl req -new -nodes -keyout kdentkey.pem \
     -out kdentreq.pem -days 365
   ```

   This command creates both a private key and a CSR, as specified by the -new option. The -nodes option tells openssl not to encrypt the key (see "Generating Server Certificates"). -keyout and -out indicate the names of the files where the private key and the CSR should be created. Finally, -days 365 says to make the certificate valid for one year.

2. If you are using a third-party CA, follow their directions for getting your certificate request signed. You will be sending them the *kdentreq.pem* file you created above. If you are acting as your own CA, you can sign the file yourself with the following command:

   ```
   # openssl ca -out kdent_signed_cert.pem -infiles kdentreq.pem
   ```

3. Once you have the signed certificate, convert it to a format that can be used by your users' email clients:

```
# openssl pkcs12 -in kdent_signed_cert.pem -inkey \
kdentkey.pem -certfile /etc/postfix/cacert.pem -out kdent.p12 \
-export -name "kdent@ora.com"
```

You will be prompted to provide a password for the file the command creates. You will have to provide your user with the password you select. The -certfile option points to your own CA certificate file. In this example, you're using the file as created by the CA.pl script. Once finished, you can provide your user with the *kdent.p12* file and the password you used when creating it.

Your user should now be able to import the file into a mail client that supports the PKCS12 format.

Configuring client-side certificate authentication

Postfix/TLS uses certificate fingerprints to identify acceptable certificates. A fingerprint is a cryptographic hash calculated from a signed certificate. Fingerprints for each certificate are stored in a standard Postfix lookup table (see Chapter 4). When a client presents a certificate, Postfix/TLS calculates the fingerprint from the certificate and compares it to those listed in its lookup table. If it finds a match, it permits the client to relay.

You need to calculate a fingerprint for each client certificate that you will accept. Many email clients can produce a fingerprint for you, or if you created the certificate, you can easily calculate a fingerprint with the openssl x509 command:

```
$ openssl x509 -fingerprint -noout -in kdent_signed_cert.pem \
| cut -d= -f2
57:8E:95:63:67:CD:2B:96:7C:0A:3A:61:46:A5:95:EA
```

To continue the calculation:

1. Obtain a list of fingerprints for each of your users' client certificates. You can generate them as described above or obtain them from your users if they can get them from their email clients.

2. Create a file to store all of the client certificate fingerprints. For this example, you'll create a file called */etc/postfix/clientcerts*

3. Edit the *clientcerts* file to add each fingerprint. Since this is a standard Postfix lookup table, you must also add a righthand value for each fingerprint, even though that value is not used. Use a value that will help you to identify the fingerprint in the future. Your resultant file should contain entries like the following for each of your users:

```
57:8E:95:63:67:CD:2B:96:7C:0A:3A:61:46:A5:95:EA    kdent@ora.com
```

4. Execute postmap against the *clientcerts* file:

```
# postmap /etc/postfix/clientcerts
```

5. Edit *main.cf* to add the following parameters:

```
relay_clientcerts = hash:/etc/postfix/clientcerts
smtpd_tls_ask_ccert = yes
smtpd_recipient_restrictions =
        permit_mynetworks
        permit_tls_clientcerts
        reject_unauth_destination
```

Note that smtpd_tls_ask_ccert has two c's for "client certificate." If you have already defined the smtpd_recipient_restrictions parameter, add permit_tls_clientcerts to the list of restriction rules.

6. Reload Postfix so that it recognizes the changes in its *main.cf* configuration file:

```
# postfix reload
```

Configuring TLS/SMTP Client

Since you may have configurations where other email servers require your server to authenticate when relaying mail, Postfix/TLS can also present a certificate when acting as an SMTP client. Note that you are limited to only one certificate for your SMTP client unless you set up additional SMTP transports in *master.cf* and configure them to use different client keys and certificates.

If you are using a self-signed server certificate, you can use the same certificate and its accompanying secret key as your client certificate. If a third-party CA signed your server certificate, it's possible that it can be used only for the SMTP server. In which case, you can generate a separate client certificate and have that signed too. Your client certificate's common name should match the hostname of your system, as specified in the myhostname parameter. Follow the same procedure that you used to create the server certificates. If you are using the same certificates, you don't have to do anything; simply configure the TLS client parameters to point to the same files as the server parameters.

The TLS patches for Postfix introduce the following parameters for dealing with TLS within the SMTP client. See the sample configuration file that comes with the TLS distribution for additional TLS parameters:

smtp_use_tls
> Turns on client TLS support. Otherwise, Postfix operates as it would without the TLS patch. Example: smtp_use_tls = yes

smtp_tls_key_file
> Points to the file containing the private key used in conjunction with your client-signed certificate. Example: smtp_tls_key_file = /etc/postfix/mailkey.pem

smtp_tls_cert_file
> Points to the file containing your client-signed certificate. Example: smtp_tls_cert_file = /etc/postfix/mail_signed_cert.pem

`smtp_tls_CAfile`
> Points to the file containing the public certificates identifying the CAs that signed your client certificate. Example: `smtp_tls_CAfile = /etc/postfix/CAcert.pem`

Assuming that you are using the same certificates that you used for your server, the procedure to enable TLS in the SMTP client is quite simple:

1. Edit *main.cf* and set the following parameters:

   ```
   smtp_use_tls = yes
   smtp_tls_key_file = /etc/postfix/mailkey.pem
   smtp_tls_cert_file = /etc/postfix/mail_signed_cert.pem
   smtp_tls_CAfile = /etc/postfix/cacert.pem
   ```

   If there are other TLS parameters that you want to set, do so here (see the TLS patches documentation).

2. Reload Postfix so that it recognizes the changes in its *main.cf* configuration file:

   ```
   # postfix reload
   ```

Now, when Postfix connects to an SMTP server that requests a client certificate, it will provide the necessary information.

CHAPTER 14
Content Filtering

A content filter is a utility that scans the headers and body of an email message, and usually takes some action based on what it finds. The most common examples are anti-virus and anti-spam programs. Viruses are commonly spread within the contents of email messages, and if you cannot detect spam based on the connecting client or envelope information, you might have better luck by inspecting the actual contents of a message. Filters might change messages, redirect them, respond to them, or tag them for later processing by another tool.

In this chapter we'll look at content filtering at your mail server, although that may not always be your best option for filtering. MTA filtering is appropriate for filtering that should occur with all or nearly all messages. If you need filtering that is configurable by user, the MTA is not the best choice for it. Other types of filtering to consider are:

Mail delivery agent (MDA)
> Configurable MDAs such as procmail or sieve allow users to manage their own delivery configuration files. Generally, MDAs expect your users to edit their own configuration files on the mail server system. If they don't have system accounts, you must provide another means for them to configure their filtering, such as through a web-based application.

Mail user agent (MUA)
> You might also consider allowing your users to take advantage of filtering capabilities within their email clients. If their client packages support filtering, this is an excellent way to provide per-user filtering for virtual users that don't have system accounts on your mail server. It has the added advantage of moving processor- and memory-intensive scanning from the server out to multiple clients.

Postfix body and header checks
> Postfix body and header checks can provide limited filtering. They cannot be configured by the user, but they are probably the simplest to implement. See Chapter 11 for information about setting them up.

A combination of MTA and MUA filters might make a nice compromise. The MTA filter can tag messages with a value to be read by users' MUA filters. Users can then configure their own filters to accept, reject, or categorize messages based on the tagged value.

An anti-virus filter is an excellent choice for MTA filtering. You can maintain it centrally and block viruses before they even enter your network. Actions that should occur for every message that enters your system are best handled by the MTA.

Postfix body and header checks, while powerful, can consider only one line of a message at a time, and they're always applied to all messages. They don't offer a convenient way to set up complex options for rejecting or redirecting messages. Anything more than simple filtering should probably not be handled within a general MTA like Postfix.

Postfix provides two approaches for configuring external filters: commands that accept the contents of email messages on their standard input or daemons that accept message contents via SMTP or LMTP. With commands, a new process is started for every message, which can be resource-intensive, particularly if the command has a high start-up cost. Daemon filters stay resident and have the potential for better performance using fewer system resources. The daemon method is somewhat more complicated to configure but provides a more robust solution.

Command-Based Filtering

The simplest way to set up content filtering is to use a program that runs as a command and accepts the contents of a message on its standard input. Postfix delivers messages to your filter command via the pipe mailer. Your filter command performs its checking and then gives the filtered message back to Postfix using the Postfix sendmail command.

For this discussion, we'll assume that the filter command operates on mail that comes in through the SMTP daemon but not on mail that is delivered locally (using the sendmail command), so that your filter can use sendmail to give the message back to Postfix without looping. Figure 14-1 illustrates the path messages follow once you put your filter in place. Rather than passing the message to a delivery agent, the queue manager invokes the filter.

Your filter program must be able to accept the message on its standard input and then deliver it to the Postfix sendmail command. If you have a filtering program that doesn't handle input and output in this way it should be easy enough to create a shell script wrapper to deal with those details. In the Postfix distribution, the FILTER_README file contains an example of such a script.

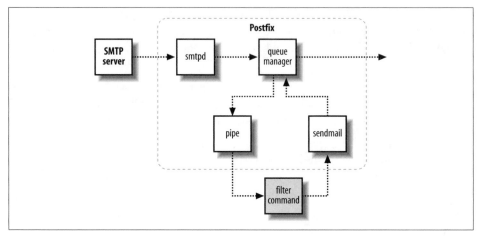

Figure 14-1. Mail-filtering command

Configuration

When you configure Postfix to use your filter program, you must specify a user that the program runs as. You should create a pseudoaccount whose sole purpose is to run the filter.

Let's set up an example configuration and assume that you have a filter program named `simple_filt` stored at */usr/local/bin* and that you have created a pseudouser called *filter* to run it. Edit your *master.cf* file to add an entry for your filter:

```
filter    unix -    n    n    -    -    pipe
    flags=Rq user=filter argv=/usr/local/bin/simple_filt
    -f ${sender} -- ${recipient}
```

The first line contains all of the standard settings for a Postfix component entry with the last column indicating that the message should be handled by the Postfix `pipe` daemon. The second and third lines are a continuation of the first because of the whitespace at the beginning. They contain options the `pipe` service will use when executing the command. The options `R` and `q`, specified as `flags`, tell the `pipe` service to prepend a `Return-Path:` header and to quote whitespace and special characters in the `${sender}` and `${recipient}` addresses that are passed to the command. See the `pipe(8)` man page for other possible options.

The `user=` option is the *filter* pseudouser that you set up for running your filter command. The `argv` option specifies the actual command along with its arguments to execute. The argument list specified here (`-f ${sender} -- ${recipient}`) can be used exactly as is by the script when it invokes the `sendmail` command to deliver the message back to Postfix. Your own filter may require different arguments, but make sure you include the items you need to send the message back to Postfix through the `sendmail` command. The `${recipient}` variable is expanded by the `pipe` daemon into multiple recipients up to the limit specified in the $filter\_destination\_recipient\_limit$ parameter when a message has more than one recipient.

In addition to the new component entry, you must also make a change to the smtpd entry in *master.cf* to turn on filtering for all messages that are delivered to the SMTP daemon:

```
smtp      inet  n       -       n       -       -       smtpd
    -o content_filter=filter:
```

Simply add the second line in the preceding example to your existing smtpd line. Don't forget the initial whitespace to indicate that it is a continuation of the previous line. The content_filter parameter is set equal to the entry you just created in *master.cf* for your filter program. Set this option here rather than in *main.cf* because it should apply to the smtpd daemon only and not for every message that enters the Postfix system. After you reload Postfix, all messages coming in over SMTP will now be handled by your filter program.

A filter of this sort, although easy to configure, is not the most efficient method of filtering. It requires that Postfix invoke a shell or interpreter and that the filter invoke sendmail to resubmit the filtered message. If your program runs into problems—disk space or memory—for example, there isn't a reliable way for it to report the exact problem back to Postfix. Daemon-based filtering described in the next section offers a more robust solution with better performance.[*]

Daemon-Based Filtering

Daemon-based filtering offers a more advanced architecture over the command-based method with lower cost in I/O and CPU usage. It can provide better error handling than is possible with the command method. If implemented as a resident process, the startup overhead per message is eliminated. A daemon-based content filter can pass email messages back and forth with Postfix using the standard SMTP or LMTP protocol. Such a filter can run as a standalone daemon or it can be started by Postfix if configured to do so in *master.cf*.

In this configuration, we want the content filter to handle all messages, whether delivered locally (via sendmail) or to the smtpd daemon. You have to configure Postfix in *master.cf* to use a special smtp client component to deliver the messages to your filter and an additional smtpd daemon to receive messages back from your filter. Figure 14-2 illustrates how a filtered message travels through Postfix to your content filter and back into Postfix for delivery. In this diagram, the filter receives mail via localhost port 10025 from the additional smtp client and submits it back to Postfix via localhost port 10026 to the additional smtpd server component.

[*] All else being equal. The performance depends largely on the content-filtering program itself.

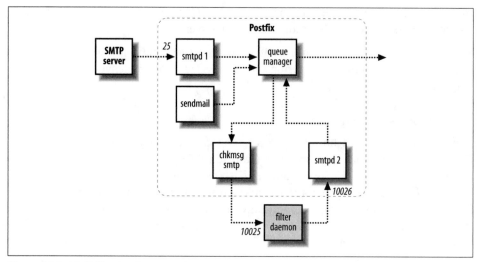

Figure 14-2. Mail-filtering daemon

If the filter wants to reject a message, it should reply with an SMTP code of 550 along with the reason for the rejection. Otherwise, it should accept the message and perform its operations before passing it back to Postfix. If your filter rejects a message, Postfix bounces it back to the sender address with the message your filter provides.

Configuration

For the purposes of this discussion, I'll assume that you are running a standalone content filter daemon that listens for incoming messages using SMTP. After processing, it sends the message back to Postfix using SMTP. The basic steps to configure this setup are:

1. Create a pseudoaccount for your filter.
2. Install and configure your content filter.
3. Edit *master.cf* to add two additional Postfix components.
4. Edit *main.cf* to add the content_filter parameter.
5. Restart Postfix so that it recognizes the changes to its configuration files.

When setting up a daemon-based content filter, make sure it does not use the same hostname that Postfix has set in its myhostname parameter, or the Postfix SMTP client will consider it an error and not deliver the message to your filter. The rest of this section walks you through the details of setting up a daemon-based content filter.

Creating a pseudoaccount

As with the simple filtering solution described earlier, you should create a pseudoaccount for your filter. The account shouldn't have access to other resources on your system. If your filter needs to write files, you should create a directory for that purpose. Your filter should be started as the designated user or configured to become that user after starting. Check your filter's configuration options. For this example, I'll assume that you've created a user called *filter*.

Installing a content filter

Your content filter package should provide you with instructions for installation and configuration. In this example, assume that the filter listens on the loopback interface on port 10025. After processing messages, the filter should pass them back to Postfix on port 10026. You should be able to configure your filter accordingly, or if your filter listens and reinjects on a different port, keep that in mind as you follow the example. If possible, test your filter first to make sure that it operates correctly before trying to connect it to Postfix.

Configuring additional Postfix components

You may encounter "mail loops back to myself" problems when creating additional SMTP components. One solution is to give the additional component a different value for myhostname.

Edit *master.cf* to add the new components you need. A second smtp component will be used to send messages to your content filter. (See "master.cf" in Chapter 4 for more information on editing *master.cf*.) We'll call this additional smtp entry chkmsg:

```
chkmsg              unix -     -     n     -     10    smtp
    -o myhostname=localhost
```

Later, when you turn on content filtering in *main.cf*, you'll tell Postfix to send the message to your filter on port 10025 using this component.

In addition to the extra smtp client, you also need a second smtpd service to receive messages back from the content filter program. The second smtpd instance is configured slightly differently from the normal one because you want Postfix to handle traffic from your filter differently from messages coming from outside. Set options with an entry like the following:

```
localhost:10026    inet  n     -     n     -     10    smtpd
        -o content_filter=
        -o local_recipient_maps=
        -o mynetworks=127.0.0.0/8
        -o smtpd_helo_restrictions=
        -o smtpd_client_restrictions=
        -o smtpd_sender_restrictions=
        -o smtpd_recipient_restrictions=permit_mynetworks,reject
```

This instance of smtpd is configured to listen on the loopback interface on port 10026. You configure your filter to send the processed messages to this service. There are several options in this example. These override the settings in the *main.cf* file and are explained below:

`content_filter`

> The default `smtpd` instance has content filtering turned on in *main.cf*. This instance of `smtpd` should not have the content filter process messages again.

`local_recipient_maps`

> Some lookup maps convert an address when it is received by the external `smtpd`. When your filter tries to reinject it, Postfix may not recognize the recipient and reject the message. Set this option to blank to make sure the filtered messages are always accepted from your filter.

`mynetworks`

> Since your filter runs on the same system as Postfix, the filter and Postfix can communicate over the local loopback interface, a pseudonetwork device not associated with any real hardware interface. The loopback interface always uses an address of 127.0.0.1. Since 127 is the first byte of its address, it's a class A network that you identify with a /8 network prefix. By setting `mynetworks` to the loopback network and `smtpd_recipient_restrictions` to permit only this network, this instance of `smtpd` accepts connections from your filter only and isn't exposed to any (potentially hostile) traffic from the network.

`smtpd_helo_restrictions`, `smtpd_client_restrictions`, `smtpd_sender_restrictions`

> You can turn off any restrictions that were already checked by the original `smtpd` instance. If you're not already using these restrictions in *main.cf*, you don't need to turn them off here.

`smtpd_recipient_restrictions`

> Finally, tell `smtpd` to accept connections on the loopback interface and reject everything else.

Turning on filtering

After you have made the necessary changes to *master.cf*, you have to configure Postfix to pass all messages it receives to your content filter. Edit the *main.cf* file to add a line like the following:

```
content_filter = chkmsg:[127.0.0.1]:10025
```

This parameter tells Postfix to pass messages to the content filter via the `chkmsg` service that you created in *master.cf*. You also tell it to send the messages to port 10025, which should match what you have configured your content filter program to use. Be sure to reload Postfix to recognize the changes in its configuration files. Once Postfix is reloaded, it will start passing all messages through your content filter for processing.

Daemon-Based Filter Example

To demonstrate setting up a daemon-based content filter, this section walks through installing Vexira AntiVirus from Central Command. Vexira is a commercial anti-virus product available on the Central Command web page, *http://www. centralcommand.com/*. Its Vexira AntiVirus for Mail servers product is written to

---

work with Postfix among other MTAs. It is available for Linux, FreeBSD, and OpenBSD platforms. If you are using a different daemon-based anti-virus solution, the configuration should be similar to the procedure presented here:

1. Install Vexira according to the documentation from Command Central. The rest of this procedure assumes that your configuration files are in /etc per the installation instructions.

2. Configure Vexira to listen on the local loopback interface on port 10024. Edit /etc/vamailarmor.conf and set the parameter ListenAddress as follows:

   ```
   ListenAddress localhost port 10024
   ```

3. Also set the ForwardTo parameter to pass messages back to Postfix over the loopback interface on port 10025:

   ```
   ForwardTo SMTP: localhost port 10025
   ```

4. Restart Vexira using the method or scripts installed on your system. See your Vexira documentation.

5. Edit the Postfix *main.cf* file to have all messages sent to the Vexira daemon for virus scanning. Edit the content_filter parameter as follows:

   ```
   content_filter = smtp:[127.0.0.1]:10024
   ```

6. Edit the Postfix *master.cf* file to add another SMTP daemon to accept messages back from Vexira after virus scanning:

   ```
   localhost:10025    inet  n     -     n     -     10     smtpd
            -o content_filter=
            -o local_recipient_maps=
            -o mynetworks=127.0.0.0/8
            -o smtpd_helo_restrictions=
            -o smtpd_client_restrictions=
            -o smtpd_sender_restrictions=
            -o smtpd_recipient_restrictions=permit_mynetworks,reject
   ```

7. Reload Postfix so that it recognizes the changes in its configuration files:

   ```
   # postfix reload
   ```

Other Considerations

You can run multiple content filters, if necessary, by chaining them. If, for example, you have both an anti-virus and an anti-spam content filter, simply configure the first one to deliver to the next one rather than immediately back to Postfix. The Postfix configuration doesn't have to change from what's presented here. Only the final filter delivers the message back to Postfix.

Be aware of any email address rewriting that occurs before your filter receives a message. When the filter resubmits a message, if the rewritten address isn't in one of the recipient maps, Postfix will reject it. You may have to turn off address rewriting in your normal SMTP server and configure it instead in your SMTP server that accepts messages back from your filter.

Some filters recommend that you configure them to accept mail in front of your normal MTA, and then they pass the messages on to your MTA after processing. You probably do not want to do this. Postfix is specifically designed to accept messages over an unfriendly network. A content filter is specifically designed to deal with processing the contents of messages and probably isn't optimized for dealing with the load and potential hazards of accepting connections from the outside. Likewise some filters want to handle the final delivery of messages without re-injecting them into Postfix. Again, Postfix offers a lot of flexibility and security in dealing with the final disposition of messages that you might lose by delegating the delivery to another package.

## CHAPTER 15

External Databases

Postfix map files provide an easy and efficient mechanism for the many lookup operations needed when handling email. In some situations, however, it can be more convenient to have the information in a database separate from Postfix. A database can provide a central repository available to many system or network services that need similar information, such as account names and passwords. A database can be useful when redundant systems running Postfix need to share the same configuration information. A central database might also be more convenient when you have multiple people who need access to edit information.

Databases can also slow Postfix performance compared to normal index files. In general, if you don't have a definite need for a database, you're better off with the standard Postfix maps. In many cases you can get the best of both options by storing information in a database and running regular scripts that update your Postfix files from the central data repository. But if your environment requires instant access to revised data, an external database configuration may be your only option.

In this chapter, we'll look at configuring Postfix to work with MySQL and LDAP. (Postfix also has support for PostgreSQL as of Version 2.1.) In either case, Postfix must be compiled with additional libraries to support the mysql and ldap map types. If you are using a prebuilt package, make sure that it has support for the type of database you plan to use. If you built your own Postfix, see Chapter 15 for information on compiling with the additional libraries.

You can easily check if your Postfix installation contains support for LDAP and MySQL with the postconf -m command:

```
$ postconf -m
static
pcre
regexp
mysql
environ
proxy
ldap
```

```
btree
unix
hash
```

You should see either ldap or mysql or both listed among the map types.

While the databases you use with Postfix may contain a variety of information, conceptually they work the same as Postfix maps. You have a key such as the recipient email address, and you expect to get back a value associated with the key such as a forwarding address. How to perform this with each type of database, MySQL and LDAP, is explained in the next sections.

It is a good practice to make sure your lookups work correctly with normal Postfix lookup tables. Then duplicate your configuration with MySQL or LDAP lookups. Make sure that you get the same results from both. In most cases, Postfix expects a lookup to return only one result. Make sure that your database queries do not return multiple result values.

MySQL

MySQL is an open source relational database system that uses Structured Query Language (SQL) for querying and managing its data. You don't have to know SQL to use Postfix with MySQL, but it will help to understand how they interact. Normally, you would use MySQL because you already have a database of information about each user such as a full name, account name, phone numbers, etc. You have to make sure your database includes the information you need to accomplish a particular task with Postfix. A common use is to map an email alias to the local account name. For this to work there must be one database column containing email aliases and another with local account names. Postfix can query your database with the recipient address of an email message as the key to look up the value of the local account for delivery. Any of the Postfix lookup table parameters can work with MySQL queries. You just have to figure out which columns contain the information you need.

MySQL Configuration

MySQL maps are specified like any other map in Postfix. You specify the map type and the file containing the mappings. In the case of MySQL, however, the file you specify is not the lookup map itself, but rather a file that contains configuration information that specifies how to get the desired value from your database:

```
alias_maps = mysql:/etc/postfix/mysql-aliases.cf
```

The file *mysql-aliases.cf* contains configuration information that specifies how to get the information from MySQL. The parameters for this file are explained below.

MySQL parameters

MySQL parameters provide the information necessary for Postfix to connect to your database server and construct an SQL statement to look up the data it needs. These parameters are placed in a MySQL map configuration file that functions like a Postfix configuration file with blanks and comments ignored. Comments are marked by a # as the first character of a line. You can have as many MySQL configuration files as needed in place of normal Postfix lookup files. All of the MySQL parameters presented here are required except for additional_conditions.

Figure 15-1 shows an SQL statement that Postfix creates using the parameters described.

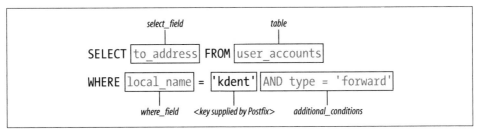

Figure 15-1. Sample SQL statement

hosts
> List of hostnames or IP addresses where a MySQL server is running. You can also indicate a Unix domain socket by preceding a path to a socket with unix:. You should list more than one host or socket only if you have multiple redundant database servers. Each host is tried in the order listed until a successful query can be made. For example:
>
>   hosts = unix:/tmp/mysql.sock, db.example.com, 192.168.150.15

user
> Account name to use when logging into the MySQL server.

password
> Password to use when logging into the MySQL server.

dbname
> The name of the database to use for the query.

table
> The name of the table to use for the query.

select_field
> The name of the column that contains the lookup value.

where_field
> The name of the column that contains the key value.

`additional_conditions`

Additional comparisons for the WHERE clause of the SQL statement built by Postfix. You must understand SQL to use this attribute. Set this parameter as if you are continuing the SQL statement. For example:

```
additional_conditions = and mail_type = 'local'
```

MySQL Example

Let's go through an example illustrating a MySQL and Postfix configuration. The *example.com* site uses a MySQL database to manage all of the users on its network. There is a database that contains a variety of information about users on the network, including names, phone numbers, etc. Among the tables in the database is one called `email_address`, which contains the pertinent information for configuring Postfix. The database structure looks like the following:

```
+-----------------+-------------+------+-----+---------+-------+
| Field           | Type        | Null | Key | Default | Extra |
+-----------------+-------------+------+-----+---------+-------+
| localpart       | varchar(15) |      | PRI |         |       |
| type            | varchar(15) | YES  |     | NULL    |       |
| to_address      | varchar(65) | YES  |     | NULL    |       |
| password        | varchar(65) | YES  |     | NULL    |       |
| last_changed_by | varchar(15) | YES  |     | NULL    |       |
+-----------------+-------------+------+-----+---------+-------+
```

This table contains all of the email addresses that Postfix should accept mail for with the `localpart` column providing the local part of the addresses. Some of the users maintain their primary email accounts on other systems, so their *example.com* addresses are aliases that forward messages to their primary email addresses elsewhere. The type column indicates whether an address is delivered locally or forwarded to another address. The value `forward` indicates that this address is an alias. If an address is forwarded, the `to_address` column contains the address to forward messages to.

Table 15-1 contains the access information needed to configure Postfix in this scenario. You should collect the same information about your own database before starting to configure Postfix.

Table 15-1. MySQL database information for Postfix configuration

Access information:	Values
Host	mysql.example.com
Database name:	user_accounts
Database table:	email_address
Database user:	kdent
Database password:	Rumpelstiltskin

In addition to the general database information in Table 15-1, you will have to determine the columns you need for the particular Postfix maps you are replacing with your MySQL table. Example 15-1 shows a sample record from the database with the relevant columns for this configuration. In this example, you'll be configuring the Postfix parameters local_recipient_maps and alias_maps.

Example 15-1. Sample record from email_address table

```
+------------+----------+-------------------+
| localpart  | type     | to_address        |
+------------+----------+-------------------+
| kdent      | forward  | kyle.dent@ora.com |
+------------+----------+-------------------+
```

Configuring local_recipient_maps

The local_recipient_maps parameter points to lists of local users that should receive email at this system. By default it points to the user accounts and aliases on the system, so that mail sent to a nonexistent user is rejected by the SMTP server. This lookup map is a bit different from others in that it doesn't require a return value to map to. It matters only that the recipient is in the lookup table or not. In this example, the MySQL database contains the list of all email accounts that should receive mail on the system. You can point the local_recipient_maps parameter to a MySQL configuration that extracts the list of email users. You'll use a file called *mysql-local.cf* for the query configuration. First, set local_recipient_maps to point to the query configuration file, indicating that the lookup type is mysql:

```
local_recipient_maps = mysql:/etc/postfix/mysql-local.cf
```

The file *mysql-local.cf* contains parameters for each of the items listed in Table 15-1, plus the select_field and where_field for this specific query:

```
#
# mysql-local.cf - local recipients for mail server.
#
hosts = mysql.example.com
user = kdent
password = Rumpelstiltskin

dbname = user_accounts
table = email_address

select_field = localpart
where_field = localpart
```

The select_field and where_field both point to the localpart column. The select_field in this case is not particularly important since you don't need a value back from the map. You don't need the additional_conditions parameter because you want every record that appears in the table. After reloading, Postfix uses the

MySQL configuration to determine local users and reject mail for recipients not listed in the MySQL table.

You can easily check your MySQL configuration file with the postmap command:

```
$ postmap -q 'kdent' mysql:/etc/postfix/mysql-local.cf
kdent
```

The -q option tells postmap to query the map using the specified key. If your query has any problems, postmap reports them to your terminal.

Configuring alias_maps

Some users do not receive their mail on this system, but rather have it forwarded to another account. By pointing alias_maps to another MySQL configuration, you can obtain the list of users that have aliases and determine what the forwarding address is. You'll use a file called *mysql-alias.cf* for this query configuration. First, set the alias_maps parameter to point to the query configuration file:

```
alias_maps = mysql:/etc/postfix/mysql-alias.cf
```

The *mysql-alias.cf* file contains the following parameters:

```
#
# mysql-alias.cf - forwarding aliases
#
hosts = mysql.example.com
user = kdent
password = Rumpelstiltskin

dbname = user_accounts
table = email_address

select_field = to_address
where_field = localpart

additional_conditions = and type = 'forward'
```

In this case, you set the select_field to to_address since that's the value needed by alias_maps to forward messages. You also specified additional_conditions because you want only the addresses that have aliases. After reloading Postfix, it uses this MySQL configuration to determine addresses with aliases and where messages should be forwarded.

Configuring virtual domains

MySQL databases are often used by sites that host many virtual domains. This last MySQL example walks through configuring virtual mailbox domains. Be sure to read Chapter 8 for information about virtual hosting in general, as this section discusses only the MySQL configuration.

In this example, you'll use a table called `email_address` from a database called customer. The table contains a record for every virtual address at all the domains the system accepts mail for. It includes the following fields that are of interest:

domain
> The virtual domain name for this record.

mail_address
> The public email address that messages can be sent to. Messages are delivered to the local virtual mail store.

mailbox
> Contains the filename for delivery into the local mail store. The name should be relative to the path set in `virtual_mailbox_base`. You can append the name with a slash for maildir-style delivery.

Example 15-2 shows a sample record from the database with the relevant columns.

Example 15-2. Sample record for virtual mailbox alias

```
+------------+---------------+---------------+
| domain     | mail_address  | mailbox       |
+------------+---------------+---------------+
| ora.com    | kdent@ora.com | ora.com/kdent |
+------------+---------------+---------------+
```

In this example, all virtual deliveries occur under the same user and group, `vmail:vmail`. If you require different user and group privileges for the different users or domains, you should have additional columns for `uid` and `gid` in your table and then create `mysql` maps for them as well.

You are using a static `uid` and `gid` for deliveries and your message store is simply a directory on the local filesystem:

```
virtual_mailbox_base = /usr/local/vmail
virtual_uid_maps = static:1003
virtual_gid_maps = static:1003
```

The list of virtual domains and mailbox maps comes from two MySQL configuration files:

```
virtual_mailbox_domains = mysql:/etc/postfix/virtual_domains.cf
virtual_mailbox_maps = mysql:/etc/postfix/virtual_mailboxes.cf
```

The *virtual_mailboxes.cf* configuration maps email addresses to the mail store file where messages should be delivered:

```
hosts = mysql.example.com
user = kdent
password = Rumpelstiltskin

dbname = customer
table = email_address
select_field = mailbox
where_field = mail_address
```

LDAP

LDAP is a protocol that provides access to directories of information. LDAP directories are composed of entries that are organized into hierarchies. You have to understand how LDAP works and how your own directory is organized to use it with Postfix. Many networks are starting to make use of LDAP for user information, which makes it a nice way for Postfix to determine what users and addresses it should accept mail for. If your organization uses an LDAP directory, you can query your existing information for your Postfix configuration.

LDAP Configuration

LDAP maps are specified with the ldap map type and can be listed along with any other maps for a given parameter. Unlike MySQL, LDAP parameters are all listed in *main.cf*. You have to invent a name for the particular LDAP configuration you are creating and specify it with the ldap map type. If you call your LDAP configuration ldapaliases, for example, set your alias maps like this:

    alias_maps = ldap:ldapaliases

The LDAP parameters for this configuration all start with the name you invented followed by the name of the parameter. Thus, the LDAP server is identified by the parameter *name*_server_host, so for the example above, the parameter is called ldapaliases_server_host:

    ldapaliases_server_host = ldap.example.com

The important LDAP parameters are defined below. The complete list is available in the *LDAP_README* file that comes with the Postfix distribution:

*name*_search_base
> The base DN from which to start the search. You have to know the naming context for your directory so that you can specify the common container for your entries. Often it is the root of the directory. Example: ldapaliases_search_base = dc=example, dc=com

*name*_scope
> The scope of the search. There are three possible options for the scope: sub, base, and one. Your directory hierarchy determines which value you need. The base option is rarely useful. With sub the entire tree under the base is searched, and with one only direct child nodes are searched. The _scope parameter defaults to sub if you don't specify another value. Example: ldapaliases_scope = one

*name*_query_filter
> The attributes and values that should form your search filter. The variable %s can be used as a placeholder for the current recipient email address. Example: ldapaliases_query_filter = (mailType=forward)

*name*_result_attribute

The attribute containing the value you want returned for this lookup. You can list multiple attributes in order of preference. Example: ldapaliases_result_attribute = email, rfc822Mailbox.

LDAP Example

A common use of LDAP with Postfix is to protect an internal mail server on a network that uses an LDAP directory of user accounts. Postfix resides on a gateway system accepting messages from the Internet, and relays them to the internal mail server. You want Postfix to reject messages for unknown users on the network so that they are never accepted on your network. By setting the local_recipient_maps parameter to query the LDAP directory, you can configure Postfix so that it knows about all of the user accounts and can reject mail for nonexistent accounts. On a large network there may be different mail systems serving different groups of users. You can also set up Postfix to forward messages to the correct mail server for a particular user by setting transport_maps to point email addresses to the correct internal mail servers.

The LDAP directory includes attributes for mail and mailHost, where mail contains the public email address for a user and mailHost is the internal server to which messages should be forwarded. A sample item in the directory looks like the following:

```
dn: uid=kdent,ou=people,dc=example,dc=com
uid: kdent
cn:  Kyle D. Dent
mail: kyle.dent@example.com
uidNumber: 1001
gidNumber: 1001
mailHost: mail1.example.com
homeDirectory: /home/kdent
mailType: forward
objectClass: people
userPassword: {crypt}hidden
accountStatus: active
```

Table 15-2 contains the LDAP directory information you need to configure Postfix in this scenario. You should collect the hostname and base DN for your own directory before starting to configure Postfix.

Table 15-2. LDAP directory information for Postfix configuration

Directory information	Values
Host	ldap.example.com
Base DN:	dc=example,dc=com

For the `local_recipient_maps` lookup, you only have to know that an address exists in the `mail` attribute. For forwarding messages to the correct internal mail server, you need the value from the `mailHost` attribute.

Configuring local_recipient_maps

The `local_recipient_maps` parameter points to lists of local users that should receive email at this system. By default it points to the user accounts and aliases that exist on the system, so that mail sent to a nonexistent user is rejected by Postfix. In this example, the LDAP directory contains the list of all email accounts that should receive mail on the system. You can set up an `ldap` lookup map for `local_recipient_maps`. In the case of `local_recipient_maps`, the value returned is not used for anything because you only need to know if the email address exists or not. Use an LDAP configuration called "ldaplocal." First, set `local_recipient_maps` to use this configuration:

```
local_recipient_maps = ldap:ldaplocal
```

The rest of the LDAP parameters for this configuration are set as follows:

```
ldaplocal_server_host = ldap.example.com
ldaplocal_search_base = dc=example, dc=com
ldaplocal_query_filter = (&(mail=%s)(accountStatus=active))
ldaplocal_result_attribute = uid
```

The `ldaplocal_query_filter` parameter compares the recipient email address to the `mail` attribute in the directory. It also checks to make sure that the `accountStatus` attribute is set to active. The result attribute is set to `uid`. For this lookup, you only need to know that the item exists, but Postfix does require a non-blank result for the lookup.

After reloading Postfix, it uses the LDAP configuration to determine local users and reject mail for recipients not listed in the LDAP directory.

You can easily check your LDAP configuration file with the `postmap` command:

```
$ postmap -q 'kdent' ldap:ldaplocal
kdent
```

The `-q` option tells `postmap` to query the map using the specified key. If your query has any problems, `postmap` reports them to your terminal.

Configuring transport_maps

When messages received by Postfix have to be relayed to the correct internal mail server, use `transport_maps`. Set `transport_maps` to use a new LDAP configuration called "ldaptransport":

```
transport_maps = ldap:ldaptransport
```

Because the LDAP directory returns just the name of the host, and you need a transport value (transport:nexthop), you can use the _result_filter parameter to specify a template for the results:

```
ldaptransport_result_filter = relay:%s
```

Also, configure the following parameters:

```
ldaptransport_server_host = ldap.example.com
ldaptransport_search_base = dc=example, dc=com
ldaptransport_query_filter = (&(mail=%s)(accountStatus=active))
ldaptransport_result_attribute = mailHost
```

Again, the ldaplocal_query_filter parameter compares the recipient email address to the mail attribute in the directory and checks to make sure that the accountStatus attribute is set to active. The result attribute is the value for the mailHost attribute, which is the email server that should receive messages for the specified user. The result is expanded in the template specified in ldaptransport_result_filter.

Be sure to reload Postfix for the new ldap transport map to go into effect.

Configuration Parameters

This appendix contains an alphabetical listing of parameters normally configured in the Postfix *main.cf* file. The brief descriptions are only meant to give you an idea of the purpose of the parameter. All of the parameters are fully documented in the sample configuration files and manpages that come with the Postfix distribution. This quick reference can point you in the right direction, but you will have to consult the body of this book or the online documentation to understand how each parameter works.

All of the parameters are listed with a type of value that should be assigned to it. Most of the value types are obvious. Those that require some explanation are described here:

Explicit list
> The parameter requires one or more items from a specific list of possible values. See the online documentation for a particular parameter to see what the possible values are.

Lookup tables
> When a parameter points to lookup tables, the tables are specified with their map type and the table name separated by a colon:
>
>   transport_map = hash:/etc/postfix/transport

Pathname
> The complete path to a file.

Template
> Some parameter values are specified as strings that contain macros:
>
>   smtpd_banner = $myhostname ESMTP $mail_name
>
> The macros are expanded into their values at the time the parameter is used. See the online documentation to find out what macros are allowed for a particular template parameter.

Time units
> Many parameters are specified as an amount of time:
>
>   queue_run_delay = 1000s

They are assigned a value and a time unit abbreviation. Time unit abbreviations are listed in Table A-1. If you leave off the time unit, each time parameter has a default unit that it assumes for the value specified. You can check the online documentation to see what the default unit is for a particular parameter.

Table A-1. Time units

Unit	Abbreviation	Example
Seconds	s	1s
Minutes	m	15m
Hours	h	4h
Days	d	5d
Weeks	w	2w

All of the parameters have a default value (although for some the default is blank). Only parameters that differ from their default values have to be specified in *main.cf*. The parameters are listed here with their default values, but they sometimes change with Postfix releases. You can check the default value for a parameter with the postconf command and its -d option:

```
$ postconf -d alias_maps
alias_maps = hash:/etc/aliases, nis:mail.aliases
```

Postfix Parameter Reference

2bounce_notice_recipient

Possible values: email address   **Default:** postmaster

"2bounce" is one of several possible error classes. Each class of error can optionally generate an error notice. 2bounce_notice_recipient designates the recipient address for "2bounce" error notices.

Example: 2bounce_notice_recipient = postmaster

access_map_reject_code

Possible values: reply code   **Default:** 554

SMTP response code sent when a request is rejected because of an access map restriction.

Example: access_map_reject_code = 554

alias_maps

Possible values: alias maps   **Default:** hash:/etc/aliases, nis:mail.aliases

List of alias databases used by the local delivery agent.

Example: alias_maps = hash:/etc/aliases, nis:mail.aliases

allow_mail_to_files

Possible values: explicit list   **Default:** alias,forward

Restricts or allows local mail delivery to external files when expanded from an alias file.

Example: allow_mail_to_files = alias, forward

allow_percent_hack

Possible values: yes/no   **Default:** yes

The percent hack is an old workaround that allowed sender-controlled routing of email messages. Nowadays, DNS and mail routing are much more reliable, but Postfix continues to support the hack. To turn off percent rewriting, set allow_percent_hack to no.

Example: allow_percent_hack = yes

alternate_config_directories

Possible values: directory   **Default:** (null)

The commands postqueue and postdrop have options to use a different directory when reading the Postfix configuration file. Any nonstandard directories you plan to use must be listed in this parameter.

Example: alternate_config_directories = /usr/local/postfix/conf

append_at_myorigin

Possible values: yes/no   **Default:** yes

Expands incomplete email addresses by appending the value from myorigin onto addresses that consist of a local part only. Changes *user* to *user@host.example.com.*

Example: append_at_myorigin = yes

authorized_verp_clients

Possible values: hosts/domains   **Default:** $mynetworks

VERP is a technique used with mailing lists to handle bounced messages. It combines the list owner address and original recipient address with a special delimiter character. authorized_verp_clients contains a list of host and domain names and IP addresses of clients that are allowed to use the feature.

Example: authorized_verp_clients = $mynetworks

berkeley_db_read_buffer_size

Possible values: bytes   **Default:** 131072

Buffer size to use when reading Berkeley DB hash or btree tables.

Example: berkeley_db_read_buffer_size = 131072

biff

Possible values: yes/no   **Default:** yes

biff is a small process that can notify local users when new mail has arrived. If you have no local users, you should turn off biff notifications since they may affect the performance of the mail server.

Example: biff = yes

body_checks_size_limit

Possible values: bytes   **Default:** 51200

Limit on the amount of a message subject to body_checks filtering.

Example: body_checks_size_limit = 51200

bounce_service_name

Possible values: service   **Default:** bounce

Service the master daemon uses for maintaining log files with status information on messages that cannot be delivered. You normally do not need to change this parameter.

Example: bounce_service_name = bounce

canonical_maps

Possible values: lookup types   **Default:** (null)

List of lookup tables used to map email addresses to their desired rewritten form.

Example: canonical_maps = hash:/etc/postfix/canonical_maps

command_directory

Possible values: directory   **Default:** /usr/sbin

Location of Postfix administrative command-line tools such as postcat and postqueue.

Example: command_directory = /usr/sbin

command_time_limit

Possible values: time unit   **Default:** 1000s

When the local delivery agent passes messages to a command, Postfix limits the amount of time the command can execute. command_time_limit indicates the time limit.

Example: command_time_limit = 1000s

content_filter

Possible values: transport   **Default:** (null)

Transport to be used as a message filter. Postfix passes messages to the named transport.

Example: content_filter = myfilter

daemon_timeout

Possible values: time unit   **Default:** 18000s

Amount of time Postfix daemons spend handling a request. When they exceed the specified time, they voluntarily die.

Example: daemon_timeout = 18000s

debug_peer_list

Possible values: hosts/domains   **Default:** (null)

For help with troubleshooting, Postfix can increase logging for particular hosts that you might be having problems with. debug_peer_list specifies a list of one or more hosts, domains, or regular expression patterns whose logging should be increased by the degree specified in debug_peer_level.

Example: debug_peer_list = example.com, mail.ora.com

default_destination_concurrency_limit

Possible values: count   **Default:** 20

Postfix allows you to set a limit on the number of simultaneous deliveries to any transport in *master.cf*. If you don't set an explicit limit for a transport, the value in default_destination_concurrency_limit is used. Note that concurrency limits are per destination as opposed to process limits, which are per transport.

Example: default_destination_concurrency_limit = 20

default_extra_recipient_limit

Possible values: count   **Default:** 1000

Limit on the number of recipients for a transport when the queue manager preempts normal delivery with a higher priority transport.

Example: default_extra_recipient_limit = 1000

default_process_limit

Possible values: count   **Default:** 100

Process limits can be configured for any transport. If you don't set an explicit process limit for a transport, the value in default_process_limit is used. Note that process limits are per transport as opposed to concurrency limits, which are per destination.

Example: default_process_limit = 100

default_recipient_limit

Possible values: count   **Default:** 10000

Limit on the number of recipients the queue manager stores in memory for a particular transport.

Example: default_recipient_limit = 10000

default_verp_delimiters

Possible values: characters   **Default:** +=

VERP is a technique used with mailing lists to handle bounced messages. It combines the list owner address and original recipient address with a special delimiter character. The default_verp_delimiters parameter specifies which characters to use when constructing VERP return addresses.

Example: default_verp_delimiters = +=

defer_service_name

Possible values: service   **Default:** defer

Service the master daemon uses for maintaining log files with status information on messages that cannot be delivered. You normally do not need to change this parameter.

Example: defer_service_name = defer

delay_notice_recipient

Possible values: email address   **Default:** postmaster

"delay" is one of several possible error classes. Each class of error can optionally generate an error notice. delay_notice_recipient designates the recipient address for "delay" error notices.

Example: delay_notice_recipient = postmaster

deliver_lock_attempts

Possible values: count   **Default:** 20

Limit on the number of times Postfix tries to acquire an exclusive lock on a mailbox file.

Example: deliver_lock_attempts = 20

disable_dns_lookups

Possible values: yes/no   **Default:** no

Normally when Postfix determines where to deliver a message, it first looks up the DNS MX records for the destination domain. If `disable_dns_lookups` is set, Postfix does not check for MX records and delivers directly to the A record it finds for the destination domain.

Example: `disable_dns_lookups = no`

disable_mime_output_conversion

Possible values: yes/no   **Default:** no

Normally Postfix converts 8-bit MIME format to 7-bit format when a remote system does not advertise 8-bit MIME support. Set `disable_mime_output_conversion` to yes to turn off the normal behavior.

Example: `disable_mime_output_conversion = no`

disable_vrfy_command

Possible values: yes/no   **Default:** no

Normally Postfix allows the SMTP VRFY command. Set `disable_vrfy_command` to yes to disable it.

Example: `disable_vrfy_command = no`

double_bounce_sender

Possible values: email address   **Default:** double-bounce

A double bounce is produced when the original sender of a message cannot be notified that the message was not delivered. The `double_bounce_sender` parameter specifies the sender address Postfix uses for mail that should be discarded if it cannot be delivered. The specified address should not be used for anything else since all messages addressed to it are silently discarded.

Example: `double_bounce_sender = double-bounce`

empty_address_recipient

Possible values: email address   **Default:** MAILER-DAEMON

The destination address for notifications when mail with a null sender (<>) cannot be delivered. For example, when a bounce notification, which uses a null sender, cannot be delivered, it is sent to the address specified in `empty_address_recipient`.

Example: `empty_address_recipient = MAILER-DAEMON`

error_service_name

Possible values: service	Default: error

Service the master daemon uses to generate error reports when a message cannot be delivered. You normally do not need to change this parameter.

Example: error_service_name = error

export_environment

Possible values: environment variables	Default: TZ MAIL_CONFIG

List of environment variables that are exported to external processes such as deliveries to the pipe service or external commands.

Example: export_environment = TZ, MAIL_CONFIG

fallback_relay

Possible values: hosts/domains	Default: (null)

List of IP addresses, hosts, or domains to receive messages when the normal destination is not found or is not reachable.

Example: fallback_relay = example.com

fast_flush_domains

Possible values: hosts/domains	Default: $relay_domains

The fast flush service allows the queue manager to retry immediate delivery of messages for a particular domain upon request. The fast_flush_domains parameter specifies a list of IP addresses, hosts, and domains that are eligible for the fast flush service.

Example: fast_flush_domains = $relay_domains

fast_flush_refresh_time

Possible values: time unit	Default: 12h

The fast flush service allows the queue manager to retry immediate delivery of messages for a particular domain upon request. The fast_flush_refresh_time parameter specifies a time interval for automatically flushing messages that have not otherwise had redelivery requested.

Example: fast_flush_refresh_time = 12h

fork_attempts

Possible values: count	Default: 5

Limit on the number of times Postfix tries to fork a process.

Example: fork_attempts = 5

forward_expansion_filter

Possible values: characters   **Default:** (see example)

When assigning path names to the forward_path parameter, you can use macros such as $user that are expanded by Postfix to determine the path for the current message. The forward_expansion_filter parameter specifies a list of characters that should be allowed when expanding macros. Characters that are not permitted are replaced by underscores.

Example: forward_expansion_filter =
         1234567890!@%-_=+:,./abcdefghijklmnopqrstuvwxyz\
         ABCDEFGHIJKLMNOPQRSTUVWXYZ

hash_queue_depth

Possible values: count   **Default:** 1

Postfix creates a structure of subdirectories for each of its queues in order to organize queue files. The hash_queue_depth parameter specifies the number of subdirectory levels below the queue directories.

Example: hash_queue_depth = 1

header_address_token_limit

Possible values: count   **Default:** 10240

Limit on the number of tokens (every word and every @ or . is a token, as defined in RFC 2822) in header addresses to be rewritten by Postfix. Excess tokens are silently discarded.

Example: header_address_token_limit = 10240

header_size_limit

Possible values: bytes   **Default:** 102400

Limit on the number of characters allowed in a message header. Excess text is silently discarded.

Example: header_size_limit = 102400

home_mailbox

Possible values: pathname   **Default:** (null)

Postfix normally delivers messages to mailbox files in the mail spool. You can change the delivery to mailbox files relative to users' home directories by specifying a path with the home_mailbox parameter. Include a trailing slash to indicate maildir-style mailboxes.

Example: home_mailbox = Mail/mbox

ignore_mx_lookup_error

Possible values: yes/no   **Default:** no

Normally when Postfix gets no response from a nameserver for an MX lookup, it tries again after some period of time. You can cause immediate lookups of A records by enabling ignore_mx_lookup_error.

Example: ignore_mx_lookup_error = no

in_flow_delay

Possible values: time unit   **Default:** 1s

Causes Postfix to pause for the specified time before accepting a new message. You would need to change this parameter only if you are experimenting with performance.

Example: in_flow_delay = 1s

initial_destination_concurrency

Possible values: count   **Default:** 5

Initial number of delivery processes for a particular destination.

Example: initial_destination_concurrency = 5

ipc_idle

Possible values: time unit   **Default:** 100s

Maximum idle time for internal communication channels. Once the maximum time has been reached, Postfix components disconnect voluntarily.

Example: ipc_idle = 100s

line_length_limit

Possible values: count   **Default:** 2048

Limit on the length of any single line in a message. Lines that exceed the limit are broken up and reconstructed at delivery time.

Example: line_length_limit = 2048

lmtp_connect_timeout

Possible values: time unit   **Default:** 0s

Limit on the amount of time the LMTP client waits to complete a TCP connection. Set the parameter to 0 to disable timeouts.

Example: lmtp_connect_timeout = 0

lmtp_data_init_timeout

Possible values: time unit   **Default:** 120s

Limit on the amount of time the LMTP client waits for a response from the server after sending the LMTP DATA command.

Example: lmtp_data_init_timeout = 120s

lmtp_lhlo_timeout

Possible values: time unit   **Default:** 300s

Limit on the amount of time the LMTP client waits for a response from the server after sending the LMTP LHLO command.

Example: lmtp_lhlo_timeout = 300s

lmtp_quit_timeout

Possible values: time unit   **Default:** 300s

Limit on the amount of time the LMTP client waits for a response from the server after sending the LMTP QUIT command.

Example: lmtp_quit_timeout = 300s

lmtp_rset_timeout

Possible values: time unit   **Default:** 300s

Limit on the amount of time the LMTP client waits for a response from the server after sending the LMTP RSET command.

Example: lmtp_rset_timeout = 300s

lmtp_tcp_port

Possible values: port number   **Default:** 24

TCP port to use for LMTP connections if the lmtp service is not found in the *services* database.

Example: lmtp_tcp_port = 24

local_destination_concurrency_limit

Possible values: count   **Default:** 2

Limit on the number of delivery processes to the same local recipient.

Example: local_destination_concurrency_limit = 2

local_recipient_maps

Possible values: lookup tables   **Default:** proxy:unix:passwd.byname $alias_maps

List of lookup tables containing all email addresses that are local. It's used by the SMTP server to reject messages for nonexistent users.

Example: local_recipient_maps = unix:passwd.byname $alias_maps

luser_relay

Possible values: email address   **Default:** (null)

Destination address that should receive all messages for unknown recipients.

Example: luser_relay = info

mail_owner

Possible values: username   **Default:** postfix

System username that owns Postfix queue files. It's also used for running Postfix daemon processes.

Example: mail_owner = postfix

mail_spool_directory

Possible values: directory   **Default:** (system dependent)

Directory where mailbox files are kept.

Example: mail_spool_directory = /var/mail

mailbox_command

Possible values: pathname   **Default:** (null)

An external command to use for final mailbox delivery. Commonly used for configuring an external local delivery agent such as procmail.

Example: mailbox_command = /usr/local/bin/procmail

mailbox_delivery_lock

Possible values: explicit list   **Default:** (system dependent)

Locking methods Postfix should use when delivering mail to files.

Example: mailbox_delivery_lock = fcntl, dotlock

mailbox_transport

Possible values: transport   **Default:** (null)

Transport to use for final mailbox delivery.

Example: mailbox_transport = cyrus

manpage_directory

Possible values: directory   **Default:** (system dependent)

Directory for Postfix manpages.

Example: `manpage_directory = /usr/local/man`

masquerade_domains

Possible values: domains   **Default:** (null)

Address masquerading hides the names of internal hosts by stripping internal hostnames off before messages are sent out from a gateway system. The `masquerade_domains` parameter specifies a list of domains that should be subject to address masquerading.

Example: `masquerade_domains = example.com`

max_idle

Possible values: time unit   **Default:** 100s

Maximum idle time a Postfix daemon process (except the queue manager) waits for a new request.

Example: `max_idle = 100s`

maximal_backoff_time

Possible values: time unit   **Default:** 4000s

Maximum time limit for Postfix to attempt redelivery of deferred messages. Each time a message is deferred, the queue manager increases the amount of time it waits to attempt delivery of that message again. The calculated increase of time is never allowed to exceed `maximal_backoff_time`.

Example: `maximal_backoff_time = 4000s`

message_size_limit

Possible values: bytes   **Default:** 10240000

Limit on the size of any message your system will accept.

Example: `message_size_limit = 10240000`

mime_header_checks

Possible values: lookup tables   **Default:** $header_checks

List of lookup tables containing patterns to match against each MIME header of incoming email messages. Each pattern is listed with the action to take if there is a match.

Example: `mime_header_checks = regexp:/etc/postfix/mime_header_checks`

minimal_backoff_time

Possible values: time unit   **Default:** 1000s

Minimum time limit on how often Postfix attempts redelivery of deferred messages. Each time a message is deferred, the queue manager increases the amount of time it waits to attempt delivery of that message again. The calculated time is never less than minimal_backoff_time.

Example: minimal_backoff_time = 1000s

mydomain

Possible values: domain   **Default:** (system dependent)

System's domain name.

Example: mydomain = example.com

mynetworks

Possible values: net addresses   **Default:** (system dependent)

List of IP or network addresses that are allowed to relay messages through your mail server. Either mynetworks or mynetworks_style can be used to designate hosts permitted to relay. mynetworks has precedence over mynetworks_style.

Example: mynetworks = 192.168.15.32/26

myorigin

Possible values: domain   **Default:** $myhostname

Domain portion to append to message email addresses that contain localparts only.

Example: myorigin = $myhostname

newaliases_path

Possible values: pathname   **Default:** (system dependent)

Full path to the Sendmail-compatibility newaliases command. newaliases is used to rebuild alias databases.

Example: newaliases_path = /usr/bin/newaliases

notify_classes

Possible values: explicit list   **Default:** resource,software

List of recognized error classes that cause a notification to be sent. Notification email addresses are configured in parameters named according to the class, *class*_notice_recipient.

Example: notify_classes = resource, software

parent_domain_matches_subdomains

Possible values: yes/no   **Default:** (see example)

List of lookup map types where lookups should match the domain itself plus all of its subdomains.

Example: `parent_domain_matches_subdomains = debug_peer_list, fast_flush_domains,`
`mynetworks, permit_mx_backup_networks, qmqpd_authorized_clients,`
`relay_domains, smtpd_access_maps`

pickup_service_name

Possible values: service   **Default:** pickup

Service the master daemon uses to retrieve locally injected messages. You normally do not need to change this parameter.

Example: `pickup_service_name = pickup`

process_id_directory

Possible values: directory   **Default:** pid

Directory for lock files used by the master daemon. The specified path is relative to the Postfix spool directory.

Example: `process_id_directory = pid`

proxy_interfaces

Possible values: IP addresses   **Default:** (null)

When a Postfix server is running on an internal network behind a proxy or NAT device, and it serves as the backup MX host for a domain, it's possible to get mail delivery loops when the primary MX host is down. The `proxy_interfaces` specifies a list of network interface addresses that receive mail via a proxy device. Postfix avoids mail loops with listed interfaces.

Example: `proxy_interfaces = 192.168.15.23`

qmgr_clog_warn_time

Possible values: time unit   **Default:** 300s

Minimum time between warnings that a particular destination is clogging up the active queue. A value of 0 disables the warnings.

Example: `qmgr_clog_warn_time = 300s`

qmgr_message_active_limit

Possible values: count   **Default:** 20000

Limit on the number of messages allowed in the active queue.

Example: `qmgr_message_active_limit = 20000`

qmgr_message_recipient_minimum

Possible values: count   **Default:** 10

Minimum number of recipients stored in memory for each message.

Example: qmgr_message_recipient_minimum = 10

qmqpd_error_delay

Possible values: time unit   **Default:** 1s

The QMQP service provides a centralized mail queue for a cluster of mail hosts. The qmqpd_error_delay specifies the length of time the QMQP server should pause before sending a negative reply to a client. The delay is meant to slow down misbehaving clients.

Example: qmqpd_error_delay = 1s

queue_directory

Possible values: directory   **Default:** /var/spool/postfix

Directory for the Postfix queue.

Example: queue_directory = /var/spool/postfix

queue_run_delay

Possible values: time unit   **Default:** 1000s

Amount of time between queue scans to check for deferred messages that are due for redelivery attempt.

Example: queue_run_delay = 1000s

rbl_reply_maps

Possible values: lookup tables   **Default:** (null)

List of lookup tables used to map RBL domain names to responses when rejecting messages because of either reject_rbl or reject_rhsbl. If an RBL domain is not listed, the default_rbl_reply provides the response.

Example: rbl_reply_maps = hash:/etc/postfix/rbl_reply

recipient_canonical_maps

Possible values: lookup tables   **Default:** (null)

List of lookup tables used to map recipient email addresses to their desired rewritten form. Operates the same as canonical_maps but only for recipient addresses. recipient_canonical_maps has precedence over canonical_maps.

Example: recipient_canonical_maps = hash:/etc/postfix/canonical

reject_code

Possible values: reply code **Default:** 554

SMTP response code to send when a request is rejected because of a client restriction.

Example: reject_code = 554

relay_domains_reject_code

Possible values: reply code **Default:** 554

SMTP response code to send when a request is rejected due to a disallowed relay attempt.

Example: relay_domains_reject_code = 554

relay_transport

Possible values: transport **Default:** relay

Transport to use for delivering relayed messages.

Example: relay_transport = relay

relocated_maps

Possible values: lookup tables **Default:** (null)

List of lookup tables that map moved addresses or domains to their new locations.

Example: relocated_maps = hash:/etc/postfix/relocated

resolve_dequoted_address

Possible values: yes/no **Default:** yes

Specifies whether or not Postfix resolves addresses whose localparts contain user-specified routing. Set to yes to have Postfix quote localparts containing special symbols such as the @ character for strict adherence to RFC 822.

Example: resolve_dequoted_address = yes

sample_directory

Possible values: directory **Default:** /etc/postfix

Directory for sample Postfix configuration files. The sample files give examples and document Postfix configuration parameters.

Example: sample_directory = /etc/postfix

sendmail_path

Possible values: pathname   **Default:** (system dependent)

Full path to the Sendmail-compatibility sendmail command. sendmail is used primarily for sending messages from a command line or from within scripts.

Example: sendmail_path = /usr/sbin/sendmail

setgid_group

Possible values: group   **Default:** postdrop

Group ID used by Postfix for mail submission and queue management. Whatever group you use should be dedicated for Postfix use only.

Example: setgid_group = postdrop

showq_service_name

Possible values: service   **Default:** showq

Service used for reporting the Postfix mail queue status. You normally do not need to change this parameter.

Example: showq_service_name = showq

smtp_bind_address

Possible values: IP address   **Default:** (null)

IP address of the interface the SMTP client should bind to when making connections to mail servers. Setting this parameter is necessary only on multihomed systems where you explicitly must use just one of the interfaces.

Example: smtp_bind_address = 192.168.15.23

smtp_data_done_timeout

Possible values: time unit   **Default:** 600s

Limit on the amount of time the SMTP client waits for a response from the server after sending the SMTP . (a single dot) indicating the end of the message contents.

Example: smtp_data_done_timeout = 600s

smtp_data_xfer_timeout

Possible values: time unit   **Default:** 180s

Limit on the amount of time the SMTP client waits while sending the message contents. If the connection stalls for more than the specified value, the SMTP client terminates the connection.

Example: smtp_data_xfer_timeout = 180s

smtp_destination_recipient_limit

Possible values: count   **Default:** (see example)

Limit on the number of recipients per message delivery going out via the SMTP client.

Example: smtp_destination_recipient_limit =
        $default_destination_recipient_limit

smtp_helo_timeout

Possible values: time unit   **Default:** 300s

Limit on the amount of time the SMTP client waits for a response from the server after sending the SMTP HELO command.

Example: smtp_helo_timeout = 300s

smtp_mail_timeout

Possible values: time unit   **Default:** 300s

Limit on the amount of time the SMTP client waits for a response from the server after sending the SMTP MAIL FROM command.

Example: smtp_mail_timeout = 300s

smtp_pix_workaround_delay_time

Possible values: time unit   **Default:** 10s

Certain older Cisco PIX firewalls contain a bug that causes them to interfere with SMTP delivery when the final period and CR/LF indicating the end of message content arrive in separate packets. Postfix can automatically detect the problem and adjust for it by waiting before sending the final period and CR/LF to give the socket send buffer a chance to empty out. The smtp_pix_workaround_delay_time parameter specifies how long Postfix waits for the socket send buffer to empty.

Example: smtp_pix_workaround_delay_time = 10s

smtp_quit_timeout

Possible values: time unit   **Default:** 300s

Limit on the amount of time the SMTP client waits for a response from the server after sending the SMTP QUIT command.

Example: smtp_quit_timeout = 300s

smtp_rcpt_timeout

Possible values: time unit

Default: 300s

Limit on the amount of time the SMTP client waits for a response from the server after sending the SMTP RCPT TO command.

Example: smtp_rcpt_timeout = 300s

smtp_skip_5xx_greeting

Possible values: yes/no

Default: yes

When an SMTP server responds with 5xx reply code, Postfix can either bounce the message or move on to any additional mail exchangers for the destination domain to see if they are able to accept the message. The parameter smtp_skip_5xx_greeting specifies whether or not Postfix should react to the reply code or move on. A value of no causes Postfix to try additional mail exchangers.

Example: smtp_skip_5xx_greeting = yes

smtpd_banner

Possible values: template

Default: (see example)

Text that follows the 220 status code in the SMTP greeting banner. If you change this parameter, be sure to include $myhostname at the start of the text, according to RFC requirements.

Example: smtpd_banner = $myhostname ESMTP $mail_name

smtpd_data_restrictions

Possible values: UBE restrictions

Default: (null)

List of UBE restrictions to apply when a client sends the SMTP DATA command.

Example: smtpd_data_restrictions = reject_unauth_pipelining

smtpd_error_sleep_time

Possible values: time unit

Default: 1s

Length of time Postfix waits initially when a client causes an error. After the number of errors exceeds the value in smtpd_soft_error_limit, Postfix increases the delay by one second for every error.

Example: smtpd_error_sleep_time = 1s

smtpd_expansion_filter

Possible values: characters

Default: (see example)

List of characters that are allowed in macro expansion by the SMTP server.

Example: smtpd_expansion_filter = \t\40!"#$%&'( )*+,-./0123456789:;<=>?@ \
ABCDEFGHIJKLMNOPQRSTUVWXYZ[\\]^_`abcdefghijklmnopqrstuvwxyz{|}~

smtpd_helo_required

Possible values: yes/no   **Default:** no

Specifies whether or not Postfix requires a client to start the SMTP conversation with the HELO/EHLO command.

Example: smtpd_helo_required = no

smtpd_history_flush_threshold

Possible values: count   **Default:** 100

Limit on the number of lines in the SMTP server command history.

Example: smtpd_history_flush_threshold = 100

smtpd_noop_commands

Possible values: explicit list   **Default:** (null)

List of SMTP commands that Postfix should accept but take no action on. Postfix always replies to these noop commands with a status of "250 Ok."

Example: smtpd_noop_commands = vrfy, expn

smtpd_recipient_limit

Possible values: count   **Default:** 1000

Limit on the number of recipients allowed in RCPT TO commands for each message. Postfix rejects RCPT TO commands once the limit is reached.

Example: smtpd_recipient_limit = 1000

smtpd_restriction_classes

Possible values: list   **Default:** (null)

List of administrator-defined restriction class names. Each defined class can be assigned to UBE parameters.

Example: smtpd_restriction_classes = myrestriction_a, myrestriction_b

smtpd_soft_error_limit

Possible values: count   **Default:** 10

Number of errors after which Postfix should increase delays to one second for every error.

Example: smtpd_soft_error_limit = 10

soft_bounce

Possible values: yes/no   **Default:** no

Specifies whether or not mail that would normally be bounced should be queued for redelivery attempts. Also converts any permanent rejection codes to temporary error codes. This parameter is useful for testing out configuration changes to make sure that no mail is permanently rejected.

Example: soft_bounce = no

strict_7bit_headers

Possible values: yes/no   **Default:** no

Specifies whether or not Postfix should accept only 7-bit text in message headers as required by the RFC. By default, if mail arrives with 8-bit text in the message headers it is rejected.

Example: strict_7bit_headers = no

strict_8bitmime_body

Possible values: yes/no   **Default:** no

Specifies whether or not Postfix should reject messages that contain 8-bit text that is not properly MIME-encoded.

Example: strict_8bitmime_body = no

strict_rfc821_envelopes

Possible values: yes/no   **Default:** no

Specifies whether or not Postfix requires envelope addresses to be within angle brackets (<>) and without extraneous information as required by the RFC.

Example: strict_rfc821_envelopes = no

swap_bangpath

Possible values: yes/no   **Default:** yes

UUCP uses the bang character (!) for routing email messages. The swap_bangpath parameter specifies whether or not Postfix rewrites the bang as an at sign (@) for Internet email routing.

Example: swap_bangpath = yes

syslog_name

Possible values: string   **Default:** postfix

Name to use with the process name in syslog records.

Example: syslog_name = postfix

transport_retry_time

Possible values: time unit   **Default:** 60s

Time to wait before attempting to use a previously unavailable delivery transport.

Example: transport_retry_time = 60s

undisclosed_recipients_header

Possible values: string   **Default:** (see example)

Header line to insert when no recipients are specified in any of the To: headers (e.g., To:, Resent-To:, Cc:).

Example: undisclosed_recipients_header = To: undisclosed-recipients:;

unknown_client_reject_code

Possible values: reply code   **Default:** 450

SMTP response code to send when a request is rejected due to the reject_unknown_client restriction.

Example: unknown_client_reject_code = 450

unknown_local_recipient_reject_code

Possible values: reply code   **Default:** 550

SMTP response code to send when a request is rejected because it is addressed to a nonexistent local user.

Example: unknown_local_recipient_reject_code = 550

unknown_virtual_alias_reject_code

Possible values: reply code   **Default:** 550

SMTP response code to send when a request is rejected because it is addressed to a nonexistent user at one of your virtual alias domains.

Example: unknown_virtual_alias_reject_code = 550

verp_delimiter_filter

Possible values: characters   **Default:** -=+

VERP is a technique used with mailing lists to handle bounced messages. It combines the list owner address and original recipient address with a special delimiter character. The verp_delimiter_filter parameter specifies which characters Postfix accepts as VERP delimiter characters.

Example: verp_delimiter_filter = -=+

virtual_alias_maps

Possible values: lookup tables   **Default:** (null)

List of lookup tables used to map virtual aliases to their destination email addresses.

Example: virtual_alias_maps = hash:/etc/postfix/virtual_alias

virtual_mailbox_base

Possible values: directory   **Default:** (null)

Base directory for virtual mailbox files. All mailbox files are found relative to the base directory.

Example: virtual_mailbox_base = /usr/local/virtual_mail

virtual_mailbox_limit

Possible values: bytes   **Default:** 51200000

Limit on the size of virtual mailbox files. For maildir-style mailboxes, it limits only individual file sizes, not the overall mailbox. The value here must not be smaller than message_size_limit.

Example: virtual_mailbox_limit = 51200000

virtual_mailbox_maps

Possible values: lookup tables   **Default:** (null)

List of lookup tables used to map virtual mailbox addresses to their mailbox files. Mailbox file paths are relative to virtual_mailbox_base.

Example: virtual_mailbox_maps = hash:/etc/postfix/virtual_mailbox

virtual_transport

Possible values: transport   **Default:** virtual

Default transport to use for delivering messages to virtual mailbox addresses.

Example: virtual_transport = virtual

Postfix Commands

Postfix command-line tools are listed below. Each one is fully documented in a manpage that comes with the Postfix distribution. This appendix is meant to give you an idea of what each command is used for. You should refer to the manpages for complete information about each of the commands:

postalias

Creates or queries alias databases.

postcat

Prints the contents of queue files, allowing administrators to display the text of a message in the queue.

postconf

Displays or changes Postfix parameters. Can display one parameter at a time, or the entire list of parameters.

postdrop

Injects a message into the maildrop directory for delivery by Postfix.

postfix

Starts and stops the Postfix system. Can also be used for other Postfix maintenance, such as checking the configuration and flushing the queue.

postkick

Sends a request to a particular Postfix service. Meant to provide a way for shell scripts to communicate with Postfix services.

postlock

Locks a specified file for exclusive access. Provides a means for shell scripts to use Postfix-compatible locking.

postlog

Logs specified information to the system-logging facility. Provides a means for shell scripts to log information easily in a style similar to Postfix.

postmap

Creates or queries lookup maps. Much of the Postfix configuration information is kept in lookup tables that are created by the postmap command.

postqueue

Provides user-level access to the Postfix queue. Changes to the queue requiring super-user privileges are managed by the postsuper command.

postsuper

Provides super-user access to the Postfix queue. Allows an administrator to delete messages, place them on hold and release them from hold, and repair the queue structure, if necessary.

Compiling and Installing Postfix

The general steps to build Postfix from the source files are to obtain the software bundle, uncompress it, compile it, and install it. The tools you need are common on nearly all distributions of Unix: gzip, tar, make, and a C compiler. Postfix generally expects the GNU gcc compiler, but you can also build it with your platform's native compiler, as long as it supports ANSI C.

Obtaining Postfix

The official Postfix web site (*http://www.postfix.org/*) has a download link that displays a list of mirrors from which you can get the software. You should select the mirror that is closest to you. Get the package you want by selecting the "Source code" link under either the Official or Experimental release (see Chapter 1). The examples here assume that you have downloaded a file called *postfix-2.0.10.tar.gz*. If the file you download is different, change the filename accordingly in the commands in the examples.

Postfix Compiling Primer

Before we move on to the specifics of building Postfix, let's take a look at some of the basics when compiling C code.

The options for a particular build are usually contained within a description file normally called *Makefile*. The make utility uses the *Makefile* to determine prerequisites, dependencies, and options to use when building a package. Using this information, make calls a compiler to create object files, and then a linker (usually called ld) to link them together into executables.

Since the Postfix distribution creates its own *Makefile*, you don't have to worry about editing that (and you shouldn't edit it, since any changes you make would likely get overwritten later). Options that Postfix needs in its *Makefile* are defined in environment variables such as CCARGS. The *INSTALL* file that comes with the Postfix distribution discusses all of the available options. We'll look at some of the more common ones here.

The following environment variables are available to set compile-time options. You should use quotes around the values to retain spaces or other shell metacharacters:

AUXLIBS

Tells the linker where to look for additional libraries that are not in the standard locations. For example, if you build support for an add-on package, you may have to indicate where the libraries are for that package.

CC

Specifies a particular compiler to use. If you want to use a compiler other than the one Postfix selects, set this variable to your compiler. Postfix normally uses gcc except on platforms where the native compiler is known to work better. You can check the *makedefs* file to see which compiler Postfix uses by default on your system.

CCARGS

Provides additional arguments to the compiler. If your compiler allows special options or your supporting files are not located in default directories, indicate those options with this variable.

DEBUG

The DEBUG parameter specifies debugging levels for the compiler to use when building the Postfix binaries. Turning on debugging produces extra information that a debugger can use. You can also turn off debugging features completely to build Postfix for a production system.

OPT

The OPT parameter specifies optimization levels for the compiler to use when building Postfix binaries. Additional optimization may increase performance but at the cost of longer compilation and more memory. You can probably accept the defaults that Postfix selects for your platform.

Compiler Options

Compiler options are set in the CCARGS variable. C source code files require header files that define certain functions and variables. The standard location for header files is the */usr/include* directory. If your header files are located somewhere else, you have to tell the compiler where to look for them. The -I compiler option is used to specify additional directories where the compiler might find header files. If you are linking with libraries from external packages, the header files might be located where the package is installed rather than in the standard location. A common convention for external packages is to install header files in */usr/local/include*. If you want to tell the compiler to look in that directory as well as the standard location when building Postfix, specify the options and directory with CCARGS:

```
CCARGS='-I/usr/local/include/'
```

Use additional -I options for each additional directory the compiler should search.

Postfix uses conditional compilation during its build, depending on which libraries or other resources are available on your system. It defines certain macros based on what it discovers about your system or based on options you have selected. The -D option provides a way to define macros at the time you compile Postfix. Add-on packages for Postfix require that you define a particular macro to tell Postfix to include it when building. For example, if you want to include support for MySQL, you define the HAS_MYSQL macro:

```
CCARGS='-DHAS_MYSQL'
```

Linker Options

Linker options are set in the AUXLIBS variable. After Postfix has compiled the object files, it links them together with required libraries into executable files. The standard location for system libraries is */usr/lib*. To tell the linker to search additional directories for libraries, use the -L option:

```
AUXLIBS='-L/usr/local/lib'
```

You must also tell the linker which specific libraries to link in. The -l option is used to name specific libraries. The library files must be in a standard location or a directory indicated with the -L option. Library archive files are named starting with *lib*, followed by their name, followed by the extension, which is normally *.a* for static libraries and *.so* or *.sl* for shared objects or shared libraries. When you use the -l option, you leave off the initial *lib* and the extension of the library file. To link with the MySQL client library for example, where the library file is called *libmysqlclient.a*, the -l option is specified as follows:

```
AUXLIBS='-L/usr/local/lib -lmysqlclient'
```

Most linkers choose runtime or dynamic libraries over the static versions. Runtime libraries are linked when a program is running rather than during compilation. At compile time, the linker adds information so the program can find the libraries when it is executed. If you always install all of your dynamic libraries in a standard location such as */usr/lib*, your system won't have any trouble finding the libraries at runtime. However, some external packages install libraries in nonstandard directories such that they cannot be found at runtime. Different systems use different conventions for locating dynamic libraries using fixed path information and environment variables. Be sure to configure your system to be able to find your dynamic libraries or make sure that the libraries are installed in your system's standard directories. Another option is to provide the actual path to specific libraries when you build your programs.

The linker uses an argument to include directories in a runtime search path for dynamic libraries. The argument differs depending on your linker and platform. The GNU linker (Linux, FreeBSD) uses -rpath, as does IRIX. Solaris, on the other hand uses -R, and HP-UX uses +b. Consult the manpage for your linker, ld(1), to see which argument you should use to set the runtime library search path.

Using the SSL library as an example, if your *libssl.so* file is located in */usr/local/lib* and you are building Postfix on FreeBSD or another system that uses rpath, define AUXLIBS as follows:

```
AUXLIBS='-L/usr/local/lib -rpath/usr/local/lib -lssl'
```

When linking Postfix with external libraries, if you have multiple versions of the libraries installed, it is very important to make sure that you link Postfix with the version you need. Also, make sure that the library version you link to corresponds to the correct version of the header files you include. Version mismatch problems are often the source of compiler errors. Sometimes the compiler does not complain, in which case your build may succeed, but you're likely to find unusual errors from Postfix at runtime that can be tricky to track down.

---

gcc and Unrecognized Linker Options

Some versions of gcc do not understand all of the linker options you might use, and generate errors when compiling. The -rpath option is a common one. The compiler generates an error like gcc: unrecognized option '-rpath'. Since this option is really meant for the linker and gcc doesn't really have to recognize it, there is an easy workaround. The gcc compiler uses the -Wl, argument to indicate that certain options should be passed to the linker and otherwise ignored. In this case, when you specify the -rpath option, do it with -Wl:

```
AUXLIBS='-L/usr/local/lib -Wl,-rpath,/usr/local/lib -lssl'
```

See the gcc(1) manpage for more information.

Building Postfix

The source file that you download is in a compressed, tar archive and must be uncompressed using the gzip command. In the same directory as the downloaded bundle, type the following:

```
$ gzip -d postfix-2.0.10.tar.gz
```

This uncompresses the file and produces a tar file without the *.gz* extension. Next, untar the file:

```
$ tar -xf postfix-2.0.10.tar
```

This creates a directory called *postfix-2.0.10* below the current directory. Set that directory as your current directory for the rest of the compilation:

```
$ cd postfix-2.0.10
```

If you accept all of the default parameters for building Postfix, compiling is as simple as executing make in the top-level directory of the distribution:

```
$ make
```

Executing make creates a *Makefile* for your particular platform, which is in turn used to compile Postfix for your system. If you don't need any changes to the default build, you can skip ahead to the "Installation" section.

Customizing Your Build

The file *makedefs* contains platform-specific information that Postfix uses when configuring the package for your system. If you are curious, you can look at the file to see which parameters Postfix uses for your platform. It identifies your environment and creates the macros and definitions that are used in the *Makefile* for building Postfix on your system. The resultant *Makefile* is invoked by the make command which in turn calls your compiler and linker to build the Postfix system. When you type make as above, all of this happens automatically, so you don't normally need to worry about this file.

If you want to change any of the parameters for your environment, you can execute the build in two steps. The command make makefiles creates a new *Makefile* based on parameters that you specify on the command line. To set specific parameters, simply define variables on the command line. For example, you can use a different compiler from the default that Postfix chooses for your environment. The following example works on an HP-UX system to be sure that make finds the correct compiler:

```
$ make makefiles CC="/opt/ansic/bin/cc -Ae"
```

You would, of course, specify the path to your own compiler plus any necessary options. If you need to specify an additional directory for header files on your system, define CCARGS to include your directory:

```
$ make makefiles CCARGS="-I /usr/local/include/"
```

And, of course, you can combine options:

```
$ make makefiles CC="/opt/ansic/bin/cc -Ae" CCARGS="-I /usr/local/include"
```

Modifying Postfix Defaults

Postfix provides a lot of flexibility through its configuration files. Nearly all of Postfix's runtime parameters, including the various directories it uses, can be set in its configuration file except, of course, the location of the configuration file itself. You can change the location by defining DEF_CONFIG_DIR within the CCARGS variable:

```
$ make makefiles CCARGS='-DDEF_CONFIG_DIR=\"/usr/local/etc/postfix\"'
```

The single and double quotation marks and backslashes are important since the value for DEF_CONFIG_DIR should itself be quoted. After compilation, Postfix looks for its *main.cf* configuration file in the directory */usr/local/etc/postfix* instead of the default directory, */etc/postfix*.

You can use combinations of all the examples above to configure the environment you need. If your command line starts to get complicated, you might want to create a simple shell script to execute it for you. See "Wrapping Things Up" later in this appendix.

Once you have used make makefiles with your specific options to create your *Makefile*, execute make to build Postfix:

```
$ make
```

Installation

After you have successfully compiled Postfix, you are ready to install it. You will have to be the *root* user in order to perform the installation steps.

You need to create a dedicated account that will own the Postfix queue and most of its processes. The account should not permit logins and does not need a shell or a home directory. Use your normal administrative tools to create an account. You can set the password to * and its home directory and shell to invalid paths (something like */bin/false* or */dev/null*). By convention the username should be *postfix*. The entry in */etc/passwd* should resemble the following:

```
postfix:*:1001:1001:postfix:/no/where:/bin/false
```

You must also create a dedicated group that is not used by any user account, including the *postfix* account you just created. By convention the group name is *postdrop*. On most systems you create groups be editing the */etc/group*. Add a line like the following:

```
postdrop:*:1007:
```

Remember that Postfix is a replacement for Sendmail, and in order to maintain compatibility it installs its own *sendmail* binary in place of your existing one. You may want to rename the existing one to save it from being overwritten. Depending on your platform your existing *sendmail* is commonly in */usr/sbin/sendmail* or */usr/lib/sendmail*. You should be able to determine the exact location of your *sendmail* by executing:

```
# whereis sendmail
```

This may list a number of files. You are looking for the binary that has no extension. Once you have found it, rename it to move it out of the way:

```
# mv /usr/sbin/sendmail /usr/sbin/sendmail.orig
```

You will also want to rename two other files that will be replaced by Postfix: *mailq* and *newaliases*. These are commonly found in the */usr/bin* directory, but you can use the whereis command to locate them if necessary. These commands might be symbolic links on your systems:

```
# mv /usr/bin/mailq /usr/bin/mailq.orig
# mv /usr/bin/newaliases /usr/bin/newaliases.orig
```

Now you are ready to run the installation script.

Make sure you are still the *root* user and still in the Postfix distribution directory. Execute the installation script:

```
# make install
```

After checking that everything is built, the installation script asks you a few questions about setting up Postfix on your system:

```
install_root: [/]
```

The *install_root* directory is the root directory of your system. The only time you would want to change this is if you are creating an installable package. Package builders often want to keep all of the files together in a separate subdirectory in order to bundle them up when creating an installable distribution:

```
tempdir: [/home/kdent/postfix-2.0.10]
```

The *tempdir* directory is a place where the installation script can write temporary files. It defaults to your current directory and cleans up after itself. If for some reason you want the installation script to use another directory, specify it here:

```
config_directory: [/etc/postfix]
daemon_directory: [/usr/libexec/postfix]
command_directory: [/usr/sbin]
queue_directory: [/var/spool/postfix]
sendmail_path: [/usr/lib/sendmail]
newaliases_path: [/usr/bin/newaliases]
mailq_path: [/usr/bin/mailq]
```

You should probably accept the defaults for the questions that involve the location of the various Postfix files. Just be sure that the default values presented by the installation script match the directories you found with the whereis command for your original copies of *sendmail*, *newaliases*, and *mailq*. If they don't, you should type in the correct path when the installation script prompts you for it.

```
mail_owner: [postfix]
```

The mail_owner defaults to *postfix*, and assuming that you followed the instructions earlier, you can accept that value. If you created an account with a different username, enter that here.

```
setgid_group: [postdrop]
```

The setgid property defaults to *postdrop*, and assuming you followed the instructions earlier, you can accept that value. If you created a group with a different name, enter that here.

```
manpage_directory: [/usr/local/man]
```

For installation of the Postfix man pages, you can accept the default or type in a more appropriate place on your system.

```
sample_directory: [/etc/postfix]
```

The sample configuration files contain explanations for Postfix parameters and should be included in your installation. If you prefer not to have them in your configuration directory, you can specify a different location here.

```
readme_directory: [no]
```

The Postfix distribution includes several README files with additional information about particular features and add-on packages. These are less critical for the regular maintenance of your Postfix server than the sample configuration files, but if you would like to include them on your system, specify a path where they should be installed. If you don't install them, they are still available in the distribution directory.

The installation script then installs all of the necessary files.

Upgrading

If Postfix is already installed on your system, you can upgrade it when you have a new compilation or version to install. It's usually best to stop Postfix before performing the upgrade. The upgrade process is not interactive but requires that the *main.cf* file exist on your system already:

```
# postfix stop
# make upgrade
# postfix start
```

Postfix checks for changed files and replaces them with newer versions from your new compilation. Be sure to check the log file after restarting Postfix.

Compiling Add-on Packages

This section walks through building Postfix with various add-on packages that are mentioned in the book. Before recompiling Postfix with any additional packages, it is important to first clean up from any previous builds. Execute the following:

```
$ make tidy
```

Now you'll be starting with a clean source tree for your new builds. Each of the examples below takes you through creating a new *Makefile*. Once you've accomplished that, simply type:

```
$ make
```

to rebuild Postfix. If your new build is successful, you can upgrade your currently installed Postfix:

```
# make upgrade
```

If you hadn't previously installed Postfix, use make install instead.

Cyrus SASL

See Chapter 12 for information on Cyrus SASL and Postfix. You can download the source for the Cyrus SASL libraries from the Carnegie Mellon web site at *http://asg.web.cmu.edu/sasl/sasl-library.html*. Note that this book assumes that you are working with SASL Version 2.x libraries. Follow the instructions for building the Cyrus SASL2 libraries. There is also a *SASL_README* file that comes with the Postfix distribution.

One issue when compiling Cyrus SASL that affects Postfix is whether or not to include support for certain Microsoft clients that authenticate using a nonstandard mechanism. The standard plain-text authentication mechanism is identified as PLAIN, but these clients use LOGIN. If you need to support such clients, be sure that the libraries are built with the workaround enabled using the --enable-login option when you run configure.

When you install the libraries, be sure to note their location. This example assumes that they are installed in */usr/local/lib* and that the header files are located below */usr/local/include*. If you are using different locations, adjust the examples accordingly.

To build Postfix with SASL support, you must define the USE_SASL_AUTH macro and specify the directories for the libraries and header files. You must also link against the *libsasl2.so* library file. Run make tidy if necessary. Build your *Makefile* with the following options:

```
$ make makefiles CCARGS='-DUSE_SASL_AUTH -I/usr/local/include/sasl' \
    AUXLIBS='-L/usr/local/lib -lsasl2'
```

Remember that if you must provide the path to your libraries to the runtime linker, include the correct runtime search path argument:

```
$ make makefiles CCARGS='-DUSE_SASL_AUTH -I/usr/local/include/sasl' \
    AUXLIBS='-L/usr/local/lib -lsasl2 -rpath /usr/local/lib'
```

If your linker uses an argument other than rpath, be sure to specify the correct one.

TLS

See Chapter X for information on the TLS patches and Postfix. You can find the web site for the TLS patches from the "Add-on Software" page of the Postfix web site. Since this add-on modifies the Postfix source, make sure you get the correct download for your version of Postfix. For this example, assume the downloaded file is called *pfixtls-0.8.13-2.0.10-0.9.7b.tar.gz*. If the file you download is different, adjust the examples accordingly.

This add-on depends on the OpenSSL library, which you must install first if it's not already on your system. Check the documentation that comes with the TLS distribution to make sure you have the correct version of OpenSSL. For this example, assume that your OpenSSL libraries are installed in */usr/local/ssl/lib* and the header files are in */usr/local/ssl/include*. If your installation differs, adjust the example accordingly.

The TLS modifications to the Postfix source are all contained in the file *pfixtls.diff*, and you use the patch command to apply the differences to your Postfix source. You should uncompress and untar the TLS patch in a subdirectory that is at the same level as your Postfix directory such that if your current directory is the one above the Postfix source, you can see both the Postfix directory and the TLS patch directory:

```
$ pwd
/home/kdent
$ ls -ld pfixtls-0.8.13-2.0.10-0.9.7b postfix-2.0.10
drwxr-xr-x   5 kdent  kdent    512 May 14  2002 pfixtls-0.8.13-2.0.10-0.9.7b
drwxr-xr-x  15 kdent  kdent   1024 May 31 17:31 postfix-2.0.10
```

From that directory apply the patch as follows:

```
$ patch -p0 < pfixtls-0.8.13-2.0.10-0.9.7b/pfixtls.diff
```

patch reports the changes as it makes them until it finishes and displays "done" on your terminal.

Go back to the Postfix distribution directory to build Postfix with TLS support. You must define the HAS_SSL macro and specify the directories for the SSL libraries and header files. You must also link against the *libssl.so* (or *libssl.a*) and *libcrypto.so* (or *libcrypto.a*) library files. Run make tidy if necessary. Build your *Makefile* with the following options:

```
$ make makefiles CCARGS='-DHAS_SSL -I/usr/local/ssl/include' \
    AUXLIBS='-L/usr/local/ssl/lib -lcrypto -lssl'
```

Remember that if you must provide the path to your libraries to the runtime linker, include the correct runtime search path argument:

```
$ make makefiles CCARGS='-DUSE_SASL_AUTH -I/usr/local/ssl/include' \
    AUXLIBS='-L/usr/local/ssl/lib -lcrypto -lssl -rpath /usr/local/ssl/lib'
```

If your linker uses an argument other than rpath, be sure to specify the correct one.

MySQL

See Chapter 15 for information on MySQL and Postfix. This add-on depends on the MySQL client library and the zlib compression library, which you must install first if they're not already on your system. This example assumes that your MySQL library is installed in */usr/local/lib/mysql* with its header files in */usr/local/include/mysql* and that the zlib library is in */usr/lib*. If your installation differs, adjust the example accordingly. There is a *MYSQL_README* file that comes with the Postfix distribution with information about building Postfix with support for MySQL.

To build Postfix with MySQL support, you must define the HAS_MYSQL macro and specify the directories for the MySQL library and header files. You must link against the *libmysqlclient.so* and the *libz.so* library files. You must also link against the *libm.so* math library file, which is standard on Unix systems. Run make tidy if necessary. Build your *Makefile* with the following options:

```
$ make makefiles 'CCARGS=-DHAS_MYSQL -I/usr/local/include/mysql' \
     'AUXLIBS=-L/usr/local/lib/mysql -lmysqlclient -lz -lm'
```

Remember that if you must provide the path to your libraries to the runtime linker, include the correct runtime search path argument:

```
$ make makefiles 'CCARGS=-DHAS_MYSQL -I/usr/local/include/mysql' \
     'AUXLIBS=-L/usr/local/lib/mysql -lmysqlclient -lz -lm \
     -rpath /usr/local/lib/mysql'
```

If your linker uses an argument other than rpath, be sure to specify the correct one.

LDAP

See Chapter 15 for information on LDAP and Postfix. This add-on depends on LDAP libraries, which you must install first if they're not already on your system. There are commercial libraries available as well as an open source package from *http://www.openldap.org/*. This example assumes that you have LDAP libraries installed in */usr/local/lib/* and LDAP header files in */usr/local/include*. If your installation differs, adjust the example accordingly. There is an *LDAP_README* file that comes with the Postfix distribution with information about building Postfix with support for LDAP.

To build Postfix with LDAP support, you must define the HAS_LDAP macro and specify the directories for the LDAP libraries and header files. You must link against the *libldap.so* library file and also the *liblber.so* library file, which defines encoding routines for the LDAP protocol. Run make tidy if necessary. Build your *Makefile* with the following options:

```
$ make makefiles CCARGS='-I/usr/local/include -DHAS_LDAP' \
     AUXLIBS='-L/usr/local/lib -lldap -L/usr/local/lib -llber'
```

Remember that if you must provide the path to your libraries to the runtime linker, include the correct runtime search path argument:

```
$ make makefiles CCARGS='-I/usr/local/include -DHAS_LDAP' \
     AUXLIBS='-L/usr/local/lib -lldap -L/usr/local/lib -llber \
     -rpath /usr/local/lib'
```

If your linker uses an argument other than rpath, be sure to specify the correct one.

Common Problems

If you run into problems, check the various README files for information about your build. Frequently, they contain information about problems you might run into. Certainly, if there is a README file specific to your platform, be sure to read it. Some possible problems are mentioned below. Exact messages vary depending on your platform and compiler, so the following are general errors similar to what you might see when building Postfix.

Compile Time

No such file or directory

Make sure that the path to your compiler is correct. If you specified a compiler by setting CC when building your *Makefile* (for example, make makefiles CC="/path"), double-check the path you typed. If the path to your compiler came from the Postfix *makedefs* file, you might need to override it with:

```
$ make makefiles CC="/path/to/your/compiler"
```

Another possibility is to have Postfix call your compiler without a path, assuming its directory is in your environment path:

```
$ make makefiles CC="cc"
```

Could not open source file

Make sure that the path to your include files is correct. The include files are normally stored in */usr/include*. If your system uses a different path for some reason, you will have to specify it with the -I option set in CCARGS:

```
$ make makefiles CCARGS="-I/path/to/include"
```

If you already specified a path with -I double-check your typing.

Unresolved (or undefined) symbol

Make sure that the library paths you specified with the -L option are correct and that you have specified the libraries themselves correctly with the -l option.

Warnings from header files

If you see errors associated with a header file like *mail_conf.h*, you may not be using an ANSI C compiler. Nearly all platforms ship with a compiler that is used to reconfigure the kernel, but they do not all include an ANSI C compiler that you can use for development. You may have to contact your vendor to get an ANSI C compiler if you want to build Postfix. Also, the GNU gcc compiler works on nearly all platforms and is available as open source software. If you are using the compiler for HP-UX, you must use the -Ae flag to compile in ANSI mode. Include it in your CCARGS variable:

```
$ make makefiles CCARGS="-Ae"
```

Don't know how to

You have probably lost your *Makefile* or never had one. You can easily create your *Makefile* by executing the command:

```
$ make -f Makefile.init makefiles
```

After that completes, try your build again.

Runtime

Error in loading shared libraries

Make sure that you specified either the -rpath or -R option when you built Postfix and that the paths specified are correct. Be sure that you are using the correct option for your platform. You may have to check the manpage for ld(1) to be sure.

Wrapping Things Up

You can mix and match any of the options or add on libraries described in this appendix to build Postfix for your environment. If your command line for building the Postfix *Makefile* is getting a little complicated, you should probably create a simple shell script that invokes the options and additional libraries you need. Creating a build script has the added advantage of documenting the options you used when you last built Postfix. Feel free to include plenty of comments to yourself to explain the reasons you are including an option or not, and how you came to that decision. The following is an example of a shell script you might use, although you will certainly need to customize it for your own environment. This example includes all of the add-on libraries we've discussed. You should exclude the ones you don't need:

```
#
# Simple script to create a Makefile to build Postfix.
#


#
# Remember to start by cleaning up or uncomment this line
# to have this script do it every time.
#
#make tidy


#
# Specify all of our options and supporting libraries
#
make makefiles \
  CCARGS='-DUSE_SASL_AUTH -DHAS_SSL -DHAS_MYSQL -DHAS_LDAP \
   -I/usr/local/include/sasl -I/usr/local/ssl/include \
   -I/usr/local/include/mysql -I/usr/local/include' \
  AUXLIBS='-L/usr/local/lib -L/usr/local/ssl/lib \
   -L/usr/local/lib/mysql -L/usr/local/lib \
   -lsasl2 -lcrypto -lssl -lmysqlclient -lz -lm -lldap -llber \
   -rpath /usr/local/lib/mysql -rpath /usr/local/lib \
   -rpath /usr/local/ssl/lib'
```

To build Postfix, type:

```
$ sh build.sh
$ make
```

The first command creates your *Makefile* with the options you need. The second executes the build.

APPENDIX D
Frequently Asked Questions

I can't seem to receive messages. What does this error mean: "<test@example.com>: mail for example.com loops back to myself"?

Postfix reports this error when a DNS reply points to your mail server, but Postfix has not been configured to accept mail for the domain. Postfix accepts mail for domains listed in mydestination, `relay_domains`, `virtual_mailbox_domains`, `virtual_alias_domains`, and domains that resolve to IP addresses listed in `inet_interfaces` and `proxy_interfaces`. Your domain must be listed in one of these parameters.

When I make changes to configuration files or lookup tables, do I have to reload Postfix?

It depends on the type of file you are changing. Changes in files that Postfix reads into memory at startup require a reload. Examples of such files are *main.cf*, *master.cf*, and any lookup table using regular expressions. DB or DBM files are not read into memory and don't require reloading Postfix when they are changed.

Is there some kind of "include" directive for main.cf?

No. Most administrators with complex configurations create a *Makefile* that will cat the necessary files together. If you have other regular administrative tasks, add them to your *Makefile* too. Your *Makefile* should have an entry that looks something like this:

```
main.cf: file1 file2 file3
        cat file1 file2 file3 > main.cf.new
        mv main.cf.new main.cf
```

Then type make `main.cf` to rebuild your configuration file.

How can I get confirmation of mail deliveries?

This is not currently available in Postfix.

How can I add or append a disclaimer (or other text) to the bottom of every email that gets sent from my mail server?

By design this is not implemented in Postfix directly. It's not the job of an MTA, and it's not as simple a problem as it seems because of MIME and digital signatures. MIME messages have a structure that can be very complex. Digital signatures attest to the fact that a signed message has not been modified. Adding a footer to the bottom of a message breaks both of these. Some people add short text to the headers of email messages, but the text is not likely to be seen by most users. The real solution is to configure your clients to add whatever text is required.

Having said that, it is possible to configure a content filter that appends the text for you. Follow the directions for configuring Postfix to work with a content filter. Your filter should be MIME-aware, and you should be aware that digital signatures will no longer work.

How can I save a copy of every message?

Specify an address in the always_bcc parameter. It will receive copies of all messages.

How can I enable quota or size limits on users' mailboxes?

This is not really a function of Postfix, although you may achieve what you're looking for with the mailbox_size_limit. Be aware that if you use maildir-style mailboxes, this parameter limits only the size of individual mail files and not the size of the entire mailbox. Mailbox quotas are best enforced by the mail store itself, which might be done through normal operating system accounting or your POP/IMAP server configuration.

When Postfix sends a bounce message, it tells the sender, "For further assistance, please send mail to <postmaster>". But I want it to include my domain name in the address, e.g., <postmaster@example.com>. How can I do that?

The idea behind this message is that users should contact their own postmasters for assistance, since the local postmaster is quite possibly the one who has to deal with the problem. If you definitely want to make the change, you have to modify the source code.

I have aliases where only the first address in the list receives messages. The others can receive mail fine when sent to them directly, but when they're part of an alias, their messages don't arrive.

If you are using an external program for delivery, it might not handle more than one address at a time. Such is the case with maildrop, for example. To make sure that Postfix passes messages for delivery one at a time, set the transport_destination_recipient_limit parameter in *main.cf* to 1. *transport* is the name of the transport method making the deliveries. If you are using maildrop, the parameter looks like the following:

```
maildrop_destination_recipient_limit = 1
```

I have a few interfaces on my system. How can I get Postfix to bind to only one of them?

Specify the IP address of the interface you want Postfix to use in the inet_interfaces parameter.

With Sendmail, I used to get a warning notice when a message couldn't be delivered for four hours or so. Can I get that with Postfix?

This is controlled by the delay_warning_time parameter. By default it's set to 0 for "never".

I'm trying to test alias lists to see which addresses are expanded from particular lists. With other mail servers, I used the EXPN command to get a full recipient list, but it doesn't seem to work with Postfix.

Postfix does not support EXPN. Because of Postfix's architecture and concern for security, the unprivileged SMTP server doesn't know anything about local aliases. It's the privileged local delivery agent that actually expands aliases at the point of delivery. If you use a mailing-list manager, it most likely has a command to tell you who is on the list, or you may have to check the aliases file on the mail server system.

What's the difference between mailbox_transport and mailbox_command?

The mailbox_transport parameter is set to a service from *master.cf*, while mailbox_command refers to an actual command on the mail server filesystem. There are a few parameters that can affect mailbox delivery. The parameters in order of preference are mailbox_transport, mailbox_command_maps, mailbox_command, and home_mailbox.

All of my internal systems relay through my mail gateway. Is there a way to remove or hide the hostnames and IP addresses of my internal systems from the messages headers before they go out?

Add header checks that match the header lines showing your internal systems and specify the IGNORE action for them.

How can I tell Postfix to forward all messages that are sent to nonexistent mailboxes to a particular user?

You can specify an address in the luser_relay parameter and disable local_recipient_maps:

```
luser_relay = info
local_recipient_maps =
```

Be careful if you do this. With the prevalence of spam, the address you specify is liable to catch a large amount of junk mail.

According to my configuration, Postfix should be replying with a permanent error code (554), but it keeps sending a temporary one (454). Why is it doing that?

You probably have soft_bounce turned on.

I have a whole bunch of mail queued up that I know I don't need. Is there any way to delete all of the queued messages?

```
# postsuper -d ALL
```

Note that the word *ALL* must be all capital letters, and that executing this command deletes *all* of the mail in your queue.

Where does Postfix log its information?

Postfix logs messages to your system's `syslogd` daemon. Check your system documentation to find the actual log file.

Postfix seems to be ignoring the MX record and trying to deliver directly to the A record system. Is this normal?

It's normal if you have:

```
disable_dns_lookups = yes
```

specified in *main.cf*. You might also have a transport map specified in brackets, in which case Postfix delivers directly to the system:

```
example.com     smtp:[mail.example.com]
```

I get a lot of spam with a blank envelope sender address. How can I block these?

You don't want to block messages based on the fact that they have a null return path. Accepting null envelope addresses is required by the standards. The technique is used to prevent looping of error notifications. You'll have to identify the spam by some other means.

I'm using header_checks *and* body_checks *to block spam, but some legitimate email is blocked by my checks. Is there any way to whitelist some mail so that the header and body checks are not applied?*

No. Header and body checks are applied to every message and should be used for simple checks that can easily be applied to all mail. If you need anything more sophisticated, you should set up a content filter that has the smarts you need.

Index

Symbols

* (asterisk), for messages in active queue, 62
\ (backslash), continuing long command lines in Unix, 12
% (command prompt), 11
$ (dollar sign)
  command prompt, 11
  in configuration variables, 32
! (exclamation point)
  marking messages in hold queue, 62
  preventing rewriting of domain names, 54
? (question mark), ending wakeup time with, 50
" (quotation marks)
  in alias definitions, 39
  lookup tables and, 33
  parameter values and, 31
(root prompt), 11
/ (slash)
  in file pointers, 32
  in regular expression keys, 37
| (vertical bar), commands as alias targets, 39

Numbers

2bounce_notice_recipient parameter, 196

A

A records, 69
  domains without, 75
  for mail exchangers, 72
  MTA routing of email with, 71
  for MX hosts, 75

access maps
  client checking with, 136, 136–139
    actions to take after checking, 137
    example configuration, 138
  regular expression tables for, 138
access_map_reject_code parameter, 196
account names, excluding from masquerading, 54
active attacks, 158
active queue, 22, 25, 58, 59
  messages marked with asterisk (*), 62
additional_conditions parameter, 186-188
address classes, 22
  masquerading all, 54
addresses, email
  address completion, turning off, 53
  as alias targets, 39
  blocking spam from (see spam)
  client-based rules, restrictions to check, 137
  correction by cleanup daemon, 25
  creating text file for mailing lists, 114
  deleting queued messages by, 63
  format in message header (RFC 2822), 14
  handling by trivial-rewrite daemon, 20
  identifying spam from, 128
  legitimate return address appropriated by spammers, 126
  rewriting, 52–55
    with canonical_maps lookup table, 33
    canonical addresses, 52
    masquerading hostnames, 54
    relocated users, 55
    unknown users, 55

We'd like to hear your suggestions for improving our indexes. Send email to *index@oreilly.com*.

user parameter, setting for MySQL, 185
users
   .forward files, checking by local delivery
      agent, 23
   NIS database of, 38
   passwords (see passwords)
   postfix user, 29
   relocated, address rewriting for, 55
   spam, labeling for, 130
   unknown, 55
UUCP, setting up gateway for, 111
uuencoding, 15

V

variable expansion, 176
variables
   configuration, 32
   specifying path with variable
      expansion, 81
Venema, Wietse, ix-x, 1
verbose logging information, 50
verp_delimiter_filter parameter, 217
Vexira AntiVirus for mail servers, 180
virtual accounts, 89
   separate domains with, 91–95
   separate password database for SMTP
      users, 154
virtual alias addresses, 22, 23
virtual aliases, 74
   catchall addresses with, 94
virtual delivery agent, 23, 92
virtual delivery transport, 78
virtual domains, 74, 89
   DNS configuration, 90
   MySQL configuration, 188
   Postfix handling of mail for, 89
virtual mailbox addresses, 22
virtual mailbox catchall address, 94

virtual mailbox domains, virtual delivery
      transport for, 78
virtual mailboxes, 74
virtual mailing list manager, configuring, 101
virtual_alias_domains parameter, 23, 90, 94
virtual_alias_maps parameter, 23, 35, 91, 93,
      100, 218
virtual_gid_maps parameter, 93
virtual_mailbox_base parameter, 92, 218
virtual_mailbox_domains parameter, 23, 91,
      94
   listing virtual domains for mail
      acceptance, 95
virtual_mailbox_limit parameter, 218
virtual_mailbox_maps parameter, 23, 92,
      218
   pointing to lookup file with valid
      addresses, 95
virtual_transport parameter, 95, 218
virtual_uid_maps parameter, 93
viruses
   anti-virus filters, 174, 175
   scanning for with header checks, 146
   Vexira AntiVirus program, 180

W

wakeup (master.cf), 50
warn_if_reject parameter, 135
warning message after content checking, 145
web site, Postfix online documentation, 57
weeks (w), 50
well-known ports (port 25 for SMTP
      servers), 16
where_field parameter (MySQL), 185, 187
whitelist applications (pre-approval for
      sending mail), 127
WHOSON, 43

About the Author

Kyle D. Dent works as an independent consultant and software developer in the New York metropolitan area. He has designed and implemented various security, network, and web-based applications for technology and financial firms. He has been working with Postfix in various settings since it was released by IBM in 1998.

Kyle grew up with computers in an IBM family, but originally started working in publishing and as a teacher of English as a Second Language. He is an avid supporter of public libraries, serving as a trustee at his local library and on the board of his regional library system. He has recently started to learn the classical guitar.

Colophon

Our look is the result of reader comments, our own experimentation, and feedback from distribution channels. Distinctive covers complement our distinctive approach to technical topics, breathing personality and life into potentially dry subjects.

The animal on the cover of *Postfix: The Definitive Guide* is a dove. Doves belong to the class Aves (birds) and the order Columbiformes (doves and pigeons), to which the now-extinct dodo bird (*Raphus cucullatus*) also belonged. Their family, Columbidae, includes over 300 species of pigeons and doves, including the common rock dove or feral pigeon (*Columba livia*).

In 1679, the French astronomer Augustin Royer discovered the dove-shaped constellation Columba. A constellation in the southern hemisphere, located near Puppis and Caelum, Columba's stars were originally part of the constellation Canis Major.

Reg Aubry was the production editor and copyeditor, and Matt Hutchinson was the proofreader for *Postfix: The Definitive Guide*. Colleen Gorman and Claire Cloutier provided quality control. Mary Agner provided production assistance. Ellen Troutman-Zaig wrote the index.

Ellie Volckhausen designed the cover of this book, based on a series design by Edie Freedman. The cover image is an original illustration created by Susan Hart. Emma Colby produced the cover layout with QuarkXPress 4.1 using Adobe's ITC Garamond font.

David Futato designed the interior layout. This book was converted by Joe Wizda to FrameMaker 5.5.6 with a format conversion tool created by Erik Ray, Jason McIntosh, Neil Walls, and Mike Sierra that uses Perl and XML technologies. The text font is Linotype Birka; the heading font is Adobe Myriad Condensed; and the code font is LucasFont's TheSans Mono Condensed. The illustrations that appear in the book were produced by Robert Romano and Jessamyn Read, using Macromedia FreeHand 9 and Adobe Photoshop 6. The tip and warning icons were drawn by Christopher Bing. This colophon was written by Leanne Soylemez and Reg Aubry.

Need in-depth answers fast?

Access over 2,000 of the newest and best technology books online

Safari Bookshelf is the premier electronic reference library for IT professionals and programmers—a must-have when you need to pinpoint exact answers in an instant.

Access over 2,000 of the top technical reference books by twelve leading publishers including O'Reilly, Addison-Wesley, Peachpit Press, Prentice Hall, and Microsoft Press. Safari provides the technical references and code samples you need to develop quality, timely solutions.

Try it today with a FREE TRIAL
Visit *www.oreilly.com/safari/max/*

For groups of five or more, set up a free, 30-day corporate trial
Contact: *corporate@oreilly.com*

What Safari Subscribers Say:

"The online books make quick research a snap. I usually keep Safari up all day and refer to it whenever I need it."
—Joe Bennett, Sr. Internet Developer

"I love how Safari allows me to access new books each month depending on my needs. The search facility is excellent and the presentation is top notch. It is one heck of an online technical library."
—Eric Winslow, Economist-System, Administrator-Web Master-Programmer

Related Titles Available from O'Reilly

Networking

802.11 Security

802.11 Wireless Networks: The Definitive Guide

BGP

Building Wireless Community Networks, *2nd Edition*

Cisco IOS Access Lists

Cisco IOS in a Nutshell

Designing Large-Scale LANs

DNS & BIND Cookbook

DNS & BIND, *4th Edition*

Essential SNMP

Hardening Cisco Routers

Internet Core Protocols

IP Routing

IPv6 Essentials

LDAP System Administration

Managing NFS and NIS, *2nd Edtion*

Network Troubleshooting Tools

Networking CD Bookshelf, *Version 2.0*

Practical VoIP Using Vocal

qmail: An Alternative to sendmail

RADIUS

Samba Pocket Reference, *2nd Edition*

sendmail, *3rd Edition*

sendmail Cookbook

Solaris 8 Administrator's Guide

TCP/IP Network Administration, *3rd Edition*

Unix Backup and Recovery

Using Samba, *2nd Edition*

Using SANs and NAS

Keep in touch with O'Reilly

1. Download examples from our books

To find example files for a book, go to:

www.oreilly.com/catalog

select the book, and follow the "Examples" link.

2. Register your O'Reilly books

Register your book at *register.oreilly.com*

Why register your books?
Once you've registered your O'Reilly books you can:

- Win O'Reilly books, T-shirts or discount coupons in our monthly drawing.
- Get special offers available only to registered O'Reilly customers.
- Get catalogs announcing new books (US and UK only).
- Get email notification of new editions of the O'Reilly books you own.

3. Join our email lists

Sign up to get topic-specific email announcements of new books and conferences, special offers, and O'Reilly Network technology newsletters at:

elists.oreilly.com

It's easy to customize your free elists subscription so you'll get exactly the O'Reilly news you want.

4. Get the latest news, tips, and tools

www.oreilly.com

- "Top 100 Sites on the Web"—PC Magazine
- CIO Magazine's Web Business 50 Awards

Our web site contains a library of comprehensive product information (including book excerpts and tables of contents), downloadable software, background articles, interviews with technology leaders, links to relevant sites, book cover art, and more.

5. Work for O'Reilly

Check out our web site for current employment opportunities:

jobs.oreilly.com

6. Contact us

O'Reilly & Associates
1005 Gravenstein Hwy North
Sebastopol, CA 95472 USA

TEL: 707-827-7000 or 800-998-9938
(6am to 5pm PST)

FAX: 707-829-0104

order@oreilly.com
For answers to problems regarding your order or our products. To place a book order online, visit:

www.oreilly.com/order_new

catalog@oreilly.com
To request a copy of our latest catalog.

booktech@oreilly.com
For book content technical questions or corrections.

corporate@oreilly.com
For educational, library, government, and corporate sales.

proposals@oreilly.com
To submit new book proposals to our editors and product managers.

international@oreilly.com
For information about our international distributors or translation queries. For a list of our distributors outside of North America check out:

international.oreilly.com/distributors.html

adoption@oreilly.com
For information about academic use of O'Reilly books, visit:

academic.oreilly.com

O'REILLY®

Our books are available at most retail and online bookstores.
To order direct: 1-800-998-9938 • *order@oreilly.com* • *www.oreilly.com*
Online editions of most O'Reilly titles are available by subscription at *safari.oreilly.com*